DESCENDANTS

OF

LORENZ AND ANNA M. HOFF/HOOFF

Ronald L. and Barbara M. Hooff

HERITAGE BOOKS
2015

HERITAGE BOOKS
AN IMPRINT OF HERITAGE BOOKS, INC.

Books, CDs, and more—Worldwide

For our listing of thousands of titles see our website
at
www.HeritageBooks.com

Published 2015 by
HERITAGE BOOKS, INC.
Publishing Division
5810 Ruatan Street
Berwyn Heights, Md. 20740

International Standard Book Numbers
Paperbound: 978-0-7884-1578-4
Clothbound: 978-0-7884-6249-8

❧ Dedication

This family ancestry is dedicated to our grandchildren, Courtney, Jamie, Brittany, Kerry, Michael, Shaun, and Ashleigh with all our love!

Contents at a Glance

Lorenz Hooff (Lawrence Hoff/Hough) 3

Laurentius Hooff (Laurence) 13

John Hooff 31

Lewis Hooff 49

James Wallace Hooff 53

Lewis Hooff II 65

Charles Rapley Hooff (1826) 61

Charles Rapley Hooff (1882) 69

Charles Rapley Hooff (1911) 71

John Carlyle Herbert Hooff 73

William Hooff 77

John Lawrence Cramer Hooff 87

William Lawrence Hooff 99

Francis Rankin Hooff 105

Edward Lee Hooff 109

Hammond Francis Hooff 117

Jessie Gordon Hooff 123

Ronald Lee Hooff 129

Philip Henry Hooff (I) 149

James Lawrence Hooff 171

Fontaine Beckham Hooff 181

Fontaine Beckham Hooff Jr. 183

Allison Armstead Hooff 185

Washington Hammond Hooff 187

Philip Henry Hooff, Jr. 191

Philip Henry Hooff, III 199

Wilson Lee Hooff 201

Mahlon Overall Hoff 205

Robert McGill Hoff 207

Robert Byrne Hoff 209

John Vowell Hooff 211

Index of Names 217

Introduction

Welcome to the *Descendants of Lorenz & Anna M. Hoff/Hooff.* We started this adventure sometime around 1977 and completed our research in 1980. We have continually updated our project whenever new information became available. This search took us to Pennsylvania, Virginia, West Virginia, Washington, D.C., and across Maryland.

The first approach we chose consisted of several visits to the National Archives in Washington, D.C. Countless hours were spent (sometimes days) scrolling through microfilm and looking through many journals and publications. On our days off from work, we started traveling to the states mentioned above to visit churches and cemeteries and examine their records.

As you begin to read our heritage, a few points must be kept in mind:

      *   West Virginia succeeded from Virginia in 1864

      *   Washington City is now Washington, D.C.

      *   Alexandra, D.C. is now Alexandria, VA

      *   We found that family members would name their children after other family members. At times this caused some confusion on tracing the line as with John and Lewis Hooff. John named one of his children Lewis, and Lewis named one of his children John. In addition, they often used their mother's family name as the middle names of their children, despite the sex of the child. Some names could be for a male or female, i.e., Francis and Rankin. In addition, we have read in very old books that naming each child the same first name was not unusual in German tradition, but different middle names. This would confuse the "devil" when he came. It was a form of protection for the children.

Through all of this, we somehow met a distant cousin (Betty Lemons) who was on the same journey as we were. We took many trips together combining our findings. Betty went on to publish the information in 1980.

In 1998 we became interested in which of our ancestors may have fought in the Civil War; this reopened our probe into history. We have updated our findings and again enjoy that feeling of excitement each time we learn something new about "us." We decided it was time to present our version of *Descendants of Lorenz & Anna M. Hoff/Hooff.*

We typed all of the documentation we found exactly as originally written, including the misspelling of words as we know them today. Even in those days they would drop an "o" out of Hooff, sometimes done in the same paragraph. Some chronicles may be confusing to the reader because of the phrases used in the 1700's and 1800's, but that makes it more interesting. The direct descendants are marked with the * symbol.

Our hope is that someday one of the *Hooff* children or grandchildren will be curious about their heritage and enjoy reading about their ancestors . . . both good and bad.

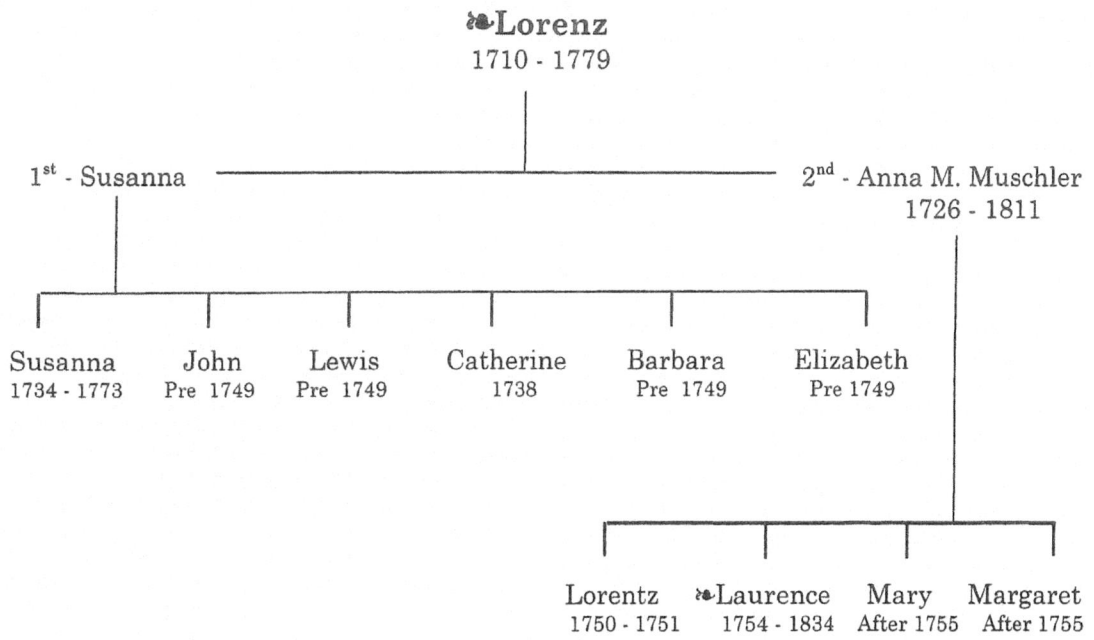

Lorenz
1710 - 1779

1st - Susanna

2nd - Anna M. Muschler
1726 - 1811

Susanna
1734 - 1773

John
Pre 1749

Lewis
Pre 1749

Catherine
1738

Barbara
Pre 1749

Elizabeth
Pre 1749

Lorentz
1750 - 1751

Laurence
1754 - 1834

Mary
After 1755

Margaret
After 1755

❧ Lorenz (Lorentz, Lawrence) Hoff, Hooff

Born: ca. 1710, possibly in Palatinate, Germany
Christened/Baptized (Baptismal name may have been John Lorentz)
Died: 1779 in Alexandria, VA.
Buried:
Father: Mother:

Spouse: 1st Susanna.   Apparently between the time Lorentz arrived in Lancaster and 1749, his first wife died. However, there is no record of this and we do not know if he was married in Germany or after arriving in Lancaster. No other information is known about Susanna.

They had six children:

Susanna. Confirmation and Holy Communion on April 27, 1751 at Holy Trinity Church. Lancaster, Pa. Per *Frederick, Maryland Evangelical Lutheran Church*, burial records: May 25, 1773, Susanna Hoffin born near Lancaster, PA in 1734. Father was Lorentz Hoff, died May 24, 1773 at about age 39 of convulsions, in Frederick, MD. Never married.

Maria Catharina (Catherine). Born June 5, 1738. Baptized August 6, 1738 at Holy Trinity Lutheran Church, Lancaster, PA. She married Alexander McDonald. Per *Frederick, Maryland, Evangelical Lutheran Church* burial records we found the following statement: On October 4, 1795, Alexander McDonald, for 31 years the honest and diligent English schoolmaster in Fredericktown. Born 1742 in Edenburg, Scotland. Married daughter of Lorentz Hoff and his wife Susanna with whom he had two daughters and one son. Died of a high fever and jaundice, with which he was bedfast for 10 days the 3rd, at 1:30 p.m., age 53 years.

Barbara who was born before 1749 in Lancaster, PA. She married Michael Paulsult.

Elizabeth who was born before 1749 in Lancaster, PA. She married Darren, and had 1 son named Henry.

John who was born before 1749 in Lancaster, PA. Cannot find any other positive information about him.

Lewis who was born before 1749 in Lancaster, PA. Cannot find any other positive information about him.

Spouse: 2nd - Anna Margaretha Muschler
Born: June 18, 1726 in Germany
Christened/Baptized:
Married: October 24, 1749 in Lancaster, PA.
Died: October 6, 1811 at age 86 years.
Tombstone reads: Anna Margaretha Hoff (Luth) wife of John L. Hoff. Born June 18, 1726. Died October 6, 1811. From *Frederick Town Herald October 5, 1811*: Died in this town Tuesday morning last after a lingering illness, Mrs. Margaret HOOFF, in the 86th year of her age.
Buried: Churchyard of Evangelical Lutheran Church, Frederick, MD
Father: Mother:

From the *Pennsylvania Society of Germans* we found writings of a Minister Soever, one of which reads "Lorentz Hoff, a widower, and Anna Margaretha Muschler, a single person, reformed, were Publically proclaimed three different Sundays, and married October 24, 1749 in my room in the presence of many people."

They had four children:

Lorentz who was born June 4, 1750. Baptized June 24, 1750 at Holy Trinity Lutheran Church, Lancaster, PA. He died July 28, 1751 and was buried July 29, 1751, age 1 year, 3 weeks, 3 days. Parents, Lorentz Hoffins and Anna Margaretha.

❧Laurentius (Laurence) who was born December 19, 1754. Baptized May 19, 1755 at Holy Trinity Lutheran Church in Lancaster, PA. See a separate chapter on Laurentius, page #13.

Mary M. who was born ca. 1755. Died April 5, 1829 at age 75 in Frederick, MD. She married Conrad Doyle and had five children: Margaret, Henry, Lawrence, John, George.

Margaret who was born after 1755. She married _____Tatezbaugh and had four children: George, Elizabeth, Lawrence, Peter.

The Hoff family came from another area of Germany and settled in Mutterstadt around 1710. The records show that they were members of the Reformed Church and were employed as "coach builders."

Lorenz Hoff embarked for America from Pfalzer, Germany aboard the ship Thistle traveling by way of the Rhien River, stopping first at Dover, England (per *German Pioneers, Vol. 2*, which has the signatures of the passengers, including Lorenz). On June 19, 1730, the ship left Dover, and after 72 days, arrived at the Port of Philadelphia, PA. On August 29, 1730. Upon arrival, all male passengers over the age of 16 years were required to sign an "Oath of Allegiance." Lorenz signed his name to both of the passengers' lists, and to the "Oath."

He was probably indentured to someone in the Lancaster, PA area for about seven years. He settled in Warwick Township, Lancaster, PA. In 1744 he was one of the Trustees for land granted by the Commonwealth of Pennsylvania for construction of Emmanuel Lutheran Church, Warwick Township, Lancaster, PA. In 1746 he received a patent for 141 acres of land in Lancaster County on which he placed a mortgage in the amount of 320 pounds. Both documents are in the name of Lawrence Hoff. Lawrence and his second wife, Margaret, entered into three deeds between 1752 and 1760, in which he is variously described as "yeoman" or wagon maker.

The family left Lancaster approximately 1760. Lawrence may have stayed in Frederick, MD and Winchester, VA for a few years. His daughter Susanna and his wife are buried in Frederick, MD.

From *Handley Library Archives Room, Winchester, VA*, we found a statement that "Lawrence Hoff was in the poll for election for Burgesses in Frederick County, VA, for or with Col. Adam Stephen." Also found in "1763 Lawrence Hoff of VA served in the French and Indian War in Capt. Isaac Parker's Co. of Infantry."

The family then moved to Alexandria, VA, Fairfax County where Lawrence built a home which he left to his wife Margaret (in 1791 she was listed as the owner of a house on Fairfax Street). We feel that Anna Margaetha is not buried with Lawrence because all burials within Alexandria City limits were stopped in 1805. There was a smallpox epidemic in the 1780's which nearly filled the local cemeteries. The earliest actual document we can find on him in Alexandria is dated 1768 (a law suit).

Virginia Colonial Soldiers by Lloyd Dewitt Bockstruck dated 1760 show a Lawrence Huff/Laurence Hoff of Capt. John Grienfields Co. of Frederick Co., VA was fined for being absent from two musters.

Note: It had been suggested that Margaret was the person who added the second "o" to the Hoff name, making it "Hooff" to differentiate between his first and second family. We are unsure if this is true because the second Laurence was using Hooff before his father's death in 1779.

From Lancaster records we found Anna's sister, Catharina Muschler married Casper Tieffenback on April 11, 1751 at Trinity Lutheran Church. Mr. Tieffenback came from Durdach Germany - near Baden.

IN THE NAME OF GOD, AMEN: I, Lawrence Hough the Elder of the Town of Alexandria in Fairfax County in the Common Wealth of Virginia being weak in body but of sound mind, memory and understanding do make and devise this my Last Will and Testament in manner and form following that is to say

FIRST I recommend my soul to Almighty God and my body to be decently Buried at the discretion of my Executrix hereinafter named next that all my just debts and Funeral Charges be justly paid and as to my worldly effects my Real as well as personal Estate I give and bequeath to my Loving Wife Margaret Hough during her natural life and to be disposed of at her death among my Children in such division as may seem meet to her my said wife. I further hereby constitute and appoint my said loving wife Margaret Hough sole Executrix of this my last will and Testament hereby removing all other wills heretofore made by me. In Witness whereof I have hereunto set my hand and Seal this fifth day of August 1776.

Lawrence Hough (Seal)

Signed and Sealed in presence of:
John Orr, Peter Wise, Conrad Doyle

At a Court Continued and held for the County of Fairfax, 18th November 1779, this Will was presented in Court by Margaret Hough Executrix herein named who made oath thereto and the same being proved by the oath of Peter Wise and Conrad Doyle is admitted to record and the said Executrix having performed what the Laws require a Certificate is granted her for obtaining a probe thereof in due form.

Test. P. Wagoner

Will of Margaret Hooff

Will book D1, pages 154 and 155, Fairfax County Courthouse, Virginia (typed exactly as seen in the book).

I, Margaret Hooff, widow and relict of Lawrence Hooff, late of the town of Alexandria, deceased, do make and ordain this to be my last will and Testament. Whereas the said Lawrence Hooff did by his last will and Testament devise unto me the said Margaret Hooff all his Estate, both real and personal, with power to dispose of the same as my death among his children in such divisions as I might think proper, therefore:

I give and devise unto Lewis Hooff and John Hooff, sons of the said Lawrence by a former marriage, the sum of five shillings, Virginia currency, each.

Item. I give and devise unto Catherine McDonald, wife of Alexander McDonald, and Barbara Pollsult, wife of Michael Pollsult, daughters of the said Lawrence Hooff also by a former marriage, the sum of five shillings, Virginia currency each.

Item. I give and devise unto Henry Darren, son of Elizabeth Darren, another daughter of the said Lawrence Hooff, the sum of five shillings, Virginia currency.

Item. As to the lot of ground in the town of Alexandria and the improvement thereon of which the said Lawrence Hooff died seized. I dispose of the same in the following manner, the said Lawrence Hooff having a son and two daughters born of him by me who lived with him until they grew up and by their labor enabled him to improve that lot without any aid or assistance from his elder children. It appears to me but just that they alone should enjoy the fruits of their own labor, but it not being possible to devise so small a piece of ground into three portions without rendering it in a manner useless to each of the persons interested in it.

I do thereby order and direct my executors hereinafter named so soon as after by death as can be (in case such power be vested in me by the aforesaid will) to sell the same for the highest price which can be got for it and the money arising therefrom I give and devise in the following manner, that is to say, I give and devise one-third part thereof unto my son Lawrence Hooff, to him, his executors and administrators forever, one-third part thereof I direct my executor to lay out to the best advantage in the purchase of a piece of ground and a small house either in town or country as to them shall seem most advisable for the use of my daughter Mary Doyle wife of Conrad Doyle, during her natural life and after her death for her children, Margaret, Henry, Lawrence, John and George, their heirs and assigns forever as tenants in common to be equally divided among them. One-third part of the money arising from the sale of the said lot of ground I direct to be put to interest upon good security or laid out in the purchase of another piece of ground as to my said executors shall appear most advisable. If the money be put to interest I direct the same be paid in equal portions unto George, Elizabeth, Lawrence and Peter Tatzebaugh, children of my daughter Margaret Tatzebaugh, as they shall severally come of age, but if my executor shall deem it more advisable to lay that money out in the purchase of ground, I direct the purchase to be made in the name of the aforesaid children, their heirs and assigns, but in case my authority under the aforesaid will of the said Lawrence Hooff is not so extensive as to enable me to direct a sale of the said lot of ground, then I do give and devise one-third of the said lot of ground and all improvements thereupon I give and devise unto my daughter Mary Doyle, wife of the said Conrad Doyle, during her natural life, and after her death I give and devise that part of the said lot and improvements unto her children, Margaret, Henry, Lawrence, John and George their heirs assigns forever to be equally divided among them, and the other third part of the said lot of ground and improvements I give and devise upon George, Elizabeth, Lawrence and Peter Tatzebaugh and to their heirs and assigns forever to be equally divided among them.

Lastly, I nominate, ordain, constitute upon my son the said Lawrence Hooff, and my friend Peter Wise, executors of my last will and Testament hereby revoking and annulling all former and other wills by me heretofore made declaring this and no other to be my true last will and Testament. In witness hereof I have hereunto set my hand and affix my seal this 22nd day of October 1793.

> Her
> Margaret Hooff (Seal)
> Mark

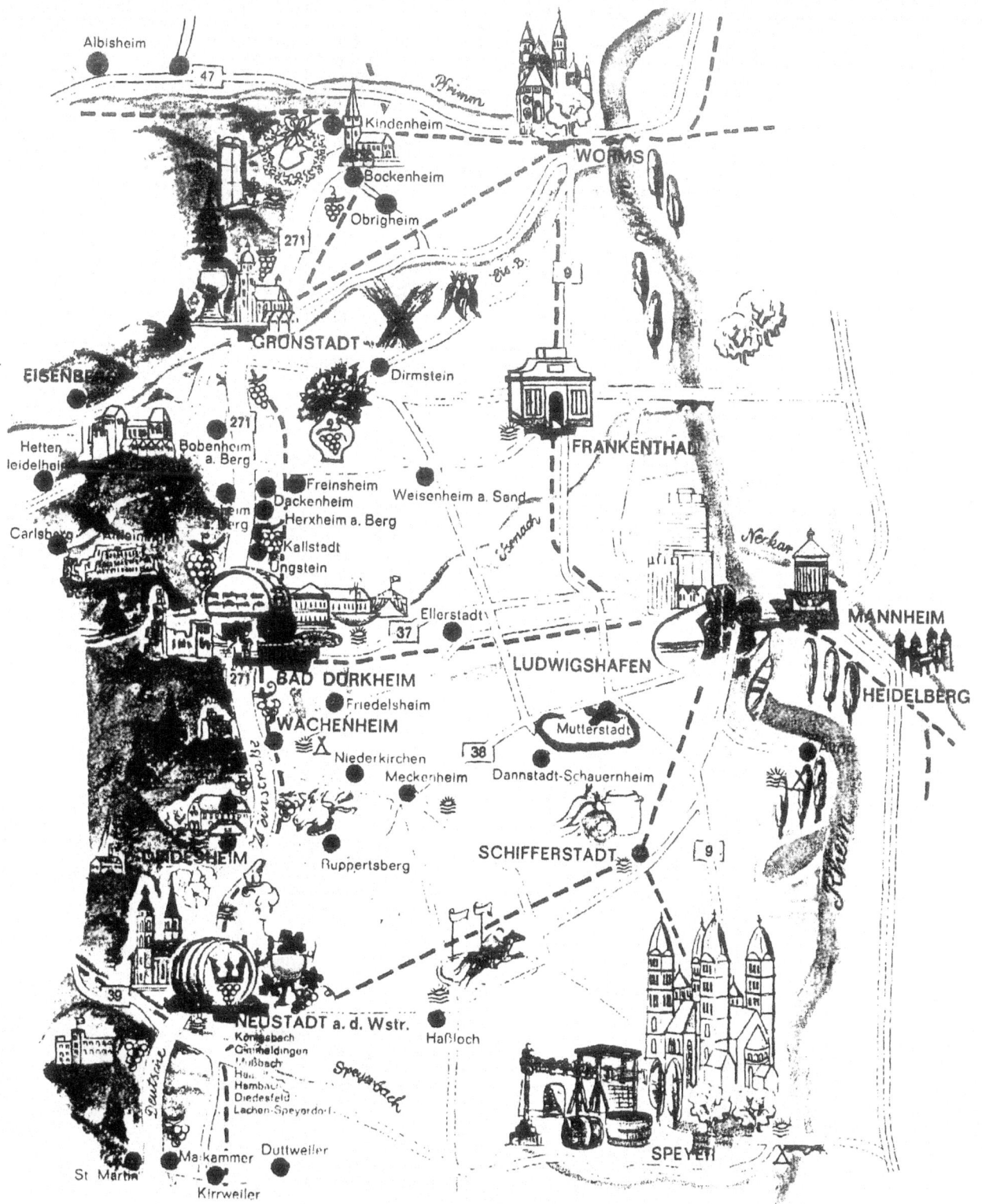

Albisheim

47

Primm

Kindenheim

WORMS

Bockenheim

271

Obrigheim

GRÜNSTADT

Dirmstein

EISENBERG

FRANKENTHAL

Hetten
leidelheim

Bobenheim
a. Berg

271

Freinsheim

Weisenheim a. Sand

Eis. B.

Dackenheim

Herxheim a. Berg

Neckar

Carlsberg

Kallstadt

Ungstein

Ellerstadt

37

MANNHEIM

LUDWIGSHAFEN

HEIDELBERG

271   BAD DÜRKHEIM

Friedelsheim

Mutterstadt

WACHENHEIM

38

Niederkirchen

Dannstadt-Schauernheim

Meckenheim

9

Rhein

DÜRDESHEIM

SCHIFFERSTADT

Ruppertsberg

39

NEUSTADT a. d. Wstr.

Königsbach
Gimmeldingen
Mußbach
Hans
Hambach
Diedesfeld
Lachen-Speyordorf

Haßloch

Speyerbach

SPEYER

Deutsche

Maikammer

Duttweiler

St. Martin

Kirrweiler

DEUTSCHE WEINSTRABE

nordlicher Teil

From Tourist Catalogue "Die Pfalz am
Rhein", Mutterstadt, Germany, 1978.

11) Aug. 29, 1730. Palatines with their families, two hundred and sixty persons, imported in the ship Thistle, of Glasgow, Colin Dunlap, Master, from Rotterdam, last from Cowes. —*Col. Rec.* III. 283.

Aug. 29, 1730. Das Schiff Thistle von Glasgow, Capitain Colin Dunlap, brachte Pfälzer mit ihren Familien, zwei hundert und sechzig Personen, von Rotterdam über Cowes.—Col.-Ber. III. 283.

Valentin Grisemer,	Hans Menigh,
Johannes Dunckel,	Nichol Fiser,
Christof Batter,	Johan Zwinger,
Christian Leman,*	Jacob Nagel,
Jeremias Hes,*	Ulrich Scherer,
Joh. Georg Ludwig Hass,	Philip Groscost,*
Bernhart Siegmund,	Casper Bittner,*
Hans Jacob Dohl,	Nickel Cünter,
Johan Peter Ohller,	Johannes Scherer,
Johan Henrich Schmidt,	Johannes Haus,*
Caspar Fiehman,	Philip Hautz,*
Steven Remer,*	Lorentz Hoff,
Rudolph Draugh,*	Thomas Hamma,
Johannes Kun,*	Jacob Stiffel,
William Keim,*	Wolfer Sperger,*
Ludwick Delman,*	Ulrich Steyner,*
Gerhart Zinn,	Thomas Hes,

AND OTHER IMMIGRANTS—1730. 63

Henrich Hes,	Frederick Peifer,
Hendrich Gutt,*	Johannes Kepplinger,
Caspar Krieger,	Felte Meidelman,
Christoph Anckenbrant,	Dietrich Beidelman,
Jean Henri Fortineaux,*	Elias Meidelman,
Frederich Reimer,	Jacob Ammon,
Peter Beswanger,*	Johan Nickel Lukenbell,*
Johan Caspar Schmidt,	Hans Simon Mey,
Johan Paulus Düttenhöffer,	Henrich Lukebill,
Johan Augustus Scherrer,	Ludwig Mohler,
Hans Georg Hofman,	Lönhart Hochgenug,
Abraham Transu,	Peter Federolff,
Casper Hartman,*	Peter Müller, *a*
Christian Shram,	Friederich Lienberger,
Leonhart Köpplinger,	Peter Frawiener,
Rudolp Andreas,	Bernhard Renn,

a *Peter Müller* was a native of Oberamt Lautern, Germany. He graduated at Heidelberg. He was a man of profound erudition—of more than ordinary powers of mind—a finished scholar, as is evident from testimony born him by the Rev. Jedediah Andrews. In a letter dated Philadelphia, 10 mo., (Oct.) 14th, 1730, "There is," says Andrews, "lately come over a Palatine candidate of the ministry, who, having applied to us at the synod for ordination, 'tis left to Tenant, Andrews and Boyd to do it. He is an extraordinary person for sense and learning. We gave him a question to discuss about *Justification*, and he answered it, in a whole sheet of paper, in a very notable manner. His name is John Peter Müller, and speaks Latin as readily as we do our natural tongue." In 1735, he connected himself with the *Siebentägers*, of Ephrata. He died Sept. 25, 1796. His remains rest at Ephrata, Lancaster County, Pa.—*Rupp's His. Lan. Co., p.* 229.

Signature of Lorenz Hoff as it appeared on the manifest of the ship *Thistle*.

Lower Lancaster County, Pa.,
showing early Townships, ca. 1740

X indicates probable location
of property of Lawrence Hoff.

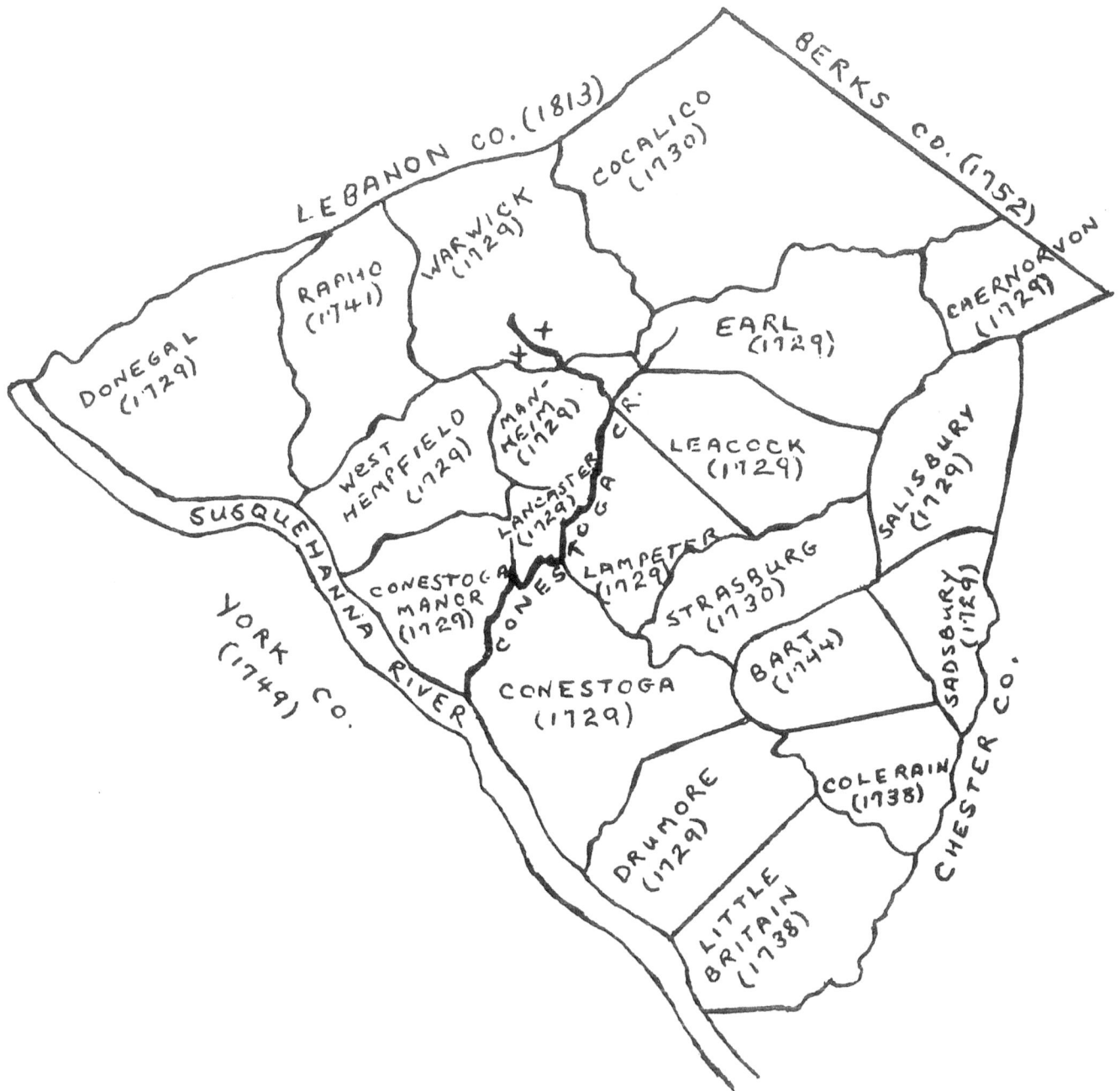

Map of Lower Lancaster County, Pa., showing early Townships, ca. 1740:

- LEBANON CO. (1813)
- BERKS CO. (1752)
- CAERNORVON (1729)
- COCALICO (1730)
- WARWICK (1729)
- RAPHO (1741)
- EARL (1729)
- DONEGAL (1729)
- MAN-HEIM (1729)
- WEST HEMPFIELD (1729)
- LEACOCK (1729)
- SALISBURY (1729)
- SUSQUEHANNA RIVER
- LANCASTER (1729)
- CONESTOGA CR.
- LAMPETER (1729)
- STRASBURG (1730)
- SADSBURY (1729)
- YORK CO. (1749)
- CONESTOGA MANOR (1729)
- CONESTOGA (1729)
- BART (1744)
- CHESTER CO.
- DRUMORE (1729)
- COLERAIN (1738)
- LITTLE BRITAIN (1738)

❧Lorenz
1710 - 1779

1st - Susanna

2nd - Anna M. Muschler
1726 - 1811

Susanna	John	Lewis	Catherine	Barbara	Elizabeth
1737 - 1773	Pre 1749	Pre 1749	1738	Pre 1749	Pre 1749

Lorentz	❧Laurence	Mary	Margaret
1750 - 1751	1754 - 1834	After 1755	After 1755

Ann Gretter
1760 - 1836

- Elizabeth
  1778
- Lawrence
  1780 - 1842
- John
  1783 - 1859
- Ann
  1785
- Peter
  1787
- George
  1789
- Lewis
  1791
- Mary Ann
  1794
- ❧William
  1796 - 1850
- Julia Maria
  1798 - 1863
- Philip Henry
  1801 - 1888
- Mary Amelia
  1803 - 1837

Laurentius (Laurence) Hooff II   Res: 521 Duke St., Alex., VA

Born: December 19, 1754 in Lancaster, PA
Christened/Baptized: May 19, 1755 at Holy Trinity Lutheran Church in Lancaster, PA
Married: 1777 in Richmond, VA
Died: Friday, May 26, 1834 in Alexandria, D.C. (now Virginia) at age 79.
Buried: St. Paul's Episcopal Church Cemetery, Alexandria, VA
Father: Lorentz Hooff   Mother: Ann Margareth Muschler

Spouse: Mary Ann Gretter
Born: July 8, 1760 probably in Richmond, VA.
Died: June 8, 1836 in Alexandria, D.C. (now Virginia) age 76
Buried: St. Paul's Episcopal Church Cemetery, Alexandria, D.C.
Father: George Michael Gretter   Mother: Elizabeth Burnett
    Born in Ober Sennigen, Bovaria   d: June 28, 1798
    d: September 1, 1796

They had 12 children:

Elizabeth Hooff - Born February 20, 1778, Alexandria, D.C. She married Judge Henry Lewis of Hagerstown, MD. They had one daughter, Mary Ann who married Robert James Scott (Robert died 1835) son of Gustavas Scott.

Lawrence Hooff III - Lawrence was born April 26, 1780 in Alexandria, D.C. He was never married. He died March 10, 1842 and is buried at St. Paul's Episcopal Church Cemetery. His tombstone reads "And in Memory of Lawrence Hooff, Jr. who died on the 10th day of March 1842 in the 62nd year of his life". St. Paul's records state: March 12, 1842 Major Lawrence Hooff (apoplexy) 62 years. His silhouette is owned by Alexandria Washington Lodge AF and AM.

An excerpt from *"Our Town" Alexandria, VA*: Lawrence Hooff, III (1780-1842) son of Lawrence II and Ann Getter Hooff and brother of John, was one of the four lieutenants of the 106 Regiment of Virginia militia who served as pallbearers at Washington's funeral, carrying the bier from the Mount Vernon mansion to the tomb. During the War of 1812, Hooff was Major of an Alexandria regiment.

An insurance record of 1805 shows him as owner of a two-story brick house on the west side of Fairfax Street, between Cameron and Queen, now 210 North Fairfax Street.

Obituary: Lawrence Hooff, a son of Lawrence was born April 26, 1780. At the funeral of Washington he was one of a detail of six Lieutenants of the 106th Regiment, Virginia Militia, to who was assigned the duty of carrying the bier from the mansion to the tomb. During the War of 1812 he was a major of a regiment raised in Alexandria. Major Hooff was a kindhearted, poplar gentleman and universally beloved. He died suddenly at Alexandria, March 10, 1842, and was buried with Masonic honors on the 12th, from the residence of his brother John, south-west corner Prince and Water (now Lee) Streets. He was a brother of Messrs. John and Lewis Hooff, for many years the cashier and teller of the Farmer's Bank of Alexandria, and of Philip H. Hooff, Esq. Lawrence Hooff was a member of Washington-Alexandria Masonic Lodge No. 22, and a pew holder of St. Paul's Church. He owned and occupied a two-story red brick house for which he paid $1.00 ground rent and $60.00 per year.

Alexander Gazette, March 6, 1909: WASHINGTON'S PALLBEARERS, Mount Vernon Chapter, D.A.R., through various committees, has about completed arrangements for the unveiling of the tablet to the memory of Gen. George Washington's pallbearers to be placed on the wall of Christ Church in this city in April next. The work of this chapter has ever been to perpetuate the memory of the heroic and historic, and this beautiful tablet a memorial to the pallbearers of George Washington (who were all revolutionary soldiers) will at the same time bear witness to the patriotism and enthusiasm of the members of the Mt. Vernon Chapter, DAR. The tablet, which is of bronze is 3 feet 6 inches by 3 feet 2½ inches, designed and cast by Jas. B. Calwell & Co. Of Philadelphia, and while handsome in the extreme, is simple and chaste in design thus being in perfect harmony with the old church on whose wall it will rest. The inscription reads: In memory of the Honorary Pallbearers of General George Washington. Fellow Townsmen, Brother Masons, Trusted Friends, Comrades, In the Cause of American independence: Col. Charles Simms, Col. George Gilpin, Col. Dennis Ramsay, Col. Philip Marsteller, Col. William Payne, Col. Charles Little. In memory also of the Lieutenants, William Moss, *Laurence Hooff*, James Turner, Jr., George Wise of the 106th Regiment of the Virginia Militia Who bore his body to the Tomb December 16, 1799. Erected by the Mt. Vernon Chapter National Society Daughters of the American Revolution of Alexandria, Virginia in 1909. Contributions for the tablet were most generously made by descendants in many states of the men whose memory is thus to be honored, and the unveiling will be by the hands of two of the most youthful of these descendants: Little Miss Margaret Douglas Reese, great, great granddaughter of Co. Dennis Ramsay, and Master John Caile Scott, great, great, great grandson of Co. Charles Simms. Hon. C.C. Carlin will introduce the prominent speakers of the occasion. It is expected that there will be many distinguished guests on this occasion, among them, Mrs. Donald McLean, president general of the society of the DAR. Entrance to Christ Church yard, where impressive services will take place, will be by card only.

Lawrence Hooff, Jr., 1780-1842, by Isaac Todd, 1804 (in Relic Rm., Geo. Washington Mem. Temple, Alexandria, Va.

Home of Lawrence Hooff, Jr.
210 No. Fairfax Street
Alexandria, VA

John Hooff - Born 1783. See a separate chapter on John, page #31.

Ann Hooff - Born September 12, 1785 and died young

Peter Hooff - Born December 3, 1787 and died young

George Hooff - Born May 7, 1789 and died young

Lewis Hooff - Born 1791. See a separate chapter on Lewis, page #49.

Mary Ann Hooff - Born February 14, 1794 and died young

William Hooff - Born 1796. See a separate chapter on William, page #77.

Julia Maria Hooff - Born July 30, 1798 in Alexandria, D.C.. Confirmed July 15, 1838 at St. Paul's Episcopal Church. Died August 20, 1863. Julia married Benjamin Lambert Wallace who was born March 11, 1797 in Kirkonell, Scotland. He died June 4, 1852 in Albany, NY and is buried there. His father was William Wallace of Scotland.

Julia Maria and Benjamin were married January 23, 1823 in Richmond, VA. She died August 28, 1863 in Albany, NY and is buried there. They had four children:

William Lawrence Wallace - Born February 22, 1824 in Richmond, VA.

Mary Ann Wallace - Born February 14, 1826 in Richmond, VA.

Jane Eliza Wallace - Born August 14, 1829 in Richmond, VA. Died October 5, 1832. Buried St. Paul's Episcopal Church Cemetery, Alexandria, D.C.

Robert Redfield Wallace - Born November 10, 1833. Baptized at St. Paul's Episcopal Church. Died February 20, 1838 in Alexandria, D.C. and is buried at St. Paul's Episcopal Church Cemetery.

Note: Plaque on back of Hooff Family Vault for Robert R. and Jane Eliza

Julia and Benjamin L. Wallace resided in Richmond, VA. It is believed that Benjamin died while they were visiting their daughter in Albany, NY and that Julia remained in Albany until her death.

Philip Henry Hooff - Born 1801. See a separate chapter on Philip Henry, page #149.

Mary Amelia Hooff - Born October 9, 1803 in Alexandria, D.C. She married James Hamilton Bennett who was born January 12, 1797 in Leesburg, VA. He died February 16, 1853 in Washington, D.C. His father was Charles Bennett, Jr. and his mother was Mary Hamilton. Mary Amelia and James were married September 4, 1823. She died October 6, 1837 in Hamilton, VA, Loudon County, age 34. They had four children.

Mary Ann Bennett - Born March 16, 1825 in Pernambuco, Brazil. Died December 9, 1907 in Baltimore, MD. She married J.G. Leche in Upperville, VA on August 1, 1843 - they had no children.

Clara Soares Bennett - Born October 3, 1831 in Union, VA. She married John Lawrence Cramer Hooff, son of William and Frances Hammond Hooff and had six children.

Julia Dulaney Bennett - Born April 16, 1834 in Union, VA. She died February 23, 1923 in Baltimore, MD. She married Alban G. Stabler April 31, 1861 in Baltimore, MD. They had no children.

An infant son born to Mary Amelia and James Hamilton Bennet died October 5, 1837 and is buried in the same casket as his mother who died the following day.

Note: James Hamilton Bennet was ambassador to Pernambuco, Brazil at the time of his marriage. He and Mary Amelia lived in Brazil for several years before returning to Virginia.

Home built by Lawrence Hooff in 1787-88 at 521 Duke Street, Alexandria, VA

The Family Record of
Lawrence & Mary A. Hooff

Lawrence   Born March   1755
Ann   "   July   1760

            Children
Elizabeth   Feb 20. 1778
Lawrence   Apl. 26. 1780
Jno   Sep 10   1783
Lewis   June 20   '791
William   "   8   '794
Julia   July 30   1798
by
father Philip Henry   Feby 23. 1801
        Mary Amelia   Oct   9. 1803

Anna, Peter, George & Mary Ann
have no record of Births.

In this Family of my Grand Father &
Mother. They were there 12 children

Record of James
Lawrence Hooff,
son of Philip Henry
Hooff and Jane
Hammond, grandson
of Lawrence, Sr.
and Ann Gretter
Hooff. Courtesy of
Mr. & Mrs. Fontaine
Beckham Hooff, II.

Lawrence Hoff (father) was born December — 1755 he died not — died May 26 — 1834

Ann ? Hoff — Mother — 1762 Grandmother died she died 7-8-1836

Elizabeth Hoff — February 26 — 1778 —

Lawrence Hoff —

John Hoff — April — 26 — 1780 —

Ann Hoff — January — 10 — 1783 —

Peter Hoff — September 12 — 1785 —

George Hoff — December — 5 — 1787 —

Lewis Hoff — May — 7 — 1789 —

Mary Ann Hoff — June — 20 — 1791 —

William Hoff — February — 14 — 1794 —

Julia Maria Hoff — June — 8 — 1796 —

Philip Henry Hoff — July — 30 — 1798 —

Mary Amelia Hoff — October — 9 — 1843 — February — 23 — 1801 —

Philip says this last letter is gone he was here to stay, so I will send this up to him, all well all join me in love to all. yours 1833

affectionately Julia Hobach 35

Laurence (Lawrence) Hooff bought 521 Duke Street, Land - Liber R. 1788-9, page 175, Deeds from Arthur Lee, 5 June 1786 to build a dwelling house within 2 years.

Laurence (Lawrence) Hooff was a merchant in Alexandria, Fairfax County, VA as early as 1783 and in 1785, signed a petition to increase the power of Congress over commerce. In 1793 he was one of the Alexandria merchants who petitioned the Assembly of Virginia for establishment of a bank within the Town. He engaged in numerous real estate transactions in Fairfax County (deed on record, Fairfax County Courthouse, others unindexed), and is said to have constructed the "Bunch of Grapes Tavern" at 201 N. Fairfax Street. It was under construction in 1777, and was later known at "Wise Tavern."

On June 5, 1786 he purchased land from Arthur Lee and built a townhouse at 521 Duke Street, which he rented to Bushrod Washington, nephew of George Washington (1789-91). It was later used as a "school for young ladies. (This lovely home is now privately owned and was on exhibit in December of 1978). In July 1786, Lawrence purchased 200 hundred acres of land from Bryan Allison. A stream running through the property is shown on early maps as "Hooffs Run." The property is now a part of the Rosemont section of Alexandria. In 1791 Lawrence Hooff was listed as the owner and occupier of a house on King Street.

Lawrence and Ann were members and pew holders of Christ Episcopal Church. Although some of the early records of the church have been destroyed, two have survived pertaining to Hooff burials in the churchyard: "April 23, 1787, Mr. Lawrence Hooff to opening a grave for his child, permission by Dr. Brown, Church Warden" and "June 11, 1790, Lawrence Hooff to opening grave for his child by permission of William Brown, Esq." It is probable that four of their children who died young were buried in Christ Church yard; Ann, Peter, George and Mary Ann. After 1805 there were no further burials within the Alexandria City limits.

In 1810 many members left Christ Church to form St. Paul's Episcopal Church. Lawrence Hooff became the first Senior Warden of the new congregation, and paid $22.00 per year for pew No. 24. He wrote a number of letters to Benjamin Labtrobe (architect of the U.S. Capitol) in regard to the church. The letters are presently in the possession of the Latrobe family.

A manuscript of the original pew holders list L. Hooff, Jr. & Co.; J. Hooff 1st Vestryman; L. Hooff, Sr., Senior Vestryman. The records of St. Paul's Episcopal Church contain the names of Hooff family members from 1810 to the present time. In 1912, the pulpit was dedicated by William C. Redfield, a descendant of Julia Hooff Wallace. The plaque reads: "In Memory of Lawrence Hooff, 1st Senior Warden of St. Paul's Episcopal Church, born December 1754, died May 1834, and Ann Gretter, July 1760 - June 1836; their sons, John Hooff, 1783-1859; Lewis Hooff, June 1791-1874, who were also wardens, and James Wallace Hooff, son of Lewis, 1825-1915."

St. Paul's Church
200 block, South Pitt Stree
Alexandria, VA

Obituary from *Alexandria Gazette, May 29, 1834*: Departed this life, on the 26th instant, in the 79th year of his age, Lawrence Hooff, Sen. One of the oldest and most respectable inhabitants of this place, after a painful and lingering illness, which he bore with that Christian resignation and meekness that distinguished him through the greater part of his long and useful life. In the character of this venerated citizen were happily blended all the social, domestic, and Christian virtues. As a husband and parent, he was uniformly kind and affectionate; as a friend, steady and sincere; an indulgent master, and a most zealous and devoted Christian; and, through the whole course of his long life, he invariably manifested that guileless manner and integrity of purpose which could not fail to endear him to all who had the pleasure of his acquaintance. He is gone to that bourne from whence none ever return, leaving behind a beloved widow and numerous offspring, who, while they lament his loss, have the consolation to believe that he died the death of the righteous. "Peace to his manes-honor to his dust ." This poor tribute of respect is paid to his memory by one who knew him well and loved him much.

Justitia

St. Paul's Episcopal Church Cemetery, Alexandria, DC - tombstone for Laurentius reads: "In Memory of Laurence Hooff who departed this life on the 26th day of May in the 79th year of age".

Tombstone reads: "In Memory of Mrs. Ann Hooff consort of the late Laurence Hooff who departed this life on the 8th day of June 1836 in the 76th year of her age."

Excerpt from the book *Our Town, Alexandria, VA*- Mrs Laurence Hooff (Ann Gretter). Mrs. Hooff was a daughter of Michael Gretter. Her husband was the first Senior Warden of St. Paul's organized in 1810, and letters he wrote Benjamin Latrobe, the architect, concerning it's construction are preserved by the Latrobe family. Laurence who died in 1834, and Ann had five sons.

Alexandria, Va.
(Alexandria Co., D. C., 1791-1846)

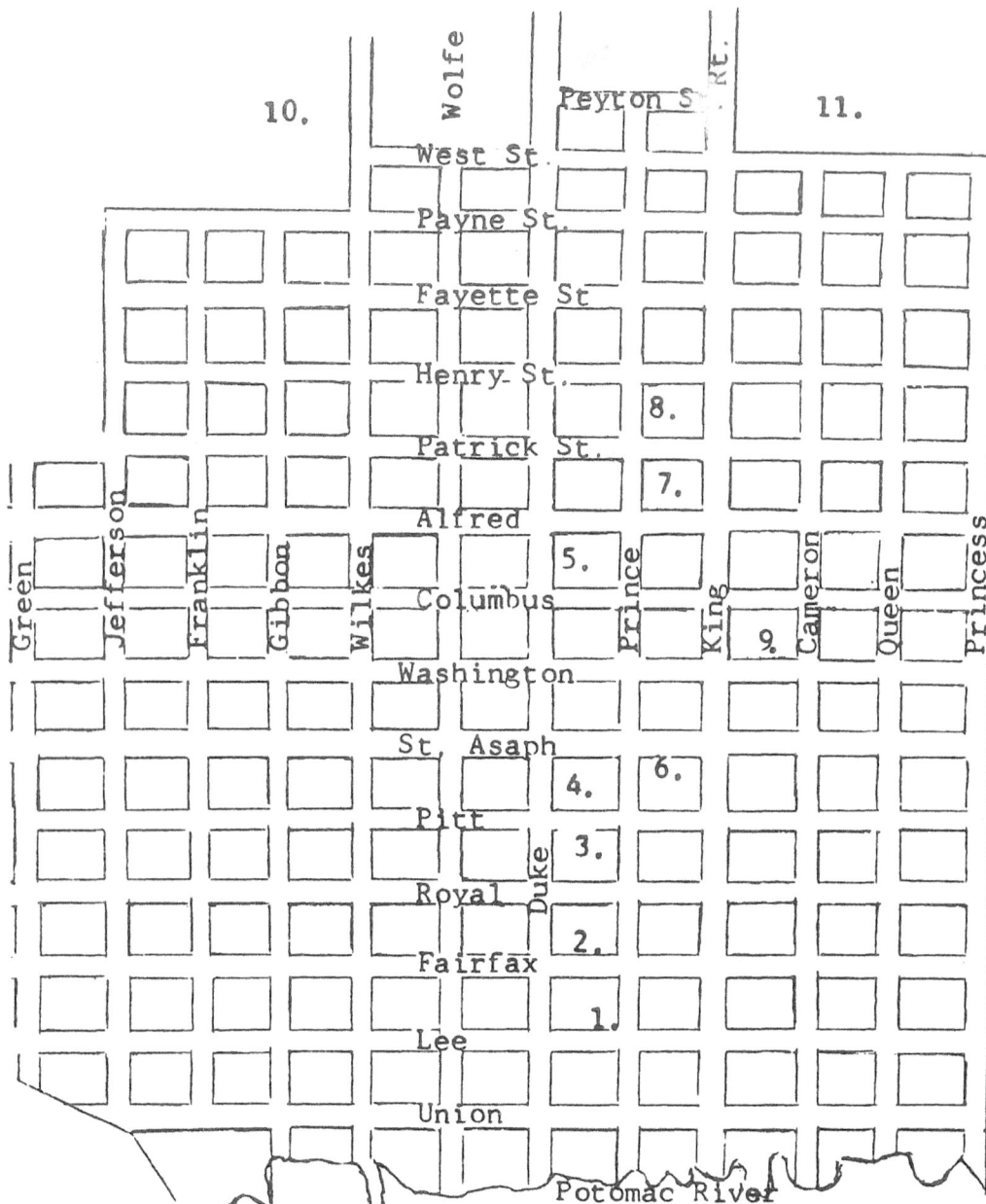

1. 200 Lee & 201 Prince Sts.,
   res. of John & Lewis Hooff
2. 210 Fx.St., res.of Lawrence
   Hooff, Jr.
3. St. Paul's Episc. Church
4. 521 Duke St., Law.Hooff, Sr.
5. 801 Duke St., Chas. R. Hooff
6. 517 Prince St., James Wallace
   Hooff (Brown-Fawcett house)
7. 916 Prince St., res. of
   Philip Henry Hooff, Sr.
8. 1016 Prince St., res. of
   Lewis Hooff
9. Christ Episc. Church
10. St. Paul's Cemetery
11. 200 acre farm of Lawrence
    Hooff, Sr.
12. 201 Fx. St., Wise's Tav.

Will of Lawrence (Laurentius, Laurence) Hooff II

Will probated in Alexandria, D.C. 1834 (copied verbatim from court records)

I, Lawrence Hooff of Alexandria, being weak in body but sound and disposing mind, do hereby make, constitute and appoint this my last will and Testament in manner and form following; that is to say - I give and bequeath unto my beloved wife Ann Hooff all my property real, personal and mixed, subject to her and her disposition only. And it is my will that no appraisement or inventory of my property should be taken - and that no Security of my wife Ann should be required of her as my Executrix, and I do hereby appoint her Executrix of this, my last Will and Testament.

As witness my hand and seal this 19th day of May 1834.

Law. Hooff

Signed, sealed and acknowledged before us these subscribers.
John A. Stewart, Geo. Wise, James Dunlap

At a session of the Orphans Court for the County of Alexandria in the District of Columbia the 4th day of May 1834 - the last Will and Testament of Lawrence Hooff deceased, was proved in due form and lay by John A. Stewart, Geo. Wise and James Dunlap in the witness hereto and ordered to be recorded.

Teste A. Moore, Regt. Wills

(Dates were copied verbatim from court record)

Will of Ann Hooff

I, Ann Hooff, of the town of Alexandria in the District of Columbia, of sound and disposing mind do make, ordain and constitute and appoint this my last will and Testament in the manner form following, to wit:

Item. I give and devise to my sons Lewis Hooff and Philip Henry Hooff and their assigns for and during the natural life of my son Lawrence Hooff, the slaughtering house, hog-house, stable and my house with the yards attached thereto as now inclosed under post rail fencing for their benefit, and at the death of the said Lawrence or his forfeiture by breach of the condition hereafter name, it is my will and desire that it be divided between by children then living and the descendants of any deceased child or children in equal portions, that is giving to the said descendants or descendant of such deceased child or children such share of shares as the parent or parents of such child or children if living would be entitled to, but upon this express condition and no other do I make this gift. That should my son Lawrence wish to use and occupy the premises aforesaid in the manner he has heretofore done or in any other manner, that my sons Lewis and Philip Henry or their assigns shall permit him to do so the said Lawrence yielding and paying them or their assigns for the use and occupation thereof the annual rent charge of one dollar and also keeping the said property in tenantable order and paying the taxes thereof and no more, and if my said son Lawrence should fail at anytime to claim the use of the said property then the same shall be rented out and during his life the rents applied as he may direct.

Item. I give to my sons Lewis and Philip Henry and their assigns a slave girl called Julia Amelia Ware, born the 21st September 1826, until the said girl arrive at the age of 28 years when she is to be free. And I do hereby declare her free when she arrives at the said age of twenty-eight years. In trust for the sole and separate use of my daughter Julia Maria during her natural life or until the expiration of the said 28 years free from the power or control of her present or any future husband and not be disposed of by her without the consent of the said Lewis and Philip Henry or of the survivors of them; and if the said Julia Maria may have.

Item. I give unto my son John Hooff a servant boy name John McKinsey Ware born the 15th June 1823, until the said boy arrives at the age of 28 years then to be free.

Item. I give unto my son Lewis Hooff a servant girl named Mary Ann Ware born the 21st January 1828, until the said girl arrives at the age of 28 years, then to be free.

Item. I give unto my son Philip Henry Hooff a servant boy names Philip Henry Ware born 19th December 1824 until the said boy arrives at the age of 28 years, then to be free.

Item. I give unto my son William Hooff, a servant girl named Adeline Ware, age on the 26th July 1834, four months, until the said girl arrives at the age of 28 years, then to be free.

Item. I give unto my sons Lewis Hooff and Philip Henry Hooff a slave girl called Laura Ware, aged on the 26th July 1834, three years until the said girl arrives at the age of 28 years, then to be free, and I do declare her free when she arrives at the age of 28 years. In trust for the sole and separate use of my daughter Mary Amelia during her natural life or until the expiration of the said 28 years free from the power and control of her present or any future husband and not to be disposed of by her without the consent of the said Lewis and Philip Henry Hooff or of the survivor of them, and if the said Mary Amelia die before the said slave attains the age of 28 years, then for residue of that time she is to be held for the use of such children as the said Mary Amelia may have.

Item. I devise to my sons Lewis and Philip Henry for and during the natural life of my son Lawrence my slave Moses and my slave Montgomery, the latter until he attains the age of 28 years which will be on the 24th February 1848. The said Lewis and Philip Henry to permit my son Lawrence to the services of the said slaves if he requires it and, if not, to pay over to him their hire. The said Lawrence paying all taxes and charges on said slaves and keeping them well and comfortably clothed. The said Lawrence being empowered to emancipate the said slaves whenever he pleases and failing to do so the said Montgomery to be free upon attaining the age of 28 years as aforesaid and if the said Lawrence die before the said Montgomery attains the age of 28 years without emancipating him by deed of will, then the said Montgomery is to be hired out for the unexpired residue of the term for the benefit of my distributees.

Item. It is my will and desire that the increase of the female slaves as heretofore devised which may born before they arrive at the age of 28 years be in like manner free when they shall respectively arrive at the age of 28 years, but until then that they be held in bondage for the benefit of my children to whom they have heretofore been given and of their children until the said increase arrive at the age respectively on the terms and in the manner hereinbefore expressed, and in like manner the future increase of my slave Caroline to be free as they arrive at the age of 28 years; in the meantime to be held for the use of my children before named, excluding my son Lawrence as to my named married daughters on the terms and in the manner before expressed.

Item. It is my will that none of my slaves herein devised shall be removed out of the County of Alexandria unless by consent of my executors hereinafter named in writing and in violation of this clause of my will I then devise the slave or slaves so removed to my sons Lewis and Philip Henry to be hired out for the benefit of themselves and for such of my distributees as shall not have concerned in such removal until said slaves or slave respectively attain the age of 28 years.

Item. My son Lawrence is hereby authorized to set free my servant woman Caroline whenever he may think proper so to do and is not to be accountable for the hire of Caroline so long as he may think proper to employ her.

Item. I do further declare that the several devises made in the preceding will for the benefit of my son Lawrence shall be subject to the following conditions, that is to say, that if my son Lawrence should at any time hereafter be legally declared bankrupt or take the benefit of any act for the relief of insolvent debtors, then his interest in and right to the said property shall wholly cease and determine and further should any execution, attachment or other legal process to subject the said property or any part thereof to any debt or debts of my said son Lawrence be levied on the said property or in the part so levied on shall cease and determine.

Item. I appoint my sons Lewis Hooff and Philip Henry Hooff executors of this my last will and Testament and direct that no security shall be required of them as such. In witness whereof I have hereunto set my hand and seal this 23rd day of August 1834.

Ann Hooff

Codicils to the last Will and Testament of Ann Hooff made and published this 8th day of October, 1834.

I will and bequeath all the rest and residue of my property both real and personal and mixed to Lewis Hooff and Philip Henry Hooff or the survivor of them and their assigns during the natural life of my son Lawrence Hooff, in trust, for the sole use and benefit of the said Lawrence during his natural life aforesaid and no longer and after his death to be equally divided amongst all my children then living or their descendants in the manner already pointed out by me in my will aforesaid.

Ann Hooff

Recorded June 24, 1836

Probated June 24, 1836, Alexandria, D.C.
Will Book 4, page 116, Alexandria, VA Courthouse

Tablets on front of Hooff Crypt

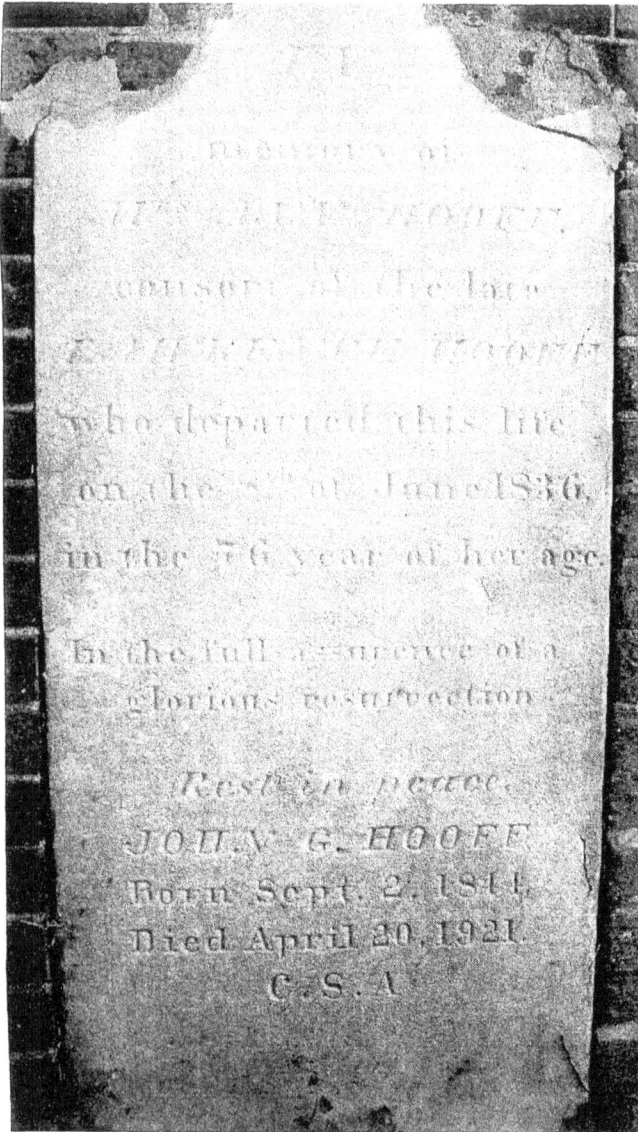

Hooff Crypt at St. Paul's Episcopal Church, Alexandria, VA.

Left side of crypt	Right side of crypt
In Memory of Mrs. Ann Hooff consort of the late Lawrence Hooff who departed this life on the 8th of June 1836 in the 76th year of her age. In the full assurance of a glorious resurrection.	In Memory of Lawrence Hooff who departed this life on the26th of May 1834 in the 79th year of his age. Blessed are the dead who die in the LORD even so with the spirit for they rest from their labours.
and	and
Rest in peace John G. Hooff Born September 2, 1844 Died September 20, 1921 C.S.A.	And in Memory of Lawrence Hooff, Jr. who died the 10th of March 1842 in the 62nd year of his age.

Marker in front of crypt:

In memory of Mrs. Jennett Hooff who departed this life the 30th day of October 1841. Age 54 years. Know my redeemer liveth.

On the left side as you look at the back of the crypt:	On the right side as you look at the back of the crypt:
In memory of Robert R. Son of Benjamin L. & Julia M. Wallace who died February 2, 1838 Age 2 months and 21 days.	In memory of Jane Eliza daughter of Benjamin L. & Julia M. Wallace Died October 5, 1832 Age 3 years and 21 days.

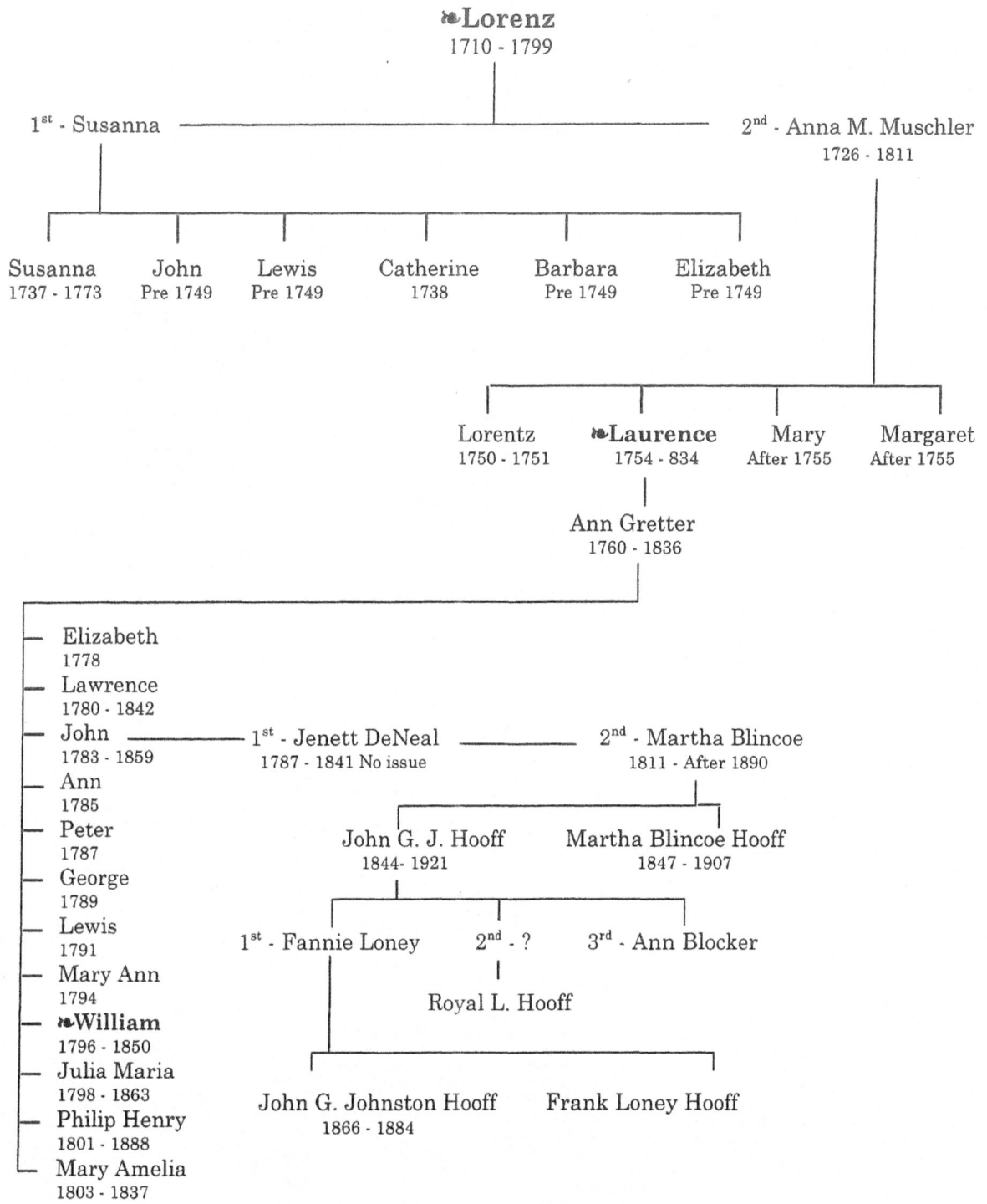

Lorenz
1710 - 1799

1st - Susanna ———————————————————————————————— 2nd - Anna M. Muschler
                                                                                                          1726 - 1811

Susanna	John	Lewis	Catherine	Barbara	Elizabeth
1737 - 1773	Pre 1749	Pre 1749	1738	Pre 1749	Pre 1749

Lorentz	**Laurence**	Mary	Margaret
1750 - 1751	1754 - 834	After 1755	After 1755

Ann Gretter
1760 - 1836

— Elizabeth
  1778
— Lawrence
  1780 - 1842
— John ——————— 1st - Jenett DeNeal ——————— 2nd - Martha Blincoe
  1783 - 1859   1787 - 1841 No issue   1811 - After 1890
— Ann
  1785
— Peter   John G. J. Hooff   Martha Blincoe Hooff
  1787   1844- 1921   1847 - 1907
— George
  1789
— Lewis   1st - Fannie Loney   2nd - ?   3rd - Ann Blocker
  1791
— Mary Ann   Royal L. Hooff
  1794
— **William**
  1796 - 1850
— Julia Maria   John G. Johnston Hooff   Frank Loney Hooff
  1798 - 1863   1866 - 1884
— Philip Henry
  1801 - 1888
— Mary Amelia
  1803 - 1837

John Hooff

Res: S.W. Corner of Prince and Lee Street, Alexandria

Born: January 10, 1783 in Alexandria, D.C.
Christened/Baptized:
Married: December 14, 1805 (Thursday) by Rev. Kemp at the residence of Jennett's father.
Died: November 21, 1859 in Alexandria, D.C., age 76.
Buried: St. Paul's Episcopal Church Cemetery, Alexandria, D.C.
Father: Laurence Hooff II   Mother: Ann Gretter

Spouse: 1st - Jennett DeNeal
Born: 1787 in Alexandria, D.C.
Christened/Baptized:
Died: October 30, 1841, age 54
Buried: St. Paul's Episcopal Church Cemetery, Alexandria, D.C. The tombstone reads: "In memory of Jennett Hooff who departed this life on the 30th day of October 1841, age 54 years." St. Paul's records show burial of Mrs. Jennett Hooff, November 1, 1841. Jennett and John had no children.
Father: William DeNeal of Fairfax County

Spouse: 2nd - Martha J. Blincoe (sister of Elizabeth Blincoe, 2nd wife of Philip Henry Hooff).
Born: 1811
Christened/Baptized:
Married: November 30, 1843 in Leesburg, VA
Died: After 1890
Father: Samson Blincoe   Mother: Martha Jones

Martha J. Hooff was a party to the pre-martial agreement entered into by Philip Henry Hooff and Elizabeth Blincoe, Martha's sister.

A document recorded January 24, 1895 (Will Book C, page 166, Loudoun County, VA) states that a curator was appointed for Martha Hooff, deceased.

They had two children:

John G. Johnston Hooff - Born September 2, 1844. Baptized at St. Paul's November 14, 1844. See a separate chapter on page #35.

Martha Blincoe Hooff - Born July 26, 1847 and baptized at St. Paul's on August 15, 1847. Married Aquila Brooke Beall on May 8, 1873 at Emmanuel Church in Baltimore, MD. She died in 1907. They had five children:

Upton Beall

Brook Beall

John Hooff Beall - married Floyd Clement Shipley (female named Floyd) and had 1 daughter named Floyd Brooke Beall who married Allen Clyde Spencer, no issue.

Louise Beall - who died in 1949

Mattie Brooke Beall - who died in Washington, D.C. and is buried in Baltimore, MD. Never married.

Obituary - "Miss Mattie B. Beall, 69, of Old Southern Family: Miss Mattie Brooke Beall, 69, retired Internal Revenue Bureau employee and one of the last members of an old Southern family, died yesterday in her home at the Argonne Apartments, 1629 Columbia Rd., N.W. She had been ill since last January. Miss Beall had spent 33 years in the tax bureau, where she was a clerk. She was retired from the bureau last March. Her only survivor is a niece, Mrs. Allen C. Spencer, 5021 N. 24th St., Arlington. Possessions that had been in her family for generations were given Miss Beall in recent years were donated by her to the Woodlawn Plantation at Mt. Vernon. Among these were a bracelet made from coffee beans grown on George Washington's farm, two knife boxes that had been originally at Mt. Vernon, and a 72-piece London Transfer tea set of soft porcelain, 200 years old. Miss Beall's parents, natives of Alexandria, were Aquila Brooke Beall and the former Martha Blincoe Hooff. Funeral services will be held at 11:00 a.m. tomorrow in Gawler's funeral home, 1756 Pa. Ave., N.W. Grave side services will be held at 1 p.m. in Baltimore."

Notes on John Hooff: John Hooff was engaged in the banking business in Alexandria for over 40 years, first as an officer of the Bank of Alexandria, later as cashier of Farmers' Bank. The Farmers' Bank occupied the 1st floor of the dwelling at the corner of Prince and Water (now Lee) Streets. John and his family lived on the upper two floors (the house believed to have been owned at one time by Lawrence Hooff, Jr. and John Hooff). He entered into several documents in Loudoun County, VA in connection with the Blincoe family, as well as others. In 1804 he was Secretary of Washington-Alexandria Lodge No. 22. In January of 1810 he was appointed to the 1st vestry of St. Paul's Church, and in 1820 was one of the Trustees of the church. John served briefly in the War of 1812.

Obituary: "John Hooff, son of Lawrence (II), was born at Alexandria January 10, 1783. At an early period of his life he was appointed an officer in the "Bank of Alexandria" and on the organization of the "Farmers' Bank of Alexandria," became it's cashier, which position he retained until the bank was merged into the "Exchange Bank of Virginia," when he became the cashier of it's Alexandria branch. In this position he remained until the 19th day of November 1859, when he died, in the 77th year of his age. He was over forty years a bank cashier, and during all this period enjoyed the confidence and respect of the community. His brothers Lewis and Philip Henry H. survived him."

Per *Leesburg, VA, Loudoun County Courthouse*: Married November 30, 1843, John Hooff to Martha I. Blincoe, Minister William N. Ward, Gospel In Protestant, Episcopal Church.

Alexandria Gazette, 1816 and 1837: Notice. The Farmers' Bank of Alexandria this day declares a dividend of profits upon its capital stock pain in, of four per cent for the last six months, payable to stockholders or their representatives, on the third instant.

By order of the Board
John Hooff, Cashier

1837 - FOR RENT-That pleasantly situated three story Brick Dwelling, at the corner of King and Columbia Streets. Possession given on the first of April next. Apply to John Hooff.

WANTED. A Sexton for St. Paul's Church. Apply to John Hooff.

A silhouette of John Hooff by Issac Todd, 1804, is in the Relic Room of the George Washington Memorial Lodge, Alexandria, VA.

John Hooff
1783 - 1859

John Hooff (1783-1859) by Isaac
Todd, 1804 (Relic Rm., George
Washington Memorial Lodge, Alex-
andria, Va.

House occupied by John Hooff at 200 Prince Street, Alexandria, VA until 1859.
After 1859 by Lewis Hooff. Farmers Bank was on the 1st floor.

John G. Johnston Hooff

Born: September 2, 1844 in Alexandria, VA
Christened/Baptized: Nov. 14, 1844 at St. Paul's Episcopal Church, Alexandria, D.C.
Married:
Died: April 20, 1921 in Bedford, VA. Age 78
Buried: St. Paul's Episcopal Church Cemetery (family vault).
Plaque reads: "Rest in Peace, John G. Hooff, born September 2, 1844, died April 20, 1921, C.S.A."
Father: John Hooff   Mother: Martha (J.) Blincoe

Spouse: 1st - Fannie (Loney or Douthitt), later secretary to Bishop of Episcopal Diocese, Western Pennsylvania Division.

They had two children:

> John Johnston Hooff - Born September 1866 in Baltimore, MD. Baptized November 16, 1866 at St. Paul's. Died May 27, 1884? Unmarried.

> Frank Loney Hooff - Born in Baltimore, MD; had 1 child, Virginia Loney Hooff who was a school teacher in Pittsburg, PA; never married.

Spouse: 2nd - (?) There was one child of this marriage:
Royal L. Hooff

Spouse: 3rd - Anna R. Blocher of Wilmington, Delaware (NOTE - Betty Lemons who did the first genealogy book on Hooff, and Wilson L. Hooff, stated that Anna R. Blocher was the wife of Royal L. - there was also a note which is typed below, stating that Anna was married to John G.J. Hooff. We cannot verify this information either way. On January 4, 1996 I went to Upper Marlboro and read Anna R. Hoff's (Bloucher) will/file. There was no indication or mention of John as being her husband or any child by her. The only mention in her will were some friends and a John O. Zorn, who contested the will. The court recognized him as her common-law husband. There was no mention of her age, date of birth, or the name of the family plot in Wilmington, DE, that she requested to be buried in after she was cremated. Anna was an employee of Larkins Products at the time of her marriage to John G.J. Hooff. She died in 1951 and was buried in the family plot in Riverview Cemetery, Wilmington, DE.

John G.J. Hooff attended Episcopal High School in Alexandria. He joined the Confederate Army in 1862 and attained the rank of Major 4th Chesapeake Battery of Maryland, attached to the staff of Gen. Pendleton. He was a member of R.E. Lee Camp, Confederate Veterans, Alexandria, VA, as well as several other organizations.

John G.J. Hooff was employed by Stabler Grocers in Baltimore, MD. In 1871 he lived at 46 Bolton Street, Baltimore, MD. He later moved to Pittsburg, PA., leaving his family in Baltimore. He is believed to have married twice more.

We also found that he was an employee of Larkin Products, then in 1903 was manager of Lamont Corliss Co., 625 F. St., Washington, D.C. (Royal Hooff was listed as clerk with the firm). The D.C. Directories for the years 1909 through 1913 list John G. Hoff Co., agents, manufacturers and brokers at 200a Q St., Washington, D.C. Royal was listed at the same address in 1913.

Obituary, April 1921: "Major John G. Hoff, a veteran of the Confederate Army, and a former Washington business man, died Wednesday at the Elks' National Home in Bedford, VA. He is survived by his wife, Mrs. Annette Hoff, who lives at 1717 Willard St., N.W., and one son, Royal L. Hoff. Major Hoff was one of the most prominent members of the Elks' organization in Washington. His health broke down about eight years ago following his retirement from the importing and exporting business. He went to a number of sanitariums, but his condition became worse. Some time ago he went to the Elks' home. He was born in Alexandria, VA, seventy-eight years ago. The family originally came to Virginia from Holland, and spelled the name "HOOFF". At the outbreak of the Civil War he enlisted in the Confederate Army, and was rapidly promoted until he attained the position of major. After the war he came to Washington and entered business. Major Hoff was a member of the Masonic Fraternity, the Confederate Veterans' Association, and Washington Lodge No. 15, B.P.O.E. The latter organization will conduct the funeral. Services will be held at Lee's undertaking establishment at 7:30 o'clock tonight. Interment will be the family burying ground at Alexandria."

John G. Johnston Hooff (1844)
4th Battery, Maryland Artillery

U.S. Archives microfilm #321, roll #13.

After researching various records we have concluded that John G.J. Hooff enlisted in the 4th Battery, Maryland Artillery on April 14, 1862 at the age of 18 years and 7 months as a private. Captured at Appomattox Court House April 10, 1865 as a Captain and aide de camp to General Pendelton. Took oath of allegiance at Harpers Ferry on May 25, 1865. Nothing can found to show his date of appointment to captain or aide de camp C.S.A. He died at the Elks home in Bedford, Va. on April 20, 1921. His obituary stated that he was a Major. Member of R.E. Lee Camp of the S.C.V. Alex. Va. and Elks #15 Lodge Washington, D.C.

Company Muster Roll

November 18, 1862 -	Was on debility from Chesapeake Battery Maryland until January 8, 1863. Listed as private. He was at C.S.A. General Hospital, Charlottesville, VA.
May/June 1863 -	Appears on company muster roll as private in Capt. Wm. D. Brown's Co., Andrews' Batt'n, Light Artillery.* Enlisted April 14, 1862 in Richmond by Capt. Forrest for 3 years or war.

*This company was organized January 1, 1862 as Capt. Joseph Forrest's Company of Virginia Artillery (Chesapeake Artillery). Subsequently it became a part of Andrews' Battalion of Light Artillery as a Maryland company under command of Capt. Wm. D. Brown and Lieut. Walter S. Chew. Still later it became the 4th Maryland Battery and served as a part of McIntosh's Artillery Battalion. These two battalions were composed of batteries from various States which subsequently served as independent commands.

Sept/Oct 1863 -	Appears on company muster roll of Lt. Walter S. Chew's Co., Andrews' Batt'n., Light Artillery.
July 22, 1864 -	Appears on receipt roll for clothing.
July 26, 1864 -	Appears on receipt roll for clothing.
August 29, 1864 -	Appears on receipt roll for clothing.
Sept. 30, 1864 through Dec. 31 1864 -	4th Maryland Battery Arty, was paid $57.
Sept/Oct 1864 -	Appears on company muster roll as absent on sick furlough
November 1, 1864 -	Private Hooff from McIntosh's Batt MD was in C.S.A. General Hospital, Charlottesville, VA. For neuralgia. He as returned to duty January 5, 1865.
Nov/Dec 1864 -	Listed on company muster roll as absent and sick at C.S.A. General Hospital, Charlottesville, VA.
Jan/Feb 1865 -	Company muster roll shows him present.

John G. Hooff, Major, 4th Chesapeake Artillery Battery

John J. Hooff, General and Staff Officers Corps, Divisions and Brigade Staffs, Non-Coms, Staffs and Bands, Enlisted Men, Staff Departments, CSA, Capt. and A.D.C.

Some of the letters written by John G. Johnston Hooff while in the Civil War, and his mother, have been preserved and are in the possession of Ann Hooff-Kline. Verbatim copies of those letters follow.

Letters of John G. Johnston Hooff
Major, Confederate States Army

Letter from John G. Johnston Hooff to his sister Mattie (Martha)

Camp Near Milford
March 14th 1863

Early's (not Ewell's) Division, Jackson's Corps

Dear Sister

I have first received your most welcome and anxiously expected letter of the 12th inst. With a P.S. by Ma. Oh! I am so thankful and glad that she is so much better. I hope and pray that the ever merciful God will yet spare her to use - do be careful and don't let her expose herself or do anything that will retard her recovery. Mrs. E. Will do everything for you that she can.

Now about the letters - the last one (but this) that I received from you was dated the 4th and received on the 10th. I had written to you on the 9th but answered yours of the 7th as soon as received (10th) and mailed it on the 11th. Why it is that you do not receive my letters regularly I cannot tell. I directed both to the care of Miss Leaton - they may come to hand after awhile.

Oh! How I do wish that I could be with you to get things for Ma - but such a thing is impossible non but Capt. Brown's favorite can get furloughs. I displeased him I think by voting for Lieut. Roberts instead of his favorite Mr. Harvey of Richmond at the recent election. Speaking in reference to the high prices of articles in Charlottesville I don't think that they can possibly be higher there than here - six eggs $1 per doz Pork $1 per lb - Bacon $1.50 - Butter $1.50 Meal $5 per bush - no vegetables to be bought for love or money. Our rations are Flour, Sugar, Rice Salt and enough fat pork to make grease to go in our bread - no meat or vegetables -now you have our bill of fare - viz Breakfast Bread & Rice - Dinner Rice & Bread. Be sure and get Ma to go out to Mrs. E's as soon as the Doctor thinks she can do so without running any risk. Do you want to know who I wrote to in Balto.? Do you think it would do you any good if I was to tell you? If so I will, it was Miss A,B,C,D,E & c&c. When does Mrs. E. Think she can send my box to me - I hope soon - I am glad to learn that you are making a neadle case for me. I hope you will put some large neadles in it as I brought only small ones and if had not previously had some 1 or 2 large ones I don't know what I would have done. I will enclose the small ones that I brought with me with one or two exceptions in this letter as they are of no use to me - please send me a darning neadle a large one too. I would give anything in the world to know what has produced such a change in Miss Bettie H - try and find out, some person must have told some stories on either you or me. I should like very much to have heard Miss Eliza telling about her troubles with the waters. It must indeed have been funny - please give my love to her also to Mr. & Mrs. I & my regards to Mrs. E. You ask me a question that can not be answered, "when do you expect to be ordered away" - Flora can tell you just as well as I can. I heard Capt. Brown say that he did not expect we would leave here for a month yet as there is every indication that the Enemy will attempt to cross at Frederickburg again, how long it may _____ I can not tell. There is one thing certain and that is this is next to my last sheet of paper. I have one or 2 more envelopes left. Easter is some distance off and I am afraid that before that time we will be leaving here. Please ask Ma if she knows where Vowel Hooff is at and what rank he holds if she does not please try & find out. But I must stop now, love to Ma - please remember me to all my friends & I remain with a heart full of Love

Your Affectionate
Bro John

Letter from John G.J. Hooff to his Mother, Martha

In Position near Hamilton Crossing
May 3rd 1863 3 P.M. Sunday

Dear Ma

I am safe thus far - were engaged yesterday morning for an hour - one wounded & this morning for about 2 hours, 4 wounded, 1 since dead. I have escaped unhurt & am quite well. Love to all I will write again as soon as possible.

In haste

Charley is safe
Your Loving & Obt. Son Jno J. Hooff

Letter from John G.J. Hooff to his Mother, Martha

Camp near Hamilton Crossing
R.F&P.R.R, May 9th 1863

Dear Ma

I wrote to you on the 29th of April from out winter quarters, on the 3rd of May from the heights before Fredericksburg and one from G_____neys Station dated the 7th. We had been sent there after ammunition and are now back to our Camp about ½ mile from Hamilton's Crossings or Station. Your dear letter of the 29th of April has just reached me and I hasten to answer it, knowing how anxious you are about me. Thanks to all Merciful God I am safe and well. Charley is well but was kicked on his nose between the eyes by one of the horses - the bones were broken but is getting on finely and hope it will be all right again shortly. He is sitting by my side, writing also.

We first went into action on Saturday morning about 9 A.M. We had redoubts to fight behind. I never was in a hotter place in my life. You could not place a stick upright in the ground as thick as my arm without it being knocked down in an instant. We ceased firing in about 3 hours. The enemy had 20 guns of heavy caliber firing on us for at the least 5 hours. It was nothing but a continual buz! buz!! buz!!! Wha! Wha!! Wha!!! all the time & when they would hit anything you hear Zip! Zip!! Zip!!! We had one man wounded his leg was cut entirely off, just above the ankle. He was standing by my side when it happened. I had just brought up an arm full of shells & had set them down & was looking at the fire of the enemy's guns when I observed his fall and some one called to me to tie my handkerchief around his leg which I did immediately & he was carried off the field. He is getting on very well. At last the enemy ceased firing and we were allowed to rest quietly for the night. Next morning we received orders to move & take a new position to the left of the one of the previous day. There it was just as hot - we had 4 men wounded going on the field. The enemy were keeping up a continual roar to prevent us from going into position but they could not do it & we soon opened fire & compelled them to cease. One of our men wounded on this day died the next - one Monday. We were under the enemies fire all day without being allowed to fire a single shot - the next and the day after we were marching all day, but now at last we are allowed to rest for a few days at the least. I intend writing to Mr. McVeigh as soon as I finish this & tell him to send the Substitute if he has got one as soon as possible - for fear we might move. I hope he has got one.

Note: Last pages missing.

Diary kept by John G.J. Hooff, July 1863, Gettysburg, PA (first four pages missing)

<u>Saturday 4th July</u> 2 of our guns were ordered into position about 6 A.M. - Nos. 3 & 4 - the other two guns Nos. 1 & 2 (No. 1 is my gun) not having men enough left to work them remained where they were. Had quite a heavy shower this morning and still continues cloudy at 9 A.M. A heavy rain about 2 P.M.. And continued all night. About 8 P.M. our two guns came back and we all moved off. Took the Fairfield road (retiring) but did not march for remained in the road all night. Capt. Brown & his Bro with James Older who were wounded and not able to be moved together with H. Buckmaster & Charley tinges who were left with them to take care of them - were left behind and are by this time prisoners in the enemies hands. Received 3 letters from Ma today dated June 19, 21st & 25th which I will answer as soon as possible.

<u>Sunday 5th July</u> still raining at 9 A.M. at which time we moved off towards Fairfield, which we made about 4 P.M. The roads are very muddy, & we were thereby compelled to march slowly. About 4 P.M. a small force of the enemy had gotten so close upon us as to open upon us with his Artillery but did very little damage. 2 of our pieces Nos. 3 & 4 were ordered into position. The others kept on and went into park at the foot of the South Mountain and about 1 mile from the village of Fairfield. Our 2 guns came back shortly after we had gotten into park. We were compelled to leave one of our caissons behind for want of horses, but before doing so we destroyed it. Charley Tinges was left behind with our wounded today near Gettysburg and is by this time a prisoner.

<u>Monday 6th July</u> moved off about 5 A.M. towards the mountains and stoped to graze our horses for a sort time. Passed by the Calidonia Springs about 3 P.M. and the Monteray Springs shortly after and reached the village of Wainsborough about 6 P.M. and turned off to the left and went into park for the night. We had

sent out a foraging party early in the morning and they have just returned bringing with them corn & chop stuff for the horses and corse corn meal for the men. All our wagons have either been captured or have gone on towards Williamsport so we have nothing to eat but what we can press from the citizens - a hog was stol for each company tonight. Made my supper of fresh pork & veal & corn bread. In or _____ the mountains saw where the enemy had captured and burnt a good many of our wagons.

Tuesday 7th July Moved off at 6 A.M. and went back to the village of Wainsborough and took the Hagerstown road. Made my breakfast off of fresh port & veal & cornbread. Marched to within 3 miles of Hagerstown Md. And stoped on the road to cook 1 days rations. Heard there was a severe fight in the town yesterday evening principally cavalry. We shiped the enemy and drove them back. Heard today that our wagons are all safe near Williamsport, Md. After cooking rations about 5 P.M. we move off to the right about 1/4 mile and went into park unhitched and unharnessed.

Wednesday 8th July Still at the same place. Commenced raining about 12 M last night and continued up to 2 P.M. today. All quiet. Slept out in the rain last night with my oil cloth thrown over me. Only got my feet wet. About 3 P.M. it cleared off and we cooked 1 days rations of flour and beef. All quiet.

Thursday 9th July Still at the same place. All quiet so far. Washed some of my clothes today. The first time that I ever did anything of the kind. There was a very heavy dew last night, but all continues quiet. Cooked one days ration of flour.

Friday 10th July About 4 A.M. received orders to harness & hitch up and be ready to move at a moment's notice. About 10 A.M. moved off towards Hagerstown Md. To change camp. Marched about one mile and went into park in a nice Camp. Unhitched and unharnessed and turned the horses out to graze, but in about on 1/4 of a hour orders came to hitch & harness up and be ready to move at a moments notice - drew one days ration of flour, no meat and had just commenced to cook when orders came to move off immediately. We started and remained in the road untill 5 P.M. when we again moved off in the direction of Hagerstown, Md. And passed through that city about 8 P.M. and marched about 2 miles when we went into park for the night and about 12 M finished cooking our rations. Heard today that Capt. Brown was certainly dead.

Saturday 11th July Got ready to move about 4 A.M. at a moments notice, but remained stationary untill about 9 ½ A.M. when we moved off and halted in a field on the right hand side of the Hagerstown & Williamsport road facing and about 2 miles from the former City and behind our Infantry which are in line. Our line extends six miles to the left resting near Hagerstown Md. The right on the Potomac. 2 Divisions are on our left. We are facing the City of Hagerstown - 12 M - heavy firing of Artillery on the right - said to be Gen A.P. Hills. 7 P.M. heavy skirmishing on the right - our men are throwing up fortifications along the whole line both for Artillery and Infantry. Had general orders from Gen. Lee dated today read to use about 7 1/2 P.M. encouraging us and congratulating us upon our previous fighting and good behavior during the recent fights and fatiguing marches.

Sunday 12th July 1863 Everything remained quiet last night. Moved off about 6 A.M. and marched back about one mile waiting for orders to take position Are now on the left of the Hagerstown road. 10 A.M. heard heavy firing on the right, but it soon ceased. 2 P.M. all quiet and ready to move at a moments notice. All the other batteries of our battalion are in position together with most all the reserve Artillery strange to say for they are always in the rear during a fight and in front during a retreat. We only carry in 3 guns. Have sent the 4th one No. 2 to the rear with the wagons as we have not enough men left to man it. Rations for 3 days including today were cooked by one man for each mess and brought up to us this morning. We are now still about 2 miles from Hagerstown, Md. - are said to be in reserve. 7 P.M. heavy skirmishing in front - believe that we drove the enemies skirmishers back. 10 P.M. all quiet - 'tis cloudy and looks like rain. Still continue in readiness to move at a moments notice. Received a letter from Ma dated the 21st and mailed from Charlestown, Va. By Dr. Alexander on the 6th of July.

Monday 13th 7 A.M. Still remain at the same place - did not rain last night. Skirmishing in front ready to move at a moments notice -raining a little. 10 A.M. Skirmishing in front very heavily has stoped raining but continues cloudy. 4 1/4 P.M. our caissons were ordered off to the rear and our 3 pieces were left to help protect the crossing of the Army over the Potomac. Moved off our 3 pieces about 7 P.M. towards

Williamsport Md and passed through that place about 10 P.M. and took a road running parallel with the Potomac and about due East South East.

Tuesday 14th July Have been marching all night and made the Potomac about 6 miles below Williamsport Md about 9 A.M. this morning and crossed the river on pontoons immediately for the first time and went into park about 1 mile from the river but did not remain over 3 hours when we moved off towards Martinsburg and went into park for the night - about 4 miles from the City. 6 P.M. the Army has al crossed some time since - all
quiet - the enemy have not attempted to follow us. Had a heavy shower about 5 P.M. but did not last long - drew & cook two days rations of flour & one of beef. All quiet.

Wednesday 15th July Moved off about 8 A.M. but did not march over 1 mile before we stoped alongside of the road for about 3 hours. Then we moved off towards Martinsburg, Va. And passed through that place about 3 P.M. and took the Winchester road and made Darksville Berkley Co. About 7 P.M. and went into park near the village having marched about 11 miles. Saw Miss Bettie but did not have an opportunity to speak to her. I saw her in her parlor talking to 2 young gentlemen and thought that I was entirely too muddy and dirty to go into ladies company. Now my dear Ma I must stop. We are making towards Winchester, Va.

Letter from John G.J. Hooff to his Mother, Martha

The fight at this place is over. I am safe and well. Charley Tinges the same. Charley Ward killed. Charley T is a prisoner.

> Bivou, 4 miles South East of
> Gettysburg, Penn.
> Sunday, 5th July 12 M

Dear Ma
   We have just parked for a short time to allow some of the troops to pass and avail myself of that time to try and write you a few lines. First. The fight of Gettysburg is over. I am well and safe, so is Charley T, thanks to the almerciful God. We had 4 killed and 9 wounded, including Capt. Brown & Lieut. Roberts, the former dangerously, and now with his brother a prisoner in the Yankey lines, also Charley Tinges, lost 10 horses. The battalion lost 70 killed & wounded including Major Lateman of Va. Who has been since Co. Andrews was wounded, our commanding officer. I have been in many hot fight but this one exceed all When I saw Capt. Brown fall I though that every one would be killed - he was on horseback at the time, cheering our boys up when he was struck. I saw him first before going into action raise up his haversack and drink something out of a canteen which he had in there and I think it was whiskey as I know he was trying to get some that morning and had sent for it but I could not swear that it was whiskey that I say him drink, but I certainly am sure that he was intoxicated or rather heated with some intoxicating liquor when we went into action, but he has paid dearly for it. He will lose one leg and the other will never be able for him to walk upon even if he recovers which all think very doubtful. He was not able to be moved so we were obliged to leave him & his brother who is also wounded in the Yankey hands - with one man to attend to them - I don't expect ever to see him again. Lieut. Plater is now the commanding officer of our Battery. He is as upright & honorable as a man can be - - never drinks. Lieut. Roberts was wounded in both arms and side - and hope he will get well soon. We had only 14 pieces engaged and the Yankees 50 - they also had the best position and were behind entrenchments - they threw shot of every description and size. They disabled three of our guns in about an hour which left us only one. It was my gun & it was the last one that fired - they blew up one of the 1st Maryland Battery casson killing one man & wounding several - the fight commenced bout 5 P.M. on Thursday 2nd of July & continued until six. When we drew off and the infantry charged the Yankey redoubts took them but could not hold them. We are now falling back to get them off from their intrenchments which if we succeed in doing I think we will gain a splendid victory. Our loss is heavy. About 10,000 killed & wounded. Must stop now have orders to move. Will finish some other time. Love to all
> Your devoted Son
> Jno Hooff

No. 1 From Bivouc Near Gettysburg, Pa.
5th July after the Battle

Letter from John G.J. Hooff to his Mother, Martha

Camp near the Orange & Alex. R.R.
2 ½ miles from Bristo Station and
14 from Centerville, October 17th, 1863

Dear Ma

At last I have an opportunity of writing a few lines to you. We have been doing such active service of late that I have not hardly had time to sleep or eat. I was in the engagement of the 14, and thanks be to the all merciful God I am again spared to you. I can not possibly see how men can go into an engagement and not perceive the interposition of the hand of the merciful God. When the iron hailes around them what keeps them from being cut in pieces but the allmerciful hand of god - and indeed it is wonderful to see how many escape, under his protection. Every one should return thanks to him for sparing their lives through so many dangers - but now dear MA as I have not time to write much I will haste and give you an account of our march and fight from the day we left the Rapidann River. I mailed a letter to you as we passed through Orange C.H. - which I hope you have received ere this.

Friday 9th Revielee at 4 A.M. Moved off at 6 for Orange C.H. en route for a ford on the Rappidan River beyond that place - passed through Orange C.H. about 4 P.M. turned to the right and about 6 P.M. crossed the Rapidann at Barneys ford and went into park 6 miles on the other side in Madison Co. about 11 P.M.

Saturday 10th Had no revielee, were awakened at 4 A.M. - moved off at 5 ½ A.M. - on the road towards Madison C.H. but soon turned off and passed to the left of that place about 1 P.M. and crossed the Robenson River at _____ about 3 P.M. it commenced raining just as we reached the river, but soon ceased. Went into park about 9 P.M. 6 miles from the river - has cleared off.

Sunday 11th Revielee at 5 A.M. - moved off at 6 ½ P.M. Gen's. Lee and Penelton passed us soon after starting - there was heavy firing yesterday evening in the direction of Culpepper C.H. but ceased about dark and has been discontinued ever since. Stewart had a fight with his Cavalry & Artillery on our right flank - which accounts for the firing heard yesterday - he drove the enemy some distance. I think that we are making a flank movement. We are to the left of Culpepper C.H., traveling N.E. about 3 P.M. went into park about 6 miles from Culpepper C.H. on the Valley turnpike to New Market to Gordonsville. 10 P.M. the wagons have just gotten up. We have had nothing to eat today. We now at 10 P.M. have orders to cook 3 days rations and be in readiness to move at 2 A.M. tomorrow. When we are to sleep I can not tell as we will not be through cooking by 2 A.M. tomorrow. Cooking utencils are so very scarce.

Monday 12th Reviele at 1 A.M. - but did not move untill 6 A.M. Crossed the turnpike to Culpepper and passed to the left of that village - passed through Rixeysville about 2 P.M. en route for Warrenton White Sulpher Springs. Crossed the Hazel river at Hazel River Ford about 3 P.M. - passed through Jeffersonville about 5 P.M. and went into park within a ½ mile of the Rappahannock River nearly opposite the Warrenton Springs about 7 P.M. Stewart captured today 500 prisoners. Saw about 200 of them principally Cavalry. They had no infantry here.

Tuesday 13th Reviele at 5 A.M. Moved off about 6 and crossed the Rappannock River at the ford opposite the Warrenton Springs. Passed through the Springs about 7 A.M. en route for Warrenton Springs. Gens. Lee, Ewell & Penelton again passed us this morning at the Springs. Reached Warrenton about 10 A.M. and went into park on the south eastern part of the town. Went into town and called on Mrs. Berkley Ward and also Mrs. Dr. Jno Ward. Saw Mrs. Sally Washington also. The Mrs' Ward were very kind and desired to be remembered with love to you. They would not let me go untill I had _____ was packed with as many niceties as I could carry - wanted me to come to see them and stay as often & and long as I could. They are greatly reduced - all their Servants have ran off - they have to cook for themselves - just to see Sue Ward making bread it was a sight. They said that our money was no use to them and could only live by selling milk and such little things.

<u>Wednesday 14th</u> Reviele at 5 A.M. - moved off at 6 towards Centerville and came up with the enemy about 9 A.M. between 3 & 5 miles from Warrenton - 8 pieces of our Battalion including our 2 went in and took a position chosen for us by Gen. Lee himself and he standing near during the whole fight, and opened on the enemy distant 3/4 of a mile. They replied immediately but in an hour we drove them off. The loss on our side was but 2 slightly wounded - none hurt in our Battery. We ceased firing in about 1 ½ hours after we opened (the enemies loss is said to be heavy) and drew off and reformed our Battalion & Division and then continued our march towards Centerville. The enemy are in full retreat. Meade is taking great care of his wagons and stores. We again came up with them about 14 miles from Centerville at 5 P.M. Gen. A.P. Hill has been fighting and pressing them hard all day. They hold their ground upon the Rail Road tonight. In yesterdays fight I escaped merely by a miracle. I saw a ball coming toward me and tried to dodge it, but it seemed that is was bound to follow me, but just before it reached me for some means I can not tell it was diverted from its course - it must have been by the hand of God and I escaped. This all occured in less than an instant. 10 P.M. Gen. Hill's infantry are fighting very hard in front, we are now on a part. of todays battlefield, expecting to be ordered to take position every moment.

<u>Thursday 15th</u> Reviele at 5 A.M. Moved off about 7th and marched about ½ mile and went into park on yesterdays battlefield - 14 miles from Centerville & 2 ½ from Bristo Station near the Orange & Alex. R.R. Our troups are busily engaged taring up the R.R., am on guard tonight.

<u>Friday 16th</u> Still at the same place all quiet. The enemy have fallen back towards Alexandria - don't think that we will follow them any farther.

<u>Saturday 17th</u> Still at same place - all quiet - no news

Now Dear Ma I think that I have told you all the news and I hope that we will soon go into a permanent camp, where I will have a plenty of time to write. How do you like Dr. Cook's. I suppose that you are there _____ this. I hope you are enjoying yourself. <u>I am Safe & Well</u>. I am very anxious to hear from you. I expect that we will move tomorrow (fallen back) - forage is so scarce about here but I must stop now. Please give my love to Mr. & Mrs Johnston & Miss Eliza - remember me kindly to Mrs. Offutt & the other ladies. My regards to Miss Rida & Miss Frazier. Love to Ginnie W and I remain with a heart full of love

> With the Greatest respect & Affection
> Your Obediant Son
> Jno J. Hooff

Letter from John G.J. Hooff to his mother, Martha

> In position near Mine Run
> Orange Co. VA November 29th 1863

Dear Ma

I received your & dear Sister's letters of the 22nd some days since but have not had an opportunity to answer them as yet. I write this to let you know that I am well and safe and hope that by the interposition of divine Providence I may be spared through the impending battle. We have been laying in front and with 3/4 mile of the enemy for the last 2 days but they do not fire upon us and we are not allowed as yet to fire upon them. We have not been engaged as yet - but would not be surprised if tomorrow would bring on a general engagement along the whole line - if they do not attack us we will attack them before tomorrow eve. Our whole battalion was near being captured day before yesterday but were saved by our infantry - the enemy ambuscaded us on the road leading to Fredericksburg and in the northern part of "the Wilderness" (of Charlottesville notoriety May 1863). We threw up redoubts in front of our guns this morning. I must close now. Will write as soon again as possible. Love to all

> In haste -
> Your obt. Son
> Jno J. Hooff

Letter from John G.J Hooff to his Mother, Martha

Camp Chesapeake Battery on <u>Piquit</u>
At Morton's Ford Rapidann River
December 5, 1863

Dear Ma

All Well! & Safe! I wrote you on the 29th the day before the fight and mailed in on the morning of the same but before the firing had commenced and hope you have received it.

Dear Ma we have again fought the enemy and I through the interposition of Divine Providence am again spared through the dangers of another battle.

At 1 ½ A.M. on the morning of November 30th the enemy opened fire upon us on the west side of Mine Creek and about 3 or 4 miles from Germana Ford - they opened with from 14 to 20 guns, 6 of them heavy siege guns - 8 of them bearing direct upon our 2 pieces and the rest to our right every now & then giving us a cross fire. We only had about 8 guns engaged upon our side Col. Andrews's finding out that it was going to end in an Artillery duel ordered us to cease firing about an hour after it had begun. Our Battery lost neither man nor beast - not even wounded. The Lee Battery on our left lost Capt. Raine & 2 privates killed & 2 wounded on our right. Captain Carpenter's Battery lost 5 killed and wounded. The last two together with the 1st Md. Battery lost about 25 horses killed & disabled. We dismounted 2 of the enemies guns, one a siege gun - and it is supposed killed & wounded a great number of them as their ambulances were very busy during & after the fight.

Our whole Battalion was very near being captured on the 27th (see account in the Richmond Examiner of the 30th) whilst moving with our division towards Germana Ford. The enemy got upon our rear & flank before we were aware of it - and but for Gen. Stewart's Brigade would have been either killed captured. The 1st Md. & a section of Capt. Carpenter's Battery's were engaged and their loss was very heavy.

We are now on Piquit at Morton's Ford, but expect to be relieved in a day or two. The enemy finding us too strong for them have fallen back towards Culpepper C. House and I think all prospect of a fight vamposed(?) for the present at least if not for the winter. I hope so! We fooled the enemy this time. All our men began fortifying themselves at every new position they took even our Batter. Every time we moved, we would go to work as soon as we reached our new position and work all night, sometimes untill we had gotten a breast-work through which no Yankee shells could penetrate. This fooled them I think, they believing were much stronger than we really were. Throwing up fortifications is something we never did before. They certainly out-numbered us 2 if not 3 to one - we about 25,000 they from 60 - 70,000. I expect that it will not be long before we go into winter quarters & I should not be surprised if it were near Charlottesville at that! I hope so! I expect to be sent up in that direction on detached service shortly for a few days. I received yesterday the shirt & 2 pair of drawers sent by our Forage Sergent, for which please accept my earnest & warmest thanks. I was glad to see that you had also sent me some pieces. I patched my shirt this morning. You ought to have seen me doing it, but nevertheless I succeeded in mending the rent at any rat. I am trying to find out where Major Young is at so that I can get the things sent by Mr. Skinner. I will send to Orange C.H. by the first opportunity about the same.

I received your & Sister Mat's dear letter of the 22d some time since & should have answered it before but between marching and throwing up fortifications I have not had the time to do so. The same excuse must be made for your dear one of the 27th which I received on the 1st day after the fight. Dear Ma, do you know that one sentence in yours of the 22d gave me more strength on the battlefield than anything else "May God strengthen you to do your duty" those words seemed in front of me during the whole fight. I felt no more afraid than if I had been setting quietly in Camp. They seemed like some guardian angel hovering around me. The shells ere falling very thick and fast, bu I heeded them not. My Mother said do your duty! It was enough. I walked from the gun tot he limber(?) Bringing up ammunition. I saw nothing but the flash from the enemies guns. I heard nothing but "May God strengthen you to do your duty." Every one thought us unusual lucky. I hope you will be able to sell my gloves. Save the money and it will help to get me a pair of boots. I must give up the idea of getting guantles as I need something to cover my feet worse than my hands. I wish January was here so that I could get my clothing money - near $100. I hope you may succeed in getting Gen. E to have me detailed he has the power if he will use it. I have heard nothing from him as yet.

There is no possible chance of getting a furlough shortly. I wish I could hear from my Blanket Jacket, etc which I left in Bowling Green last Spring with Mr. Thomas Shumate. If Tinges should be going or any one else in that direction please get him to enquire for Mr. Thomas Shumate or Mrs. Bowler & get the articles that I left with the former at the Hotel when I pass through there last winter.

When Tinges comes down please send me some paper & envelopes & stamps as I am out of all, some kind friend helped himself to nearly all I had of the former. Please also sen one lb. Of chewing tobacco by him. I can not get any worth having here and even that is at too high a price. Don't forget about the articles left in Bowling Green. I have written and rewritten about them but can get no reply. I need the blanket very much.

Tell Tinges not to come down untill we get a little more settled or at least until he hears from me. I must now close, so good bye, love to all. Remember me to all enquiring friends & with a heartfull of love I remain in haste

With the greatest respect & affection - Jno Hooff

Letter from John G.J. Hooff to his Mother, Martha

Camp of the Chesapeake Battery in
Position Before Petersburg
July 1st, 1864

My dearest Ma

I wrote to you on the 28th & again on the 29th, now for fear they should fail to reach you owing to the _____ in the mails, will still again. I wrote to you day before yesterday (29) to sell my black coat and appropriate the proceeds to buying me a pair of pants from the Government, if possible, as you can get them there much cheaper than in the Stores, and hope you will give it (coat) to your wash woman or some other trusty person to sell for you as soon as possible, and if you have any over buy me enough calico for one or two shirts. My coat ought to bring from $150 to $200 at the rate things are selling at present. I have tried again and again to draw a pair of pants from the Government, but find it impossible to get a pair did my life depend on it. If my coat does not bring enough sell also my black pants. Neither will be of any use to me as I will have outgrown them by the time I shall need such things, so much that it will be impossible for me to wear them even could I get them on - so they may as well to get me something that I can now wear and need.

I hope this fight will soon be over for it seems impossible that things can continue thus much longer. All day yesterday there was both Artillery and Infantry firing along the whole lines. We were firing at the average of every 10 minutes through the day up to 3 P.M. when a general engagement seemed to have taken place along the whole line occasioned report sayes by the enemy charging our works in the immediate front of Petersburg 3 times, but were each time repulsed with heavy loss. We then were firing as rapidly as possible and soon ran out of ammunition, 100+ odd rounds, but at night we were replenished and today have been laying quiet up to this time. 2 P.M. Yesterday the enemy were throwing mortar shells at us but thanks be to God we have had no one hurt, though at one time yesterday the shells were falling very fast and thick and being mortar shells there is no protection from them that we can make as they often fall right down in our pitts and the only way we can avoid them is to watch them when they are fired and run from under them if they happen to be coming towards you - there are 32 and 64 pounders - and when they explode it is in a thousand pieces - the latter 2 inches at a time - but I do not hear of any damage they have done the City except sending them through some unoccupied houses which are more exposed than others.

Some think that the great attack will come off on the 4th. If it does I hope it may be their final one and pray God that it will be a victory to our arms - and then I think there will be some prospect of peace, but if we should be so unfortunate as to lose the day I am afraid peace would be farther off than ever.

You may possibly imagine how actively we have been engaged since we left Hanover Junction on the 24th, when I tell you that my clothes were never so soiled in all my life. Not being able to do I could not get at my clothes and have only been able to take off my shirt wash it and hang it up to dry. My drawers I wear none, as the pair I had on were so far gone that I was compelled to cast them away and will have to go without any until I can get at my clothes which I hope will be shortly. They are in the rear chest of one of our caissons which have been in the rear all the time as we only dismount 3 chest and send the carriages & horses out of danger. I have just heard that there is a letter for me back at the carriages and I am going back there tonight to get it if possible hoping he has good news in it from you - and then I will be able to get my clothes - so good by until then.

Saturday, July 2d I had all my walk last night, back to the carriage, 2 miles for nothing the report that a letter was there for me proved to be a mistake, it was my letter to you of the 29 which had just been sent off and so I was compelled to walk back again without experiencing the great and _____ pleasure it always gives me to receive a letter from you. Oh! Dear Ma you can not possibly imagine one half my disappointment when I was told that it was a mistake and that there was none for me, but I had to swallow it as there was not possible help to be obtained, but I got my clothes which consisted of a soiled shirt and drawers, but not getting near so bad as the ones I had one. I took a good bath when I got and put them on and now feel much better and as soon as I can get some soap suitable for the purpose intent to try and wash them - and I hope I may succeed with them as well as I have done with most things I have attempted - for instance mending my pants. I have just gotten through putting two (2) good sized patches in my pants and think I have accomplished it well as all say so and it is my second attempt of the kind. I wish you could see them. I really think you would be surprised at my tailoring - my motto is that There is no such word as fail - do you not think it is a good one?

I made an effort yesterday to get a pass for 5 days to come and see you. _____ kindly forwarded my application, but I have not the least hope that it will be approved by Gen. Lee - if through God's mercy I should be so fortunate as to get it I will be greatly surprised, I tried it on the proverb that no risk no gain. As yet I have heard nothing from it and can only trust in God's mercy that I may get it approved. If so I shall come immediately, but do not put yourself to any trouble to get me a place to stay for there are 9 chances against 10 that I will not get it.

How is dear little Sister, dearer to me than ever. Oh! I hope and pray God that she has entirely recovered and is now quite well again. Dear Ma do know that her last two or 3 letters make me feel like the little one and like I should look up to her instead of her to me. I feel as if she was some years my senior - instead of being near 2 years younger.

Dear Ma do not get that haversack. I can do without it now, but do not forget to try and sell my coat, but Ma let me beg of you not to get me a pair of pants without you do sell it. I would have written to you before to sell it and send me a pair of pants but was afraid that you would buy me a pair without selling my coat and please do not do so now. But now I must close. Remember me to my friends and I must say good bye for the present and with a heart full of love I remain as ever

Your Affectionate Son
Jno J. Hooff

McIntosh's Artillery
3rd Corps

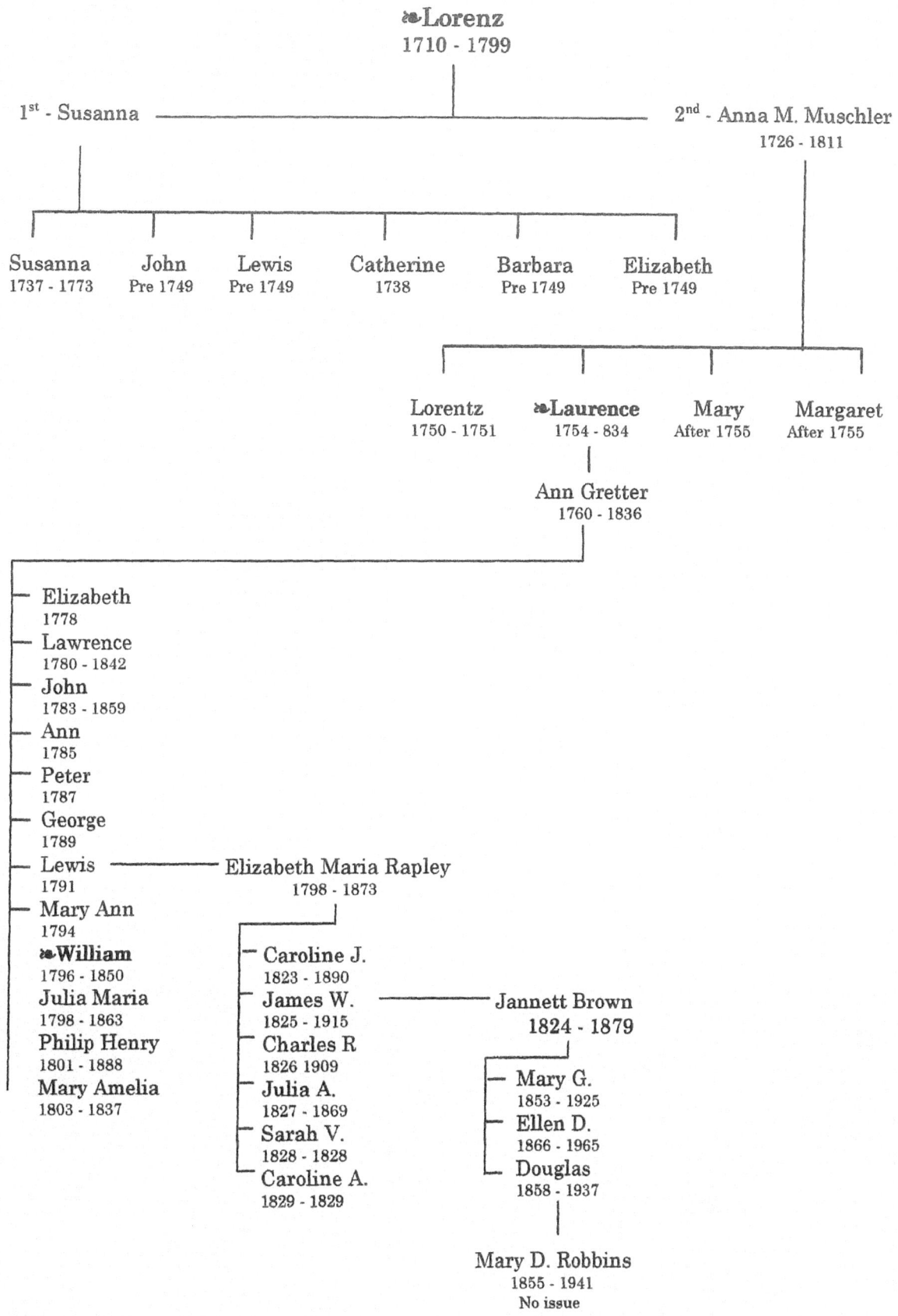

Lorenz
1710 - 1799

1st - Susanna ———————————————— 2nd - Anna M. Muschler
1726 - 1811

Susanna   John   Lewis   Catherine   Barbara   Elizabeth
1737 - 1773   Pre 1749   Pre 1749   1738   Pre 1749   Pre 1749

Lorentz   **Laurence**   Mary   Margaret
1750 - 1751   1754 - 834   After 1755   After 1755

Ann Gretter
1760 - 1836

Elizabeth
1778

Lawrence
1780 - 1842

John
1783 - 1859

Ann
1785

Peter
1787

George
1789

Lewis ——————— Elizabeth Maria Rapley
1791   1798 - 1873

Mary Ann
1794

William   Caroline J.
1796 - 1850   1823 - 1890

Julia Maria   James W. ——————— Jannett Brown
1798 - 1863   1825 - 1915   1824 - 1879

Philip Henry   Charles R
1801 - 1888   1826 1909

Mary Amelia   Julia A.   Mary G.
1803 - 1837   1827 - 1869   1853 - 1925

                   Sarah V.   Ellen D.
                   1828 - 1828   1866 - 1965

                   Caroline A.   Douglas
                   1829 - 1829   1858 - 1937

Mary D. Robbins
1855 - 1941
No issue

Lewis Hooff

Born: June 20, 1791 probably 521 Duke St., Alexandria, D.C.
Christened/Baptized:
Married: June 10, 1821 in Norfolk, VA
Died: June 1, 1874 in Alexandria, D.C., age 83.
Buried: St. Paul's Episcopal Church Cemetery, Alexandria, D.C.
Father: Laurence Hooff II   Mother: Ann Gretter

Spouse: Elizabeth Maria Rapley
Born: 1798 near Norfolk, VA
Died: September 16, 1873 in Alexandria, D.C.
Buried: St. Paul's Episcopal Church Cemetery, Alexandria, D.C.
Father: Abraham Rapley   Mother: Letitia Moon
    b: 1770   b: 1774
    d: September 4, 1854   d: December 15, 1848

They had six children:

Caroline Jannett Hooff - Born July 17, 1823 in Alexandria, D.C. She died November 8, 1890 in New York. She married William Lawrence Wallace June 12, 1851 at St. Paul's. William was born February 22, 1824 in Richmond, VA; he died August 11, 1890. He was the son of Julia M. Hooff and Benjamin Wallace.

James Wallace Hooff - Born 1825. See a separate chapter, page #53.

Charles Rapley Hooff - Born 1826. See a separate chapter, page #61.

Julia A. Hooff - Born about 1827 in Alexandria, D.C. at 1016 Prince Place. She died September 1, 1869. She never married.

Sarah Virginia Hooff - Born February 27, 1828. Christened March3, 1828. She died May 4, 1828.

Caroline Ann Hooff - Born July 5, 1829 in Alexandria, D.C. Christened July 8, 1829. She died July 9, 1829 and is buried in the family vault at St. Paul's Episcopal Church Cemetery.

Lewis was a Banker Commission Merchant. He was a Vestryman and Senior Warden of St. Paul's Episcopal Church, Alexandria, D.C.

The following declaration was taken from original records of St. Paul's: A Declaration, or the Canonical Test, required to be signed by each member of the vestry. "I do believe the Holy Scriptures of the old and new testaments, to be the word of God, and to contain all things necessary to salvation, and I do yield my hearty assent and approbation to the doctrines and worship of the Protestant Episcopal Church in these United States."
    Signed Lewis Hooff
        J. Wallace Hooff   Signed approximately 1866

Lewis Hooff was a commission merchant, and Teller for the Alexandria branch of the Exchange Bank of Virginia. He was a vestryman of St. Paul's Episcopal Church before 1832, and continuously served the church until 1871, at which time he resigned his position as Senior Warden. He resided at 1016 Prince St.; 212 S. Fairfax St.; after 1859, in the double house at 201 Lee/200 Prince Sts., Alexandria, VA.

Obituary from *Alexandria Gazette, June 2, 1874*: Death of Mr. Lewis Hooff - Another of our old citizens has departed this life. Mr. Lewis Hooff died last night at the residence of his son, J. Wallace Hooff at the ripe old age of eight-three years. Mr. Hooff was a true Christian, a most worthy gentleman, and possessed the confidence and esteem of his fellow citizens. For many years he was the teller in the Branch of the Exchange Bank of Virginia in this city, now the First National Bank, which position he filled with fidelity until old age and infirm health compelled him to retire. Mr. H. was a member of St. Paul's Episcopal Church, from whence his funeral will take place tomorrow at 2 p.m.

Home of
Lewis Hooff
1016 Prince Street
Alexandria, VA

Lewis Hooff
1791 - 1874

Elizabeth Maria Rapley
1798 - 1873

James Wallace Hooff   Residence: 517 Prince Street, Alexandria, D.C.

Born: February 21, 1825 in Alexandria, D.C.
Christened/Baptized: February 26, 1832 at St. Paul's Episcopal Church, Alexandria, DC
Married: February 17, 1853 at St. Paul's Episcopal Church by Rev. James T. Johnston
Died: November 30, 1915 in Alexandria at the age of 90 years old.
Buried: St. Paul's Episcopal Church Cemetery in the Brown's Lot
Father: Lewis Hooff   Mother: Elizabeth Maria Rapley

Spouse: Jannett Brown
Born: August 24, 1824 at 517 Prince Street, Alexandria, D.C.
Christened/Baptized:
Died: September 12, 1879 at age 55
Buried: St. Paul's Episcopal Cemetery in the Brown's Lot
Father: John Douglass Brown   Mother: Mary Goulding Gretter

They had three children:

Mary Goulding Hooff - Born December 1, 1853 at 211 Fairfax St., Alexandria D.C.
Christened February 5, 1854 at St. Paul's Episcopal Church. Married Edward Stabler Fawcett, a
dentist at NE corner of Prince and Washington St, Alexandria, D.C. Edward was born March 22, 1846
at 307 S. Asaph St. in Alex., DC. He died March 21, 1901 at 517 Prince St., Alex., DC and is buried at
St. Paul's Episcopal Church Cemetery. His father was Willis Fawcett (b: 1809, d: 1879); mother was
Susan Stabler (b: 1811, d: 1852). Mary died February 20, 1925 at Emergency Hospital, Wash. D.C., and
is buried at St. Paul's Episcopal Church Cemetery. They had 11 children:

Wallace Hooff Fawcett - Born August 4, 1876 in Alexandria. Died October 10, 1938. Unmarried.

Janet Brown Fawcett - Born March 1, 1878 in Alexandria. Married Lewis Cheeseman on November
21, 1906. Died January 4, 1952.

Susan Stabler Fawcett - Born October 24, 1880 in Alexandria. Died October 2, 1955. Unmarried.

Edward Stabler Fawcett - Born February 23, 1883. Died February 16, 1935. Unmarried.

John Douglas Fawcett - Born November 9, 1884 in Alexandria. Died January 11, 1886.

Ellen Douglass Fawcett - Born September 18, 1886 in Alexandria. Died April 11, 1965. Unmarried.

Lewis Hooff Fawcett - Born July 21, 1888 in Alexandria. Died June 6, 1971. Unmarried.

Malcolm Goulding Fawcett - Born January 22, 1891 in Alexandria. Died July 9, 1892.

Richard Hartshorne Fawcett - Born April 29, 1892 in Alexandria. Died July 8, 1918. Unmarried.
2nd Lt. A.S. Res. Mil Aviator WWI.

Mary Goulding Fawcett - Born March 18, 1894 in Alexandria. Died February 15, 1948. Unmarried.

Laurence Gretter Fawcett - Born November 21, 1898 in Alexandria. Married February 21, 1942 to
Mary Edith Lloyd. Mary died April 6, 1970 and is buried at St. Paul's.

Douglass Hooff - Born September 18, 1858 in Alexandria, VA. He was christened February 6,1859 at St. Paul's Episcopal Church. He died May 30, 1937 in Frederick, MD, and is buried at Mt. Olivett Cemetery, Frederick MD. He married Mary Douglas Robbins, (b: March, 1855 - d: March 26, 1941, and is buried at Mt. Olivett). She was the daughter of Rev. Chandler Robbins and Jannett Brown. Douglass and Mary were married on November 18, 1885 at St. Paul's by Rev. George H. Norton. They had no children.

Rev. Douglas Hooff was listed in the class of 1881 Virginia Theological Seminary in Alexandria, VA. He served in Virginia, Michigan (Detroit), Maryland, Baltimore and Frederick. He was in the records of All Saints Church, Frederick, Maryland between September 18, 1910 and May 30, 1936. He was Rector of the All Saints Church. The recessed chapel was built in his memory, given by his friends in Frederick, MD.

Ellen Douglass Hooff - Born November 3, 1864 at 517 Prince St., Alexandria. Ellen married Benjamin Lawrence Wallace on November 6, 1890 at St. Paul's Episcopal Church by Rev. Douglass Hooff. Benjamin was born January 19, 1866 in Tarrytown, NY. His father was William Lawrence Wallace; mother was Caroline Goldsborough Gardner. Benjamin died May 24, 1944 and is buried in Sleepy Hollow, N. Tarrytown, NY. Ellen died March 3, 1947 and is buried in Sleepy Hollow, N. Tarrytown, New York. They had four children:

Caroline Goldsborough Wallace - Born February 27, 1892

Janet Hooff Wallace - Born October 24, 1893

Margaret Douglass Wallace - Born August 26, 1895 in Tarrytown, NY. She married R. Perry Richardson on, April 25, 1917 at Dobbs Ferry, NY.

James Lawrence Wallace - Born February 22, 1903. Married Cynthia Louise Bigelow on July 30, 1932 in Shrewsbury, Mass. No issue.

Notes: The following declaration was taken from original records of St. Paul's Episcopal Church: A Declaration, or the Canonical Test, required to be signed by each member of the vestry. "I do believe the Holy Scriptures of the old and new testament, to be the word of God, and to contain all things necessary to salvation, and I do yield my hearty assent and approbation to the doctrines and worship of the Protestant Episcopal Church in the United States."

Signed Lewis Hooff
      J. Wallace Hooff   Signed approximately 1866

James Wallace Hooff was born at 1016 Prince Street, Alexandria, D.C. and attended the Benjamin Hollowell School at Aaronic Street. He was employed by his uncle, Philip Henry Hooff, before beginning a long career with the federal Government in 1861. During the Civil War his headquarters was the U.S. Army Commissary at 201 Prince Street (now the Athenaeum). He was a Vestryman of St. Paul's Episcopal Church in 1865 and was active in the church until his death in 1915, at which time he was a Senior Warden. He lived for a short while at 212 S. Fairfax Street, and after 1858, at 517 Prince Street. During his younger years he frequently went to Charles Town by stagecoach to go hunting with relatives there.

Obituary from The Star in 1915: "Alexandria, VA, November 30, JAMES WALLACE HOOFF, one of Alexandria's oldest and best known residents, died at 5 o'clock this morning at the home of his daughter, Mrs. Mary G. Fawcett, 517 Prince Street, at the age of ninety years. His death followed a short illness. For more than half a century, Mr. Hooff had been employed in the quartermaster's office of the War Department, being one of the oldest employees in point of service and age in that department. He resigned his position November 1, this year. Mr. Hooff was a vestryman of St. Paul's P.E. Church for fifty years, and at the time of his death was senior warden. He began his services as vestryman in 1865. He was born in Alexandria February 21, 1825, and entered the War Department December 1, 1861, in a clerical capacity, and continued as such until November 1, 1915. He leaves one son, Rev. Douglas Hooff, rector of All Saints' Church,

Frederick, MD and two daughters, Mrs. Mary G. Fawcett, widow of Edward Fawcett, this city, and Mrs. B.L. Wallace, Dobbs Ferry, NY. Mr. Hooff was a brother of the late Charles R. Hooff, for many years cashier of the First National Bank. Arrangements for the funeral have not been completed."

Family of Ellen Douglas Hooff and Benjamin Lawrence Wallace, ca. 1905
Sitting in front - Janet and Margaret Douglas Wallace
Sitting in chair - Ellen Hooff Wallace, James Lawrence Wallace
Standing - Caroline Goldsborough Wallace
Sitting in chair - Benjamin L. Wallace

James Wallace Hooff and
Mary Goulding Hooff ca. 1860

INTERMENT NO. _____   FREDERICK, MD., 6/2 1936

THE UNDERSIGNED HEREBY MAKES APPLICATION FOR PERMIT TO INTER REMAINS OF DECEASED (NAME BELOW) IN MOUNT OLIVET CEMETERY, FREDERICK, MD.

NAME OF DECEASED *Douglas Hooff*

DIED AT *Frederick Md.*   OCCUPATION *Minister*

DATE OF DEATH *May 30/36*   DATE OF BIRTH *Sept. 18 - 1858*

AGE *77yrs. 8 mos. 12days*   DISEASE *Carcinoma*

MARRIED, SINGLE OR WIDOWED *Married*   NAME OF WIFE OR HUSBAND *Mary Robbins Hooff*

FATHER OF DECEASED *James W. Hooff*

MOTHER OF DECEASED (MAIDEN NAME) *Janette Brown*

PARTY RESPONSIBLE FOR PAYMENT

ADDRESS OF SAME

C. E. Cline & Son UNDERTAKER

INTERMENT NO. _____   FREDERICK, MD., Feb. 28 1941

THE UNDERSIGNED HEREBY MAKES APPLICATION FOR PERMIT TO INTER REMAINS OF DECEASED (NAME BELOW) IN MOUNT OLIVET CEMETERY, FREDERICK, MD.

NAME OF DECEASED *Mary Douglas Hooff*

DIED AT *Frederick Maryland*   OCCUPATION *Retired housewife*

DATE OF DEATH *March 26 - 1941*   DATE OF BIRTH *March 2 - 1855*

AGE *86 years - 3 days*   DISEASE

MARRIED SINGLE WIDOWED *Widowed*   MAIDEN NAME OF WIFE NAME OF HUSBAND *Douglas Hooff*

FATHER OF DECEASED *Rev. Chandler Robbins*

MOTHER OF DECEASED (MAIDEN NAME) *Laura Florian*

PARTY RESPONSIBLE FOR PAYMENT

ADDRESS OF SAME

C. E. Cline & Son UNDERTAKER

Lorenz
1710 - 1799

1st - Susanna ——————————————— 2nd - Anna M. Muschler
1726 - 1811

Susanna 1737 - 1773
John Pre 1749
Lewis Pre 1749
Catherine 1738
Barbara Pre 1749
Elizabeth Pre 1749

Lorentz 1750 - 1751
Laurence 1754 - 834
Mary After 1755
Margaret After 1755

Ann Gretter
1760 - 1836

- Elizabeth
  1778
- Lawrence
  1780 - 1842
- John
  1783 - 1859
- Ann
  1785
- Peter
  1787
- George
  1789
- Lewis ——————— Elizabeth Maria Rapley
  1791   1798 - 1873
- Mary Ann
  1794
- **William**
  1796 - 1850
- Julia Maria
  1798 - 1863
- Philip Henry
  1801 - 1888
- Mary Amelia
  1803 - 1837

- Caroline J.
  1823 - 1890
- James W.
  1825 - 1915
- Charles R ——————— Rebecca Janey
  1826 1909   1829 - 1881
- Julia A.
  1827 - 1869
- Sarah V.
  1828 - 1828
- Caroline A.
  1829 - 1829

- Lewis
  1852 - 1916
- Caroline
  1854 - 1937
- Charles R.
  1864 - 1865

Charles Rapley Hooff

Born: August 5, 1826 in Alexandria, D.C.
Christened/Baptized: Feb. 26, 1833 at St. Paul's Episcopal Church, Alexandria, DC
Married: September 29, 1851 at St. Paul's Episcopal Church
Died: July 29, 1909 at age 83.
Buried: St. Paul's Episcopal Church Cemetery, Alexandria, D.C.
Father: Lewis Hooff   Mother: Elizabeth Maria Rapley

Spouse: Rebecca M. Janney
Born: January 29, 1829
Christened/Baptized:
Died: October 27, 1882 in Alexandria at age 54
Buried: St. Paul's Episcopal Church Cemetery, Alexandria, D.C.

They had three children:

Lewis Hooff - Born 1852. See a separate chapter, page #65.

Carrie (Caroline) Hooff - Born 1854 and died 1937. Never married.

Charles Rapley Hooff - Born April 30, 1864. Died February 5, 1865 at 1 year old. Buried at St. Paul's Episcopal Church Cemetery.

Tombstone reads: In memory of Rebecca wife of Charles R. Hooff. Died in Alexandria, VA October 27, 1882 - and Charles R. infant son of Charles R. and Rebecca Hooff born April 30, 1864, died February 5, 1865. (Mother and son are buried in the same site).

Charles Rapley Hooff was the second son of Lewis and Elizabeth Maria Rapley Hooff. He was born at 1016 Prince Street, Alexandria, and attended the Benjamin Hallowell School on Oronoco Street in Alexandria. He was director of the Exchange Bank of Alexandria; President of the First National Bank of Alexandria between the years 1900 - 1909. In 1852 he built and occupied the three story brick house at 801 Duke Street, moving later to 502 Quaker Lane.

Obituary, Alexandria Gazette, Saturday, October 29, 1881: "Mrs. Rebecca Hooff, wife of Charles R. Hooff, Esq, cashier of the First National Bank of this city, died at the resident of her husband, on Seminary Hill, last night. She a most estimable lady."

Obituary, Alexandria Gazette, July 29, 1909: "The Late Charles R. Hooff: As was stated in the Gazette yesterday, Mr. Charles R. Hooff, whose critical illness had been mentioned, died at his home near the Episcopal Theological Seminary at 4:15 o'clock that afternoon. His death occurred about the time the Gazette was being put to press, and too late for printing more than the bare announcement of his demise. Mr. Hooff was a son of the late Lewis Hooff and was born in this city nearly 83 years ago. He entered the Old Exchange Bank when in his teens, and was identified with the bank's successor at the time of his death, having spend nearly three score years in that establishment. Toward the close of the Civil War, when the Exchange Bank was merged with the First National Bank, Mr. Hooff became a cashier, a position he filled until about eight years ago when he was elected president of that institution. All his energies were concentrated in the duties of the position he occupied, and throughout his long life he faithfully fulfilled every requirement of the arduous burdens incident to the strenuous life of a banker. The deceased, from the nature of his calling, enjoyed an extensive acquaintance, and his kindly deportment toward all with whom he came in contact made him many life-long friends. He had been a member of the Episcopal Church all his life, and was constant and faithful to all it's requirements. It can truthfully be said of the deceased that he died with a conscience void of offense toward God and man. About two years ago, while at Atlantic City, Mr. Hooff began to show the effect of the weight of years, and his condition for a time caused considerable anxiety to his relatives and friends, he having sustained a fracture of the hip by a fall there. He, however, rallied and later resumed his duties in the bank, but he was seen to be failing, and his many acquaintances as well as those with whom he was associated realized that the fires of life were burning low and that it was but a matter of a short time when the wheels of life would stand still.

Mr. Hooff is survived by two children, Mr. Lewis Hooff and Miss Carrie Hooff; one brother, Mr. James Wallace Hooff and three grandchildren. His wife, who was a Miss Janney, died several years ago. The funeral will take place at 4 o'clock Saturday afternoon from the chapel of the Episcopal Seminary, and the interment will be in St. Paul's Cemetery."

Notice of Funeral, Alexander Gazette, Friday, July 30, 1909: "The front of the First National Bank building has been tastefully draped in mourning in respect to the memory of the late president, Mr. Charles R. Hooff. The funeral, as heretofore stated, will take place tomorrow evening at 4 o'clock from the chapel of Episcopal Theological Seminary, and the interment will be in the family lot in St. Paul's Cemetery. The clerks in the bank will be the active pall-bearers, and the directors, cashiers and Col. Arthur Herbert and Mr. I. Elchberg will act as honorary pall-bearers. The services will be conducted by Rev. Douglass Hooff, a nephew of the deceased and Rev. S.A. Wallis, of the Theological Seminary."

Home of
Charles R. Hooff and Rebecca Janney Hooff
801 Duke Street (formerly 1 South Columbia Street)
Alexandria, VA

Lewis Hooff (II)

Born: 1852 in Rappahannock, VA
Christened/Baptized:
Married: February 2, 1882 in Rapphannock, VA by Rev. Douglass Hooff
Died: 1916 in Atlantic City, NJ at age 64
Buried:
Father: Charles Rapley Hooff (I)   Mother: Rebecca Janney

Spouse: Mary Agusta Shackleford
Born: February 9, 1858 in Montpelier Dovedale, Albermarle Co., VA.
Christened/Baptized:
Died: January 5, 1946 in Lynchburg, VA at age 88
Buried: Ivy Hill Cemetery, Alexandria, VA
Father: Hudson Zachariah Shackleford   Mother: Harriet V. Barnes

They had three children:

   Charles Rapley Hooff - b: 1882. See a separate chapter, page #69.

   Louise Hooff - Born 1885. Married Carleton Barnwell, an Episcopal Clergyman. They had 1 child, Mary Janney who died young.

   Mary Hooff - Born 1887. She married Benjamin Janney Rudderow, Vicar of Holy Trinity Memorial Chapel, Philadelphia, PA. They had one child, Elizabeth who married Hobart H. Heinstance, no issue.

   Lewis Hooff was engaged in the banking business. He lived in Sperryville, VA, and in his later years, at 339 Quaker Lane, Alexander, VA.

   Obituary: "Mary Agusta Hooff, wife of the late Lewis Hooff died Saturday at the Memorial Hospital, Lynchburg, VA. Mrs. Hooff was born at Dovedale, Albermarle, Co. Virginia February 9, 1858, the daughter of the late Hudson and Harriet Shackleford. She is survived by a son, Charles R. Hooff, Alexandria; two daughters, Mrs. Carleton Barnwell, Lynchburg, VA, and Mrs B. Janney Rudderow, Philadelphia, PA, also by two brothers, Henry Barnes Shackleford and Rapley Shackleford of Montpelier, Rappahannock, VA, and three sisters, Mrs. George W. Macon, Charlottesville, VA; Mrs. Johnson Strother, and Mrs Lewis P. Nelson, Culpeper, VA. Funeral services were held at 11 a.m. Monday at the residence of her son, Charles R. Hooff, Quaker Lane, and were conducted by the Rev. Wm. E. Thompson of Emmanuel-Church-on-the-Hill. Interment was in Ivy Hill Cemetery."

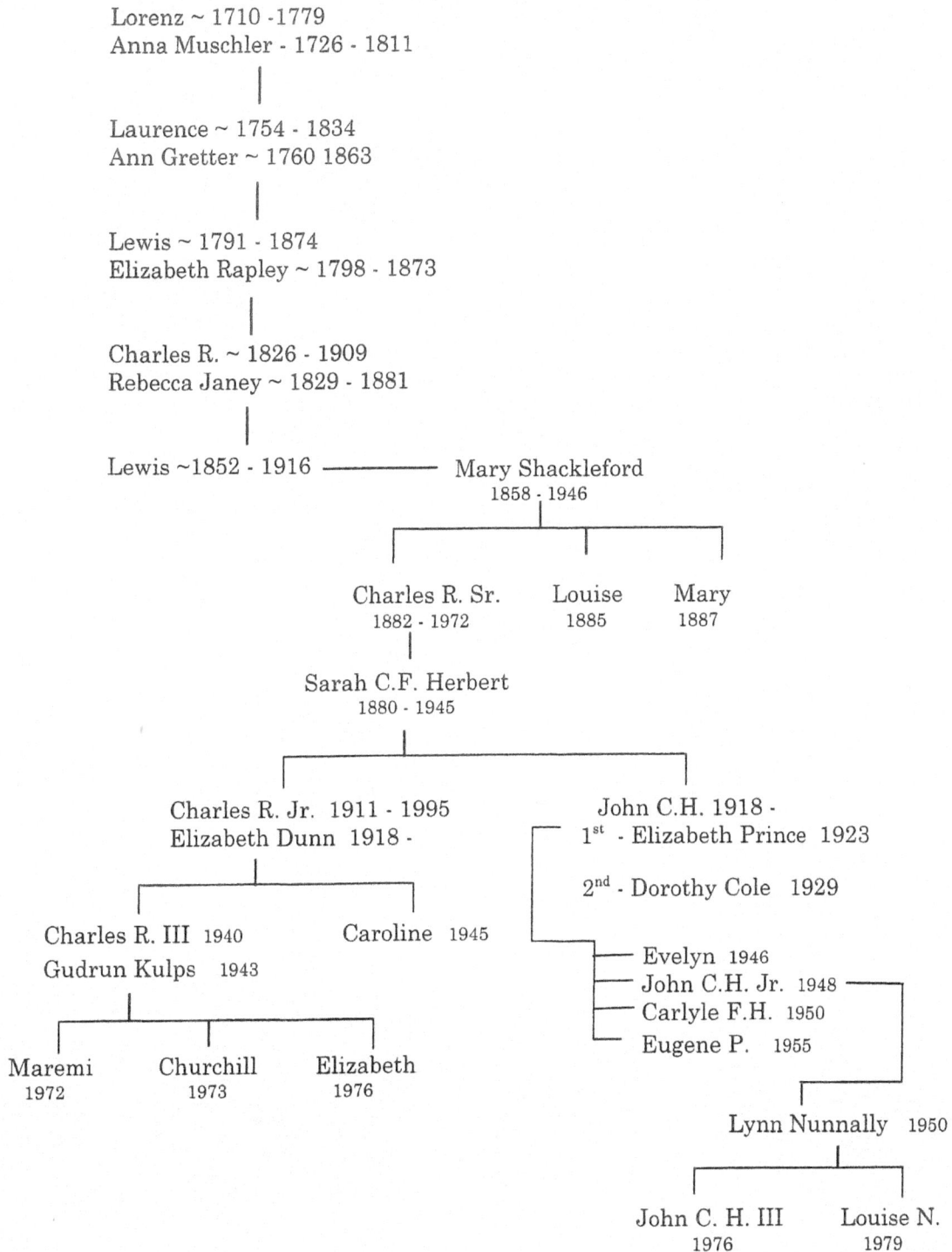

Lorenz ~ 1710 -1779
Anna Muschler - 1726 - 1811

Laurence ~ 1754 - 1834
Ann Gretter ~ 1760 1863

Lewis ~ 1791 - 1874
Elizabeth Rapley ~ 1798 - 1873

Charles R. ~ 1826 - 1909
Rebecca Janey ~ 1829 - 1881

Lewis ~1852 - 1916 ———————— Mary Shackleford
1858 - 1946

Charles R. Sr.   Louise   Mary
1882 - 1972   1885   1887

Sarah C.F. Herbert
1880 - 1945

Charles R. Jr. 1911 - 1995   John C.H. 1918 -
Elizabeth Dunn 1918 -   1st - Elizabeth Prince 1923

                                     2nd - Dorothy Cole 1929

Charles R. III 1940   Caroline 1945   Evelyn 1946
Gudrun Kulps 1943   John C.H. Jr. 1948 ——
                                              Carlyle F.H. 1950
                                              Eugene P. 1955

Maremi   Churchill   Elizabeth
1972   1973   1976

                                     Lynn Nunnally 1950

                              John C. H. III   Louise N.
                              1976   1979

Charles Rapley Hooff, Sr.

Born: November 6, 1882 in Sperryville, VA
Christened/Baptized:
Married:
Died: April 25, 1972 in Alexandria, VA, age 89 years old
Buried: Ivy Hill Cemetery, Alexandria, VA
Father: Lewis Hooff   Mother: Mary A. Shackleford

Spouse: Sara Carlyle Fairfax Herbert
Born: July 1880 in Baltimore, MD
Christened/Baptized:
Died: August 1945 at age 65
Buried: Ivy Hill Cemetery, Alexandria, VA
Father: Gen. James Rawlings Herbert, C.S.A.

They had two children:

   Charles Rapley Hooff - Born: 1911. See a separate chapter, page #71.

   John Carlyle Herbert Hooff - Born May 19, 1918. See a separate chapter, page #73.

   Charles R. Hooff, Sr. was manager of U.S. Fidelity and Guaranty Co. Of Washington, D.C. He bought (ca. 1911-1912) and resided at "Oaklands", an estate in Prince George's County, Maryland, which his wife, Sarah C.F. Herbert, was descended. They later moved to 502 Quaker Lane, Alexandria, VA. Both were active in the restoration of "Old Town."

   An article from the *Rambler, September 21, 1919*, giving the history of Montpelier/Oakland in Prince George's County, Maryland stated: "The present mistress of Oakland is Sarah Carlisle Fairfax Herbert Hooff, wife of Charles R. Hooff of the United States Fidelity and Guaranty Company where they have lived for several years. They have four sons, Mark Alexander Hooff, who has been nominated for the West Point Military Academy; Courtland H. Hooff, Charles R. Hooff, Jr., and the baby, James Carlisle Herbert Hooff." An excerpt from a second article in the Rambler, October 12, 1919 stated " then two of Mrs. Hooff's sons, Mark Alexander Smith and Courtland H. Smith, joined the party to show the Rambler the way to Montpelier. Mark is a college athlete of the foot ball kind and soon goes to West Point. Courtland was on the track team of the University of Virginia." It is unknown where Mark and Courtland Hooff came from. These two newspaper articles are the only time these two names were ever appear.

   Obituary: "Charles R. Hooff, Sr., Retired Executive: Charles R. Hooff, Sr. 89, retired manager of the Washington office of the United States Fidelity and Guaranty Company, died Monday at his home, 502 Quaker Lane, Alexandria, VA. A native of Sperryville, VA., Mr. Hooff and his late wife, the former Sara Carlyle Herbert, had been leaders in the early restoration of Alexandria's Old Town. Mr. Hooff, who retired in the late 1930's as manager of the United States Fidelity and Guaranty Company, was a master of the hounds for the Old Cameron Hunt Club, was a member of the Society of Colonial Wars. Mr. Hooff's survivors include two sons, Charles R. Jr. and John C.H., both of Alexandria; six grandchildren and two great-grandchildren. The family has requested that expressions of sympathy be in the form of contributions to the Heart Fund.

Sarah Carlyle Fairfax Herbert Hooff
1880 - 1945

Sarah Carlyle Fairfax Herbert Hooff

Charles Rapley Hooff, Jr.

Born: April 11, 1911 in Baltimore, MD
Married: October 14, 1938 at Holy Trinity Memorial Chapel, Philadelphia, PA
Christened/Baptized:
Died: March 3, 1995 at age 84 in Alexandria, VA.
Buried:
Father: Charles Rapley Hooff Sr.   Mother: Sara Carlyle Fairfax Herbert

Spouse: Elizabeth Taylor Dunn
Born: May 8, 1918 in Bristol, PA
Christened/Baptized:
Died:
Father: Huston Dunn   Mother: Elizabeth Elmslie Taylor

They had two children:

> Charles Rapley Hooff III - Born April 21, 1940 in Philadelphia, PA. He married Gudrun Kulps on October 14, 1967 in Taipei, Taiwan. Gudrun was born March 15, 1943 in Chefoo, Shanung, China. Charles R. Hooff III attended the Colorado School of Mines and graduated from George Washington University, Washington, DC. He is vice-president and secretary of Charles R. Hooff, Inc. Of Washington, DC and president of Duke Enterprises, and the Alexandria Waterfront Restoration Co. He and his family live in Alexandria, VA. They have four children:
> Maremi Hooff - Born December 10, 1972 in Winston-Salem, NC.
>
> Churchill Houston Hooff - Born August 26, 1973 in Washington, DC.
>
> Elizabeth Janney Hooff - Born July 4, 1976 in Washington, DC.
>
> Carlyle Hooff - Born 1981

Caroline Hooff - Born April 12, 1945 in Philadelphia, PA. She married Gary Stephen Bierman, August 29, 1970. They had 1 child, Gary Stephen, Jr. born May 7, 1974 in Alexandria, VA. Apparently Caroline had remarried - current last name is Norman; whether she had more children is unknown. Caroline Hooff attended Garland Junior College in Boston, Mass, and is presently employed as a tour guide for "Historic Alexandria" for Smithsonian Associations.

Charles Rapley Hooff, Jr. and his wife resided in Alexandria, VA and were featured in the July 1979 issue of Washington Dossier, "Alexandria, VA., In Search of Its Own Identity" by Rita Kempley. They hostedf the Hooff family reunion in August 1979.

Obituary from the *Washington Post, March 1995*: Charles R. Hooff Jr. Dies at 83; Realty Broker, Preservationist. Charles R. Hooff Jr., 83, a real estate broker who had worked in the preservationist movement in Old Town Alexandria, died March 3 at his Alexandria home after a heart attack.

Since the end of World War II, Mr. Hooff had worked in a family real estate business, which in 1949 became Charles R. Hooff, Inc. It specialized in residential real estate but also had done some commercial work. Mr. Hooff helped establish the cooperative multi listing service that is widely used by Northern Virginia real estate brokers.

He was born in Baltimore and grew up in Alexandria, where he was captain of the baseball team and a graduate of Episcopal High School. He graduated from the University of Virginia, where he was baseball captain in 1935. He later played semi-professional baseball in the Shenandoah Valley League.

Later, he worked for Maryland Casualty Co. In Philadelphia. During World War II, he served in the Navy in the Pacific. He was commander of an amphibious landing ship and participated in combat operations at Iwo Jima and Okinawa.

In his Old Town preservation work, Mr. Hooff was a key figure in saving the historic Lloyd House for the wrecker's ball.

He was an organizer of Security Savings, now part of Providence Savings & Loan, and was a founder and director of International Fueling Co., an aircraft fuels company. He was a director of Burke and Herbert Bank & Trust Co.

Mr. Hooff was a founding member of the Alexandria Businessman's Club. He was a member of Belle Haven Country Club, the City Tavern Club, the Metropolitan Club, the Old Dominion Boat Club, the Society of Colonial Wars, Sons of the American Revolution, the Historic Alexandria Foundation and the American Legion.

Survivors include his wife of 57 years, Elizabeth Hooff, and two children, Charles R. Hooff III and Caroline Norman, all of Alexandria; a brother John Carlyle Herbert Hooff of Sperryville; and five grandchildren.

John Carlyle Herbert Hooff

Born: May 19, 1918 in Baltimore, MD
Christened/Baptized:
Married: July 1945 in Grand Island, Nebraska
Died: March 27, 1999 of congestive heart failure at age 80 in Culpepper,VA.
Buried: Woodstock, VA
Father: Charles Rapley Hooff Sr.   Mother: Sara Carlyle Fairfax Herbert

Spouse: 1st - Elizabeth Prince
Born: September 29, 1923 in Tuolumne, California
Christened/Baptized:
Died:
Buried: Alexandria, VA
Father: John Roger Prince   Mother: Evelyn Russell

They had four children:

Evelyn Hooff - Born November 7, 1946 in Alexandria, VA. She married John Bauserman on February 15, 1963 in Elkton, MD. They had 1 son named John Jr. b: October 7, 1963 in Alexandria, VA. Evelyn married her 2nd husband William Crickenberger (b: March 3, 1947) on March 2, 1978. They have three children:
    Campbell Davis Crickenberger (female)- Born July 3, 1979.

    William A. Crickenberger- Born 1981

    Cassie Brooke Crickenberger - Born 1983

John Carlyle Herbert Hooff Jr - Born June 28, 1948 in Alexandria, VA. He married Lynn Nunnally (b: June 13, 1950 in Richmond, VA) on September 9, 1972 in Richmond. Lynn is the daughter of Moses W. and Alice Nunnally. They have three children:
    John Carlyle Herbert Hooff III - Born: August 30, 1976

    Louise Nunnally Hooff - Born September 23, 1979

    Alexander Rapley Hooff - born 1984

Carlyle Fairfax Herbert Hooff - Born May 3, 1950 in Alexandria, VA. Graduate of Lake Erie College. Married Peter Carrington Williams on November 11, 1978 at St. Paul's Episcopal Church in Alexandria, VA. Peter is a graduate of University of Virginia, Georgetown University School of Law, L.L.M. from University College in London, England.

Eugene Prince Hooff - Born December 9, 1954, in Alexandria, VA. Married Nancy Griffith on December 18, 1981 in Alexandria, VA. Nancy is the daughter of Robert S. Griffith and Helen Canaler Griffith of Altanta, GA. Eugene and Nancy have two children:
    Eugene Prince Hooff, Jr., born August 16, 1982

    Robert Easley Hooff, born December 5, 1985.

Eugene is a graduate of University of Virginia. He resides in Atlanta, GA and is the president of Real Estate Valuation, Inc.

Spouse: 2nd - Dorothy Cole Marshall who was born October 31, 1929 in Brookly, NY.
Father: Frank W. Cole   Mother: Dorothy Ackerman
There were married July 18, 1969 in Fairfax, VA.

John Carlyle Herbert Hooff was a graduate of the University of Virginia. He was a 1st Lieutenant in the Army Air Corps (1941-46). He is a member of the family real estate and insurance firms, Charles R. Hooff, Co., Alexandria, and Charles R. Hooff, of Washington, DC. He and his wife were residents of Alexandria and Rappahannock, VA.

Obituary from *Washington Post, March 27, 1999:* HOOFF, JOHN CARLYLE HERBERT, 80, of Alexandria, VA, died of congestive heart failure. Born May 19, 1918 in Baltimore, MD. He was from an Alexandria, VA family and lived there for most of his life. Mr. Hooff attended Episcopal High School in Alexandria. After graduating from U of VA, he served in the Army Air Corps as a navigator during World War II in the North African, European and Pacific theaters. When returning to civilian life after WWII he entered the real estate and development business in Alexandria as Executive Vice Present of Charles R. Hooff, Inc. and President of Hooff and Nell Builders.

He was a developer of Yates View and Cameron Mews in Old Town Alexandria and Indian Bluff Island. He is survived by his wife, Dorothy Cole Hooff; two sons, John C.H. Hooff, Jr., Eugene Prince Hooff; two daughters, Evelyn Hooff Crickenburger and Carlyle Fairfax Herbert Hooff; two step sons, John Marshall, Jr., and Robert A. Marshall and 11 grandchildren.

A memorial service will be held Thursday, April 1, 1999 at Trinity Episcopal Church in Washington, VA at 1 p.m. with the Rev. Jennings Hobson officiating. Interment will be private.

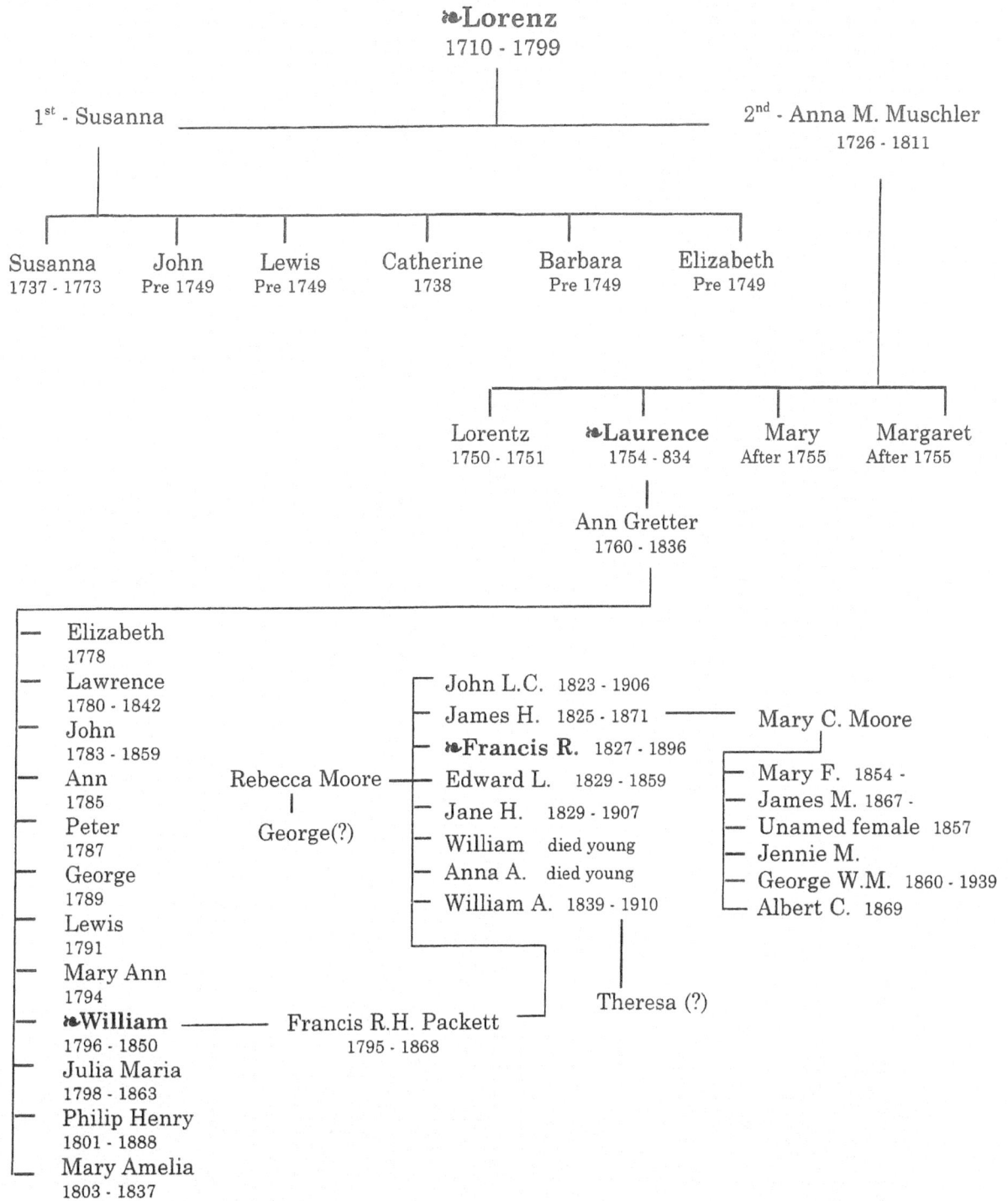

Lorenz
1710 - 1799

1st - Susanna ———————————————————————————— **2nd - Anna M. Muschler**
1726 - 1811

Susanna	John	Lewis	Catherine	Barbara	Elizabeth
1737 - 1773	Pre 1749	Pre 1749	1738	Pre 1749	Pre 1749

Lorentz	**Laurence**	Mary	Margaret
1750 - 1751	1754 - 834	After 1755	After 1755

Ann Gretter
1760 - 1836

Elizabeth
1778

Lawrence
1780 - 1842

John
1783 - 1859

Ann
1785

Peter
1787

George
1789

Lewis
1791

Mary Ann
1794

William ——————— Francis R.H. Packett
1796 - 1850   1795 - 1868

Julia Maria
1798 - 1863

Philip Henry
1801 - 1888

Mary Amelia
1803 - 1837

Rebecca Moore ——————

George(?)

John L.C.   1823 - 1906

James H.   1825 - 1871 ——————— Mary C. Moore

Francis R.   1827 - 1896

Edward L.   1829 - 1859

Jane H.   1829 - 1907

William   died young

Anna A.   died young

William A.   1839 - 1910

Theresa (?)

Mary F.   1854 -

James M.   1867 -

Unamed female   1857

Jennie M.

George W.M.   1860 - 1939

Albert C.   1869

❧ William Hooff

Born: June 8, 1796 in Alexandria, D.C.
Christened/Baptized:
Married: March 5, 1822 in Charles Town by Rev. Mr. Smith
Died: April 10, 1850 at 54 years old in Charles Town, WV.
Buried: Zion Episcopal Churchyard, Charles Town, WV. A tombstone reads: "William Hooff Died April 10, 1850 in the 54th year of his age."
Father: Laurence Hooff II   Mother: Ann Gretter

Spouse: Francis (Fannie) Rankin Hammond Packett
Born: November 8, 1795 in Charles Town, WV (Mt. Hammond)
Christened/Baptized:
Died: October 2, 1868 at age 73 in Charles Town, WV
Buried: Zion Churchyard, Charles Town, WV. Tombstone reads: Fannie R. Hooff born November 8, 1795 died October 2, 1868. Wife of William Hooff.
Father: Maj. James Hammond   Mother: Mary (Polly) Rankin

Francis was the widow of Lt. John Packett, whom she married March 14, 1817 in Jefferson Co. The following article was written about her: Mrs. Packett was considered a remarkable woman, as Miss Fannie Hammond, when engaged to Lt. Packett, and before the battle of Lake Erie. She rode on horse back, accompanied only by her colored maid and a man servant, to a place on Lake Erie where the ship "Ariel" was stationed by Lt. Packett, to see him before the memorable battle was fought 1813, for she was determined to see Lt. Packett before this battle." She had two children with Lt. Packett:

Mary Ann Packett - Born ca 1818; marr: Erasmus Tate, no issue. After the death of her husband she made her home with her stepbrother, John Lawrence Cramer Hooff, and left her estate to his children.

John Bainbridge Packett - who married Lucy Washington and had six children. Lucy was a great granddaughter of Dr. Samuel Washington. "Locust Hill" in Jefferson Co. WV was built in 1840 as a wedding present for Lucy.

William and Francis had eight children:

John Lawrence Cramer Hooff - Born 1823. See a separate chapter, page #87.

James Hammond Hooff - Born 1825. See a separate chapter, page #101.

❧Francis Rankin Hooff -b: 1827. See a separate chapter page #105.

Edward Lee Hooff - born 1829 in Charles Town, WV. He died July 30, 1859 in Shreveport, LA. Buried in Zion Churchyard in Charles Town, WV. He was a Episcopal Clergyman, and attended the College of William and Mary in 1852-53. He married Rebecca Moore (Mason Co. Marriage Records, page 16, show Edward L. Hoof marrying a Rebecca Miller on July 25, 1856) on June 25, 1856. His wife and child (George?) predeceased him.

Jane Hammond Hooff - born January 7, 1831. She was baptized at Zion Church in Charles Town on August 29, 1852. She died December 29, 1907 in Washington, D.C. She is buried at Zion Churchyard. Unmarried.

William - died young

Ann Amelia Hooff - Died on Sunday, December 28, 1834. She was 4 months and 17 days old.

William and Ann Amelia we assume are buried at Zion in unmarked graves in the same plot as their parents, William and Francis.

William Albert Hooff - Born July 7, 1839 at Zion Church. Died April 28, 1910 in Washington, D.C. Buried in Zion Churchyard in Charles Town, WV. Married Theresa _____ , they had no issue.

William Albert Hooff (1839 - 1910)
Confederate Army, Company G,
Botts Grays Second Virginia Regiment

Virginia Library in Richmond, VA. - Partial roster of Co. G., 2nd Regiment, "Stonewall" Brigade dated April 1862, shows William A. Hooff, 2nd Virginia Infantry. Co. G, Botts Greys, private, 21 years, in this company for three years. Also shown on this roster is his brother Francis R. Hooff and his cousin James L. Hooff, also privates.

National Archives Veterans Service Records

Company Muster Roll

April 18/June 30, 1861 - Age 22- Farmer-Enlisted Apl.18,1861 at Charlestown by Capt. L. Botts
Mustered into service, May 11, at Harpers Ferry by Capt. L. Botts
Miles to place on muster-in 11 miles

July/August 1861 Present - Enlisted Apl. 18,1861 at Charlestown by Capt. L. Botts for 12 months
Last Paid- June 30,186? by Paymaster Field

Sept./Oct. Present - Enlisted Apl. 18, 1861 at Charlestown by Capt. L. Botts for 12 months
Last Paid- Aug.31,186?- by A.Q.M. Har??au -Special Duty Gen. Smith's Headquarters

Nov./Dec.1861 Present - Enlisted Apl. 18,1861 at Charlestown by Capt. L. Botts for 12 months
Last Paid- Oct.31,196? by Capt. Lewis

Apr. 30/Oct. 31,1862 - Present-Enlisted Apl.18,1861 at Charlestown by Capt. Botts for War
Last Paid-Apr.30,186? by Capt. Stonebraker

Nov/Dec. 1862 Present - Enlisted Apl. 18,1861 at Charlestown by Capt. Botts for War
Last Paid- Oct.31,186? by Capt. Elhort

Jan/Feb.1863 Absent - Enlisted Apl.18, 1861 at Charlestown by Capt. L. Botts for War
Last Paid-Dec.31,186? by Stonebraker - Absent- Hospital nurse by order of Gen. Paxton- Feb.16,1863

Mar/Apr. 1863 Absent - Enlisted Apl.18,1861 at Charlestown by Capt. L. Botts for War
Last Paid-Feb.28,186? by Capt. Cary - Absent- Ward Master in Hospl., at Richmond

May/June 1863 Absent - Enlisted Apl.18,1861 at Charlestown by Capt. Botts for War
Last Paid-Feb.28,186? b y Capt. Cary - Absent-Ward Master in Hospital, Richmond

July/Aug. 1863 Absent - Enlisted Apl.18,1861 at Charlestown by Capt Botts for War
Last Paid-Feb.28,196? by Capt. Cary - Absent- Ward Master in Hospital, Richmond

Sept./Oct. 1863 Absent - Enlisted Apl.18,1861 at Chas. Town by Capt. Botts for War
Last Paid-Feb.28,1863 by Capt Cary - Absent-Ward Master at Hospital in Richmond

Nov./Dec. 1863 Absent - Enlisted Apl.18,1861 at Charlestown by Capt. L. Botts for War
Paid-Oct.31,186? by Major Cary - Absent- Ward Master at Hospital, Richmond

Jan./Feb. 1864 Absent - Enlisted Apl.18,1861 at Charlestown by Capt. Botts
Last Paid-Dec.31,186? by Major Cary - Absent- Ward Master in Hospl. in Richmond

Mar./Apr.1864 Present -	Enlisted Apl.18,1861 at Charlestown by Capt. Botts for War
	Last Paid-Dec.31,1863 by Maj. Cary - Present- Re??????? from duty at
	hospl to his company Mar.14,1864.
Sept./Oct.1864-	Enlisted Apl.18,1861 at Charlestown Prisoner since May 19,1864

Prisoner of War at Point Lookout, MD. Date of arrival at Belle Plains, Va. May 23, 1864
Captured - Spotsylvania CH. May 20,1864
Exchanged - Marshall 1865

Hospital Muster Roll

General Hospital No. 4, (Baptist College Hospital) Richmond, Va.

Mch/Apr 1863	Enlisted-Ap 19,1861 at Charlestown Va by Capt Botts War
	Attached to Hospital Mar 12, 1863 as Guard
	Last Paid, Feb 28, 1862 - Present
	Detailed by Genl Lee Jan 30, 1863
May/June, 1863	Enlisted-Ap 10, 1862 at Charlestown Va by Capt Botts War
	Attached to Hospital Mar 12, 1863 as Guard
	Last Paid Maj J B Carey Apl 30,1863 - Present
	Detailed by Genl Lee Jan 30 1863
July/Aug, 1863	Enlisted-Ap 10,1862 at Charlestown Va by Capt Betts War
	Attached to Hospital Mar 12, 1863 as Guard
	Last Paid Maj J B Cary July 1, 1863 - Present
	Detailed by Genl Lee June 30 1863
Sept/Oct, 1863	Enlisted-Apl 10, 1862 at Charlestown by Betts War
	Attached to Hospital Mar 12,1863 as Guard
	Last Paid Maj J B Carey Sept 1,1863 - Present
	Detailed by Genl Lee June 30 1863
Nov/Dec, 1863	Enlisted-Apl 10, 1862 at Charlestown by Capt Betts
	Attached to Hospital Mar 12, 1863 as Guard
	Last Paid J B Carey Nov 1,1863 - Present
	Detailed by Genl R E Lee June 30 1863

Register of General Hospital No.4

General Hospital No. 4 (Baptist College Hospital) Richmond, Virginia
"Morning Reports of Attendants," for Dec, 1863 Returned to duty by Ex. Board Feb 18th and reported Feb 21st M. Rep?

"Report of Examining Board for Attendants at General Hospital No. 4," for March 1864
Brigade - Jones as Guard   Remarks: Return to duty

"Muster Roll of detailed men in Gen'l Hosp'l No.4, and the duty in which such men are employed." How employed: Guard   Remarks: Disabled

Register of Medical Directors Office

Medical Director's Office, Richmond, Va.
Hospital Gen No 4 - Complaint Debility - Admitted Jan 20,1863

Medical Director's Office, Richmond, Va.,
"Details."   Received Sept 2, 1863 - Dated Jan 30, 186?
Remarks: Appl returned to Surg. Genl.

Medical Director's Office, Richmond, Va.
   "Furloughs and Leaves of Absence" Received Sept 15, 1863 - Dated Sept 14, 1863
     Remarks: Furlough sent to Winder Hosp
   "Furloughs and Leaves of Absence." Received Feb 19, 1864 - Dated Feb 19,1864
     From G. H. No 4   Remarks: Appd & fwd

Register of Attendants in General Hospital No. 4, at Richmond, Va. Dated April 22 1863
     How employed: Guard   Complaint: Disability   Detailed: Jan.30, 1863   By: Gen Lee

Sept.3,1863   Receipt for clothing at General Hospital # 4 Richmond, Va.
Sept.12,1863   Detail per Special Order # 217/20 (doesn't say anything else about detail)
Sept. 21,1863   Receipt for clothing at General Hospital # 4 Richmond, Va.
Oct.24,1863   Receipt for clothing at General Hospital # 4 Richmond, Va.
Dec.12,1863   Receipt for clothing at General Hospital # 4 Richmond, Va.

Rolls of Prisoners of War paroled at Point Lookout, Md.,and transferred to Aiken's Landing, Va., March
     14, 1865, for exchange. Not Dated.
     Where captured: Spottsylvania   When captured: May 20, 1864

List of prisoners of war paroled April 13 to 18, 1865, at various places in Virginia and
     West Virginia. Date: Apl. 16, 1865.   By whom given: St. R. R. Granger
     Where given: A. P??.g. Winchester, Va.

NOTE: There are other copies of "letters" from different officers, including medical officers, that I cannot not completely read. These are dated between January 1863 and September 1863. The reason for the letters is clear; William is in perfect health, however, at the thought of a battle he becomes physically ill to the point that he does not function. These officers feel he would better serve as a guard/attendant in a hospital. He was assigned to General Hospital #4 (Baptist College Hospital)

National Archives

   William A. Hooff, Co. G 2nd VA Infantry, Private

   William A. Hooff. Born July 1839. 5'8", dark complexion, grey eyes, dark hair. Farmer. Enlisted 2nd VA Inf. Botts Grays, April 18, 1861 at Charles Town in Co. G as Pvt. Detailed as nurse to General Hospital #4 Richmond, March/April 1863 - January/February 1864. Returned to regiment March 14, 1864. POW at Salem Church May 12, 1864 (Point Lookout). Exchanged March 14, 1865. Paroled at Winchester, Va. April 16, 1865. Age 25-Height 5'8" - Complexion Dark - Hair Dark- Eyes Gray

We first found William in Virginia (West Virginia succeeded from Virginia in 1864) personal property tax records in Richmond, VA, between 1816 and 1818 in Charles Town, WV. He did not appear again until March 4, 1822 when he married Francis Rankin Hammond Packett, widow of Lt. John Packett and mother of two children. William's property was on the Charles Town-Berryville Turnpike. He put land in trust to some people but transaction did not state the reason. Between 1828 and 1846, William appeared in the Charles Town Courthouse deed books as selling and buying land to and from various people. One of the transactions show William Hooff of Jefferson County, VA, sold 200 acres of land to Philip Henry Hooff of Alexandria, VA on April 18, 1828. In 1824 William appeared as administrator of John Packett's will, book 4, page 140. In 1830 Fannie Hooff appeared as Admix. John Packet, Will book 6, page 271. Except for a few dates, we know very little about him.

Since the law did not require births or deaths to be registered prior to 1853, it is difficult to find birth dates, death dates or the names of his children. We had to go by land transactions, census, and wills where children were named. The records from Charles Town Courthouse between 1860 and 1870(?) were destroyed by fire.

Philip Henry Hooff married William's sister-in-law, Jane Baxter Hammond in Charles Town on June 23, 1823.

Will of William Hooff

Charles Town, WV Will Book #2, page 199 and 292

The last Will and Testament of William Hooff, deceased. In order to prevent my securities, Thos. Rawlins and John B. Packett, from having any money to pay for me as guardian of my children it is my request that my Executor shall sell the interest in the Negroes I came in possession of by the death of my two children, William and Ann Amelia. Should that not be sufficient, he is directed to sell all or part of my interest in the farm I reside on. Provided my children should claim of said securities any money that may be due from me to them.

Witness my hand and seal this 10th day May 1845

William Hooff (seal)

William Hooff's personal and property holdings were appraised March 23, 1850:

Francis Hooff	Wheat farm consisting of 75 acres, various pieces of farm equipment, 1 cow, 1 cradle and few house-hold items.
John Hooff	2 scythes
James L. Hooff	Wheat shut

Francis Rankin Hammond (William's wife) was born at "Mt. Hammond," a stone mansion on the banks of the Shenandoah River, Berkley Co., VA (now Jefferson Co., WV). She was the daughter of James Hammond and Mary (Polly) Rankin, and granddaughter of Benjamin Rankin and Judith Lee. She and her sister, Jane Baxter Hammond (who later married Philip Henry Hooff), and their two brothers, were beneficiaries under the will of Judith Rankin, and each of the girls inherited a farm in Berkley Co., and money from their father (whose will was written September 4, 1803; he died December 13, 1803; will process completed in 1817)

Francis (Fannie) lived with her children Francis (Frank) Rankin, Jane Hammond and William Albert on her late husband William's farm until her death. Fannie and her children appear in the Mt. Zion Church records as being active in the church after William's death. We do not know why she was not active before his death or why he was not active in the church.

Obituary of Frances Rankin Hooff, *The Jefferson Co. Free Press, October 1868, Charles Town, WV*
"At her residence in this County on Thursday night last, October 1st, Mrs. Fannie (Rankin) Hooff, relict of the late William Hooff, in the 73rd year of her age. The deceased was born and raised in this County and was the daughter of Mr. James Hammond of Mt. Hammond, a home proverbial for its hospitality in years past. Mrs. Hooff was first married to Lt. Packett of the U.S. Navy, who distinguished himself with Commodore Perry on Lake Champlain, and she was the mother of Mr. John Bainbridge Packett and Mrs. Mary A. Tate, formerly Miss Packett. A number of her children by Mr. Hooff survive to lament her death, among them our townsman, Mr. John L. Hooff. The esteem in which she was held was attested by the large concourse of surviving friends who followed her remains to the grave.

William and Fannie R. Hooff are buried in Zion Churchyard, Jefferson Co., WV. Lt. Packett is also buried there, but his grave is unmarked and the location not known, though it is supposed he is buried under the present Chapel of the Church.

Obituary of Jane Hammond Hooff, Charles Town, WV, January 1908. "On Sunday night December 29th, Miss Jane H. Hooff at her home in Washington City, age about 80 years. The deceased was born and raised in this county. She was a sister of the late John L. Hooff, and a half sister of John Packett of this county. She is survived by one brother, Mr. Albert Hooff of Washington City. Funeral services were held Wednesday morning at 11 o'clock from Zion Episcopal Church, Charles Town, conducted by Rev. J.S. Alfriend, assisted by Rev. A.C. Hopkins."

Note - Jane Hammond Hooff came to Washington City (now D.C.) with William Albert and Francis R. Hooff, her brothers, and the family of Francis after the death of their mother. The 1907 DC directory list Jane H. Hooff, the Astoria, Washington, D.C.

Obituary of William Albert Hooff - Charles Town, May 1910
"Mr. W. Albert Hooff, formerly of this county, but for many years past a resident of Washington, D.C., died in the Georgetown University Hospital in that city on Thursday, April 28th. His remains were brought here Monday. Services were conducted in Zion Church at 11 o'clock by Rev. J.S. Alfriend, assisted by Rev. Dr. A.C. Hopkins of the Presbyterian Church. Mr. Hooff served in the Confederate Army, Company G. Botts Grays, 2nd Virginia Regiment. The Confederate Veterans attended the funeral in a body. He is survived by a widow. He was a brother of the late John L. Hooff and half-brother of the late John Packett of this county. The pallbearers were: Col. R.P. Chew, Messrs. John Porterfield, C.H. Moore, Thos. R. Moore, Geo. B. Hooff, and G.H. Page. Funeral Director, Chas. L. Young."

The 1910 DC directory list Albert W. Hoff 400 12th St., SW. The 1911 DC director lists Theresa Hoff, widow of William A. Hoff at 400 12th St., SW.

"Mt. Hammond" built ca. 1745, Jefferson Co. WV (formerly Berkley Co.), birth place of Frances Rankin Hammond (Mrs. William Hooff), Jane Baxter Hammond (Mrs. Philip Henry Hooff, Sr.), and Thomas Rankin Hammond, grandfather of Susan Rankin Hammond (Mrs. Francis Rankin Hooff). Benjamin Rankin left the house and land to his daughter "Polly". After her marriage to James Hammond it was called "Mt. Hammond."

James Hammond was born in Belfast Ireland, ca. 1766, and came to America in 1782. He first settled in Baltimore, MD with his brother John, and later moved to Jefferson Co. He was the son of Henry Hammond and Jane Baxter of Aghalee, Ireland.

Benjamin Rankin was a Captain of the Militia in Berkeley Co., VA, and served under Lt. Col. Washington (1781-1783). He was one of the Trustees for the founding of Charles Town in 1786. He married, ca. 1767, Judith Lee (probably the daughter of the 4th Charles Lee and Leeanna, Jones, daughter of William Jones and Leeanna Lee). Benjamin Rankin was born 1740, died January 1787. Judith Lee was born ca. 1748, died June 1, 1809.

I, Mary Ann Tate, of Jefferson County, West Virginia, conscious of the uncertainty of life, do make this my last will and Testament.

First, I direct my Executor hereinafter named, as soon as possible after my decease, to pay all my debts and funeral expenses.

Second, I bequeath to John L. Hooff Jr., the son of my brother John L. Hooff, all of the property of which I may die possessed, the money of the said property to be paid to said John L. Hooff Jr when he arrives at the age of twenty one years, - until that time said money to be left in the hands of my Executor hereinafter named to be invested by him, and should I depart this life before said John L. Hooff Jr. arrives at the age of twenty one years, then my Executor is authorized and empowered to use the interest of said money, for the education and maintenance of said John L. Hooff Jr., _____ should John L. Hooff Jr. depart this life before he arrives at the age of twenty one years, then - said money is to be equally divided among Amelia Hooff, William L. Hooff and Mary B. Hooff - or the survivor or survivors of them - same being children of my brother John L. Hooff.

Third, I hereby direct that John L. Hooff be discharged from all his indebtedness to my estate, should any exist at the time of my death.

Fourth, I hereby appoint Cleon Moore of Charles Town, West Virginia, Executor of this my last will and Testament _____ in testimony whereof I hereunto set my hand this 22nd day of October 1884.

Mary Ann Tate

Witness:
Rebecca Kearsley
Cleon Moore

State of West Virginia, County of Jefferson Sct'
In the Clerk's Office of the County Court, May 20th 1927.

A writing bearing date on the 22nd day of October 1884, purporting to be the last will and Testament of Mary Ann Tate, deceased, was this 20th day of August 1887, offered for probate in said office and on the same day in said office, the said Will was
partly proved by the oath of Cleon Moore of the subscribing witnesses thereto and ordered to lie in said office for further proof.

Teste
W.F. Alexander
Clerk of said Court

A copy, Teste:
/s/ <u>W.F. Alexander</u>   Clerk

Recognizing the uncertainty of life and wishing to place on record my wish as to the disposition after my death of one one hundred Dollar Jefferson County Bond belonging to me and now is the possession of Sam'l Howell Cashier of the First National Bank of Jefferson at Charles Town, West Virginia. I do hereby declare it to be my wish that after my death said bond shall be sold and the proceeds divided equally between Mary Strather Hooff and Amelia Bennett Hooff children of John L. Hooff.

In witness Whereof I have signed and sealed and declared this instrument as my will bequeathing the said One hundred Dollar bond to the said Mary Strather Hooff and Amelia Bennett Hooff, share and share alike. Signed this July 13th 1887 at Charles Town Jeffrson County.

Mary Ann Tate   (Seal)

Sam'l Howell:
Adele L. Howell: Witnesses.

State of West Virginia, County of Jefferson

Filed in the Clerk's Office of the County Court of Jefferson County, WV by Sam'l Howell this 17th day of July 1897.

William F. Alexander

a copy, Teste;

/s/ <u>W.F. Alexander</u>

Mary Ann Packett Tate
(Step-daughter of William Hooff)

Lorenz - 1710
Anna Muschler - 1726

|

Laurence - 1754
Ann Gretter - 1760

|

William - 1796
Francis R.H.Packet - 1795

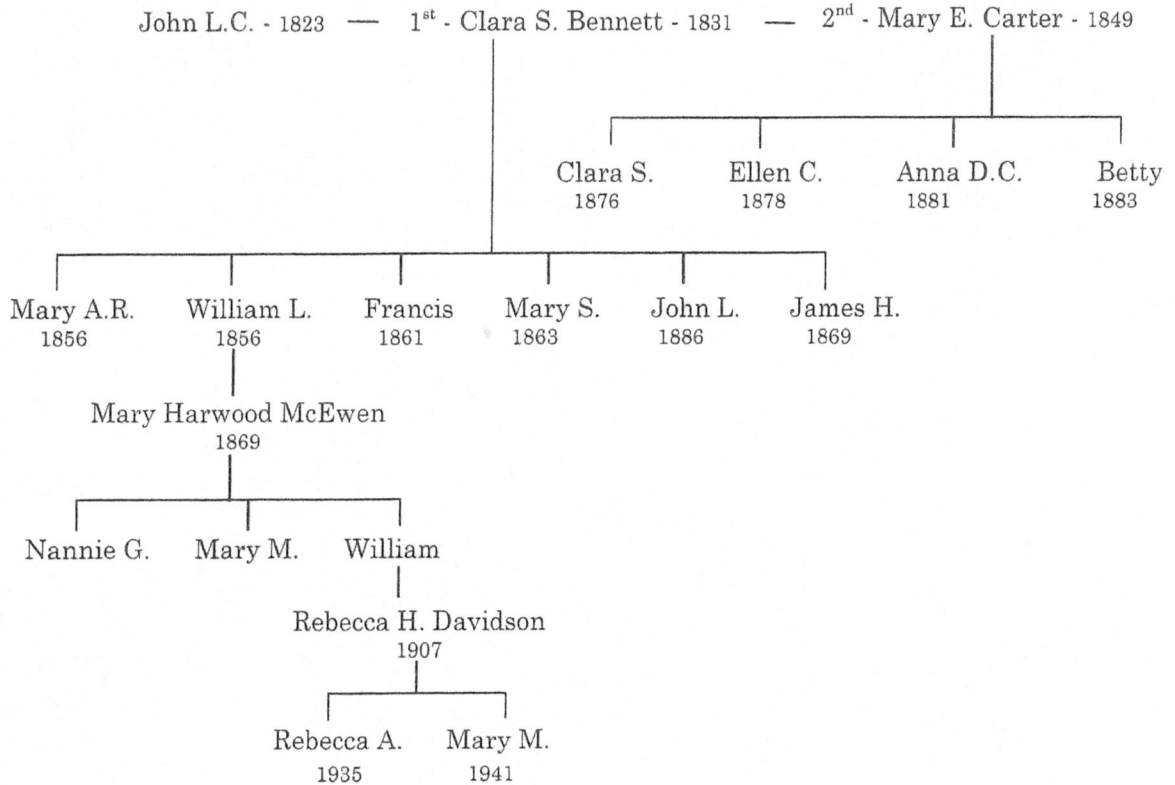

|

John L.C. - 1823 —— 1st - Clara S. Bennett - 1831 —— 2nd - Mary E. Carter - 1849

Clara S.   Ellen C.   Anna D.C.   Betty
1876   1878   1881   1883

Mary A.R.   William L.   Francis   Mary S.   John L.   James H.
1856   1856   1861   1863   1886   1869

Mary Harwood McEwen
1869

Nannie G.   Mary M.   William

Rebecca H. Davidson
1907

Rebecca A.   Mary M.
1935   1941

John Lawrence Cramer Hooff

Born: May 16, 1823 in Charles Town, WV
Christened/Baptized: Confirmed on May 1, 1887 at Zion Church, Charles Town, WV
Married: 1st - January 15, 1855 in Baltimore, MD
Died: October 8, 1906 at age 83 years, 3 months, 22 days
Buried: Zion Church Cemetery, Charles Town, WV
Father: William Hooff   Mother: Francis Rankin Hammond Packett Hooff

Spouse: 1st - Clara Soares Bennett
Born: October 3, 1831 in Union, VA, Loudoun Co.
Christened/Baptized: October 5, 1834 at St. Paul's, Alexandria, VA
Died: October 4, 1871 in Baltimore, MD at age 41 years and 1 day
Buried: Zion Church Cemetery, Charles Town, WVA. Tombstone reads: "Clara S. Hooff, wife of J. L., died October 4, 1871."
Father: James Hamilton Bennett   Mother: Mary Amelia Hooff (daughter of Laurentius (Laurence II), sister of John Lawrence Cramer Hooff's father).

They had six children:

Mary Amelia Bennett Hooff -Born September 11, 1856 in Charles Town. Baptized June 14,1857. Confirmed April 3, 1872 at Zion Church, Charles Town, WVA. Unmarried.

William Lawrence Hooff - Born 1859. See a separate chapter, page #99.

Frances (Fannie) Lee Hooff - Born July 11, 1861 and died June 6, 1862. Buried at Zion Churchyard, Charles Town, WV. Tombstone reads: "Fannie Lee, daughter of John L. And Clara S. Hooff, born July 11, 1861, died June 6, 1862"

Mary Stabler Hooff - Born April 16, 1863. Baptized June 3, 1866 at Zion Episcopal Church, Charles Town, WVA. Died April 24, 1957 in Baltimore, MD and is buried at Zion Churchyard, Charles Town, WVA. Unmarried.

John Lester Hooff - Born January 30, 1866. Baptized February 27, 1867 at Zion Church, Charles Town, WVA. Died April 16,1951 in Baltimore, MD and is buried at Zion Churchyard, Charles Town, WVA. Unmarried.

James Hamilton Hooff - Born October 19, 1869. Baptized June 19, 1870 at Zion Church, Charles Town, WVA. Died August 10, 1870; buried Zion Churchyard, Charles Town, WVA.

Spouse: 2nd - Mary Elizabeth (Mollie) Carter
Born: March 25, 1849 (found same date but 1842)
Christened/Baptized:
Married: August 3, 1875 in Cumberland, MD.
Died: January 7, 1894
Buried: Edge Hill, Charles Town, WVA
Father: Issac Newton Carter   Mother: Ann Margaret Kearsley
    Issac N. Carter owned Carter House, a large hotel in Charles Town.

They had four children:

Clara Soares Hooff - Born September 30, 1876. Baptized June 3, 1877 at Zion Church in Charles Town. Died July 15, 1962 and is buried at Zion Church Cemetery, Charles Town, WVA. Unmarried.

Ellen Carter Hooff - Born October 14, 1878. Baptized August 14, 1879 at Zion Church, Charles Town, WVA. Died March 1954 in Norfolk, VA and is buried at Forest Lawn Cemetery in Norfolk. Unmarried.

Anna Douglas Campbell Hooff - Born April 19, 1881. Died September 30, 1962 in Washington, DC. And is buried at Zion Churchyard, Charles Town, WVA. Unmarried. (Anna struck her sister Clara several times with her cane. Clara died two days later in a hospital from the injuries. Anna went to trial for Clara's death, however she was found to be incompetent. She died two months after her sister).

Bettie Beall Hooff - Born November 9, 1883. She married Anselm Bailey Urquhart. Died November 1967 in Oxnard, CA and is buried at Forest Lawn Cemetery in Norfolk, VA. They had two children: John Carter born September 13, 1913 and Mary Francis born October 6, 1922.

Wedding Announcement, August 1875: "MARRIED - HOOFF-CARTER. On the 3rd instant, at the residence of her brother-in-law, Mr. Campbell of Cumberland, MD, by the Rev. E.B. Raffensberger, Mr. John L. Hooff of Charles Town, WV, to Miss Mollie E. Carter, of the former place. We wish them all we should hope for ourselves on such a voyage."

Obituary, January 1894: "Again has death rudely broken in upon a family circle and laid low its very light and joy - the wife and mother. In the death on Sunday last of MRS. MOLLIE E. HOOFF, wife of Mr. John L. Hooff, of this town, a husband and four young daughters are left to mourn the desolation of a home which she made bright and happy by her loving presence and gently ministrations. Though for some years in delicate health and a constant sufferer, she bore up so bravely and so effectively hid her pain that few even of her most intimate associates realized her condition or dreamed that the end was so near, that there were a few days of speechless agony, of trial, only to open them in a world of bliss immortal "a rest for the weary." The funeral was held in the Presbyterian Church of which she had been a long member, on Tuesday morning, Rev. Dr. A .C. Hopkins officiating."

Obituary, Charles Town, WV, October 1906: "MR. JOHN L. HOOFF, one of the oldest citizens of this place died at his residence on Monday night at 11 o'clock, aged 84 years. His long life was spent in his native county and for many years he had resided in town. He was well known, and until the infirmities of age confined him to his home, was prominent in business and a familiar figure on the streets. He was twice married, both wives having died before him. He is survived by two sons, William and John, of Baltimore, and six daughters, Misses Amelia and Mary of Baltimore, Clara and Bettie of Charles Town, Ellen of Norfolk, and Annie of Washington. One brother, Albert, and one sister, Miss Jane H. Hooff of Washington, also survive. Funeral services were held yesterday afternoon in Zion Church, conducted by Rev. J.S. Alfriend, assisted by Rev. Dr. A.C. Hopkins. Interment in the Churchyard."

Tombstone reads: John L. Hooff, May 16, 1823 - October 8, 1906.

Obituary of John Lester Hooff, *Charles Town, April 1951*: "John Lester Hooff, Died in Baltimore. John L. Hooff died on Monday at the Ardeligh Nursing Home in Baltimore, MD. Born in Charles Town, he was the son of the late John L. Hooff, a local merchant, and Clara Bennett Hooff of Loudoun County, VA. When a young man Mr. Hooff left Charles Town and settled in Baltimore where he was associated with the Jordan Stabler Company, a wholesale grocers, for a number of years, and later became a partner. Upon their liquidation, he joined Harper-McGraw wholesale Grocers, and was with them until ill health forced his retirement. Mr. Hooff never married, and was a frequent visitor to his old home town of Charles Town, and was well known through the county. Surviving are five sisters, Miss Mary Hooff of Baltimore, MD, Misses Clara S. and Ann, both of Washington, D.C., and Miss Ellen C. Hooff and Mrs. A.B. Urquhart of Norfolk, VA. The body was brought to the Melvin T. Strider Funeral Home from Baltimore Tuesday afternoon, where it remained until Wednesday afternoon, when it was taken to Zion Episcopal Church for services at 2:30 P.M. with the Rev. Temple Wheeler of the Children's Haven and the Rev. Stanley Hauser of Zion Church in charge. Burial was made in Zion Churchyard. Bearers for Mr. Hooff were Jay Wsong, Thornton Perry, William Wyson, Ted Lowery, Paul Cain and Jon Finley."

Obituary of Ellen Carter Hooff, March 1954 "Died at her home in Norfolk, VA. MISS ELLEN CARTER HOOFF. She was born and reared in Charles Town. She went to Norfolk when a young girl and has been living here ever since. She was the daughter of the later John L. Hooff and Mary Carter Hooff. She was a lovely Christian. To know her was to love her. She leaves four sisters, Clara and Anna Hooff of Washington, and Mrs. A.R. Urquhart of Norfolk, and Miss Mary S. Hooff of Baltimore, MD. Interment was in Norfolk, Friday, March 19th."

John Lawrence Cramer Hooff
1823 - 1906

Clara Soares Bennett Hooff
1831 - 1871

Mary Amelia Bennett Hooff
daughter of John Lawrence Cramer Hooff
and Clara Soares Bennett Hooff

John L. Hooff
son of
John Lawrence Cramer Hooff
and
Clara Soares Bennett Hooff

Baptism record of Ellen Carter Hooff
daughter of John Lawrence Cramer Hooff and Mollie Carter Hooff

"**Suffer the little Children to come unto Me, and forbid them not; for of such is the Kingdom of God.**"— *St. Mark X, 14.*

This Blank is intended to be filled up by Parents, or others bringing Children for Baptism and should be returned to the Rector before the time fixed for its administration ; which may be upon any Sunday, or other Holy Day, immediately after the last lesson at either Morning, or Evening Prayer.

Place, *Charlestown* Date, *August 10 1879*

Name to be given Child } *Ellen Carter*

Date of its birth, *October 14 1878*

Place of birth, *Charlestown*

Names of Parents, *Luther L. Hooff* *Mollie C. Hooff*

Names of Sponsors *Mrs. Rebecca Hearsby* *Amelia B. Hooff*

✠ ———————————————————— ✠

¶ *"The People are to be admonished, that it is most convenient that Baptism should not be administered but upon Sundays and other Holy Days, or Prayer Days. Nevertheless (if necessity so require) Baptism may be administered upon any other day."*

¶ *"There shall be for every Male-child to be Baptized, when they can be had, two Godfathers and one Godmother : and for every Female, one Godfather and two Godmothers ; and Parents shall be admitted as sponsors, if it be desired."*

¶ *"The Minister of every Parish shall often admonish the People, that they defer not the Baptism of their Children longer than the first or second Sunday next after their birth or other Holy Day falling between, unless upon a great and reasonable cause."*

¶ *"And also they shall warn them, that without like great cause and necessity, they procure not their Children to be baptized at home in their houses."*

RUBRICS FROM THE OFFICES FOR BAPTISM.

Anna Douglas Campbell Hooff
daughter John Lawrence Cramer Hooff
and Mollie Carter

Left to right - Clara, Annie, Mollie, Bettie, Ellen -
wife and daughters of John L.C. Hooff and Millie Carter Hooff

Anna Douglas Campbell Hooff's home in
Charles Town, WV.
Taken approximately 1910.

Ancestry of Mary Stabler Hooff (from bible records)

I am the daughter of John Laurence Hooff of Charles Town, Virginia, now West Virginia, born May 16, 1823 (died October 4, 1906) and his wife Clara Soares Bennett, born in Union Loudon Co., VA, October 3, 1831 (died October 4, 1870 in Baltimore). Married in Baltimore January 15, 1855.

Children:
        Amelia Bennett - unmarried
        William Laurence - married Mary McEwen of Frankton, TN
        Fannie Lee - deceased
        Mary Stabler - unmarried
        John Lester - unmarried - b: January 30, 1886, d. April 16, 1951, buried at Zion
        James Hamilton - died in infancy

Note: Beside the above is a Notary Seal and the following statement: State of Maryland, City of Baltimore, sworn to before me, a Notary Public on this 22nd day of September 1925 by Mary Stabler Hooff, above statement. M. Gewal (?) Dora, Notary Public.

John Laurence Hooff was the eldest child of William Hooff born in Alexandria, VA, June 8, 1796, died in Jefferson Co., VA, April 10, 1850. Married March 4, 1821 in Charles Town, WV to Frances Rankin Hammond, widow of Lt John Packett, USN who commanded the Ariel in the Battle of Lake Erie.

The above William Hooff was a son of Laurence Hooff 2nd of Alexandria, born December 1755, died May 26, 1834. Married Ann Gretter, born July 8, 1760, died June 8, 1836. Ann Gretter was a daughter of George Michael Gretter, born about 1742, died November 23, 1796. Married in Philadelphia 1751. Married Elizabeth Burnett, born (?), died June 6, 1798, both he and his wife died in Alexandria, VA. The Gretter family came from Stullgard.

The Hooff family was of Dutch origin, coming from Holland to Lancaster, PA; from there going to Alexandria, VA. The first part of this paper is taken from Bible records of the Hooff family, but the above few lines are being from Pennsylvania records, I believe.

William Laurence Hooff, 2nd child of John Laurence and Clara S.B. Hooff, lives in Nashville, TN (the rest of this page is missing)

Bible Records

Descendant of Mary Stabler Hooff through the Bennett and Hamilton lines:

Clara Soares Bennett, wife of John Laurence Hooff, was born in Union, Loudoun Co. VA, October 3, 1831, died in Baltimore on October 4, 1870. Married her cousin John L. Hooff on January 15, 1855 in Baltimore, MD. Clara Soares Bennett was the second child of James Hamilton Bennett, born in Leesburg, VA on June
12, 1791, died in Washington, D.C. on February 16,1853. Married in Alexandria, VA on September 4, 1823 to Mary Amelia Hooff, born October 9, 1803, died in Cuton, Loudoun Co., VA on October 6. 1837. The children were:

Mary Ann - born in Brazil on March 16, 1823 and died in Baltimore on December 9, 1907. Married in Upperville, VA on August 1, 1843 - no children of this union.

Clara Soares - born October 3, 1831 in Union, VA and died in Baltimore October 4, 1870. Married January 15, 1855 to John L. Hooff.

Julia Dulant - born April 16, 1834 in VA and died February 23, 1923 in Baltimore. Married in Baltimore April 31. 1861 to Alban Gilpin Stabler. No children of this union.

James Hamilton Bennett was council to Pernawbuco, Brazil during The administration of President Monroe took his bride to Brazil and remained there until after the birth of their first child.

My mother was named for a Portuguese lady friend of my grandmother Bennett.

Charles Bennett Sr., was the ancestry whose service as Captain of Revolutionary forces as sent some time ago to D.A.R. He was a vestry man of old Shelbourne Parrish and I have understood all the family owned and lived on land that was part of the original Tankerville Tract. A cousin in Loudoun Co. gave a great deal to me, information on the Bennett and Hamilton families.

I have not given the names of children of Charles Bennett, Jr., and his wife Mary (Hamilton) Bennett. I have a copy from the Bennett Bible (which was lost), one bore the Christian name of Sydnor and lived in Loudoun Co., VA.

I will have the Bible records verified. It is said the marriage of Charles Bennett, Sr. and Duanna Sydnor was recorded in Richmond Co., VA.

James Hamilton Bennett, born January 12, 1797 and died February 16,1853, was the eldest son of Charles Bennett, Jr., born about 1769, died December 20,1822 in Leesburg, VA. He married Mary Hamilton, born 1774, died June 15, 1822. Mary Hamilton was the daughter of James Hamilton who was born 1720, died in Leesburg in 1775. Him and his second wife Jean McGeath, married in 1768 after the death of his first wife Priscilla. Jean McGeath Hamilton, widow of James Hamilton, married Joshua Daniels.

James Hamilton's will is on record in Loudoun co., VA. Book B, page 111. The above was one of the prominent men of the county when it was cut off from Fairfax in 1757. Was one of the trustees of the town of Leesburg, a member of the vestry of Shelbourne Parrish, a member of the House of Burgesses from 1758 to 1771. "Hammonds" Page 146-188 are other sources. A Justice of the Peace and captain of colonial troops in 1757.

Charles Bennett, Jr., was the son of Charles Bennett, Sr., born 1745, died 1820. Married in 1767 to Duanna Sydnor. Born in 1747, died 1812. His will is recorded in Leesburg. Their children were:
Charles Jr. - b: June 16, 1769, d: December 26, 1811. Married 1792 to Mary Hamilton, born 1774, died June 15, 1822.

Duanna Bennett married John A. Binns.

Winifred Bennett born 1771, died 1843, married John Hamilton in 1793.

Elizabeth Bennett born 1775, married James Hamilton (the above Hamilton's third child of James Hamilton and Jean McGeart)

FAMILY

Births, When & where

John Lawrence Bernan Hooff
was born at Charlestown Va
May 16th 1823. —————

Clara Sibell Bennett was born at
Union Va. October 3rd 1831 —————

Amelia Bennett Hooff was born
at Charlestown Va September
11th 1856 —

William Lawrence Hooff was born April
1st 1859 —

Fanny Lee Hooff was born July 11th 1861.

Mary Stabler daughter of J. L. &
C. S. Hooff was born April 16th 1863

John Lester son of J. L. & C. S. Hooff
was born Jan 30th 1866 —————

James Hamilton Hooff
was born Octob 19 1869

Mary Amelia Bennett Hooff
dau. of John L.C. and
Clara S. Hooff.

RECORD

Marriages, when & where.

In Baltimore on Monday
Morning January 15th by the
Rev E. P. Phelps. John Lawrence
Hooff to Clara S. Bennett. 1855

Deaths, when & where.

Mary Amelia Bennett departed
this life October 6th 1837 at Hamilton Va- in the 34th year of her age.

James Hamilton Bennett departed
this life

Frances Rankin Hooff the mother
of John L Hooff departed this life
Oct 1st 1868 aged 73-

William Hooff departed this life
April 10th 1856 in the 54th year of his
age.

Lawrence Hooff Sr. the father of William
Hooff and Mary Amelia Bennett, departed
this life May 26th 1834 in the 79th year of his age.
Ann Hooff wife of Lawrence Hooff Sr
died June 8th 1836 in the 76th year of her age

William Lawrence Hooff

Born: April 1, 1859 in Charles Town, WV
Christened/Baptized: June 19, 1859 at Zion Church, Charles Town, WV
Married: June 8, 1899 in Franklin, TN
Died: June 20, 1936 in Iuka, Mississippi at age 77.
Buried: Iuka, Mississippi. There is a memorial marker in Zion Episcopal Churchyard, Charles Town, WV
Father: John Lawrence Cramer Hooff   Mother: Clara Soares Bennett

Spouse: Mary Harwood McEwen. (Mary Harwood McEwen Hooff married Harry Hardeman Graham after William's death).
Born: July 3, 1869 at "Aspens" near Franklin, TN
Christened/Baptized:
Died: March 31, 1961 at age 92
Buried: Cave Hill Cemetery in Louisville, KY
Father: James Knox Polk McEwen   Mother: Nannie Shute

They had three children:

Nannie T. Hooff - Born September 10, 1900. Died September 22, 1900

Mary McEwen Hooff - Born February 2 , 1905 in Franklin TN. Married Holland Nimmons McTyeire III on September 28, 1929. One son named Holland IV, b: September 25, 1930.

William Lawrence Hooff Jr. - Born September 26, 1907, and died October 1985 in Chattanooga, TN. Married Rebecca Huey Davidson (b: December 3, 1907) on July 2, 1932. Rebecca was daughter of Archie Davidson and Ida Ashby.
    They had two children:

Rebecca Ann Hooff - Born December 24, 1935. Married Clinton Wayne York (b: August 23, 1929) on June 9, 1956.

Mary McEwen Hooff - Born April 24, 1941. Married Andrew Ray Cullum III on April 16, 1960.

William Lawrence Hooff, Sr.
Son of John L.C. Hooff

James Hammond Hooff

Born: January 2, 1825 in Charles Town, WV
Christened/Baptized:
Married: June 1, 1853 in Mason County, WV
Died: November 25,1871 in Point Pleasant, WV at age 46.
Buried:
Father: William Hooff   Mother: Francis Rankin Hammond Packett

Spouse: Mary Catherine Moore-Miller
Born: ca 1827 in Shenandoah, VA
Christened/Baptized:
Buried:
Died:
Father: Morgan Moore   Mother: Mary Allen

They had six children:

   Mary Francis (Fannie) Hooff - Born April 3, 1854 in Mason Co., WVA. Baptized May 24, 1854 at Christ Church. Married Jonthan W.C. Armstrong on December 30, 1875 in Mason Co., WVA.

   James Mayen Hooff - Born June 5, 1867. Baptized May 3, 1868 at Christ Church. Married Lana Lois Mahone on April 4, 1916 in Point Pleasant Baptist Church, Mason Co., WVA.

   Unnamed female - Born July 26, 1857 in Mason Co. WV. (Possibly named Ida who married _____ Sharp)

   Jennie Moore Hooff - Married Henry Marion Sanders on May 29, 1890 in Mason Co. WVA.

   George William Moore Hooff - Born May 17, 1860 in Mason Co. WVA. Baptized January 5, 1870. Died June 1, 1939. Married Adelia G. Miles, div. 1901. Will recorded in Mason Co., WVA. Left estate to Cora Saunders, Frank Sharp and Katie Miller Bowling.

   Albert C. Hooff - Born October 22, 1869 in Mason Co. Baptized January 5, 1870 in Christ Church.

   Mary Katherine Moore Miller married James H. Hooff after the death of her husband Joseph M. Miller (b. July 15, 1822, son of Reuben M. and Atlantic Ocean (Walton). Joseph Miller's mother was the 2nd wife of Mary Catherine's farther, Morgan Moore.

   Joseph M. Miller was killed on the 8th of January 1848 in a steamboat explosion below Gallipolis on the Ohio River. Mary Catherine and Joseph has one son, Joseph Samuel Miller, born on April 24, 1848, three months after his father died. Joseph Samuel Miller married Mattie J. Shaw on January 11, 1872 and had one daughter, Katie Ruffner Miller. Katie married William P. Bowling on December 11, 1895; they had four children.

   James Hammond Hooff attended the Winchester Medical College, and the University of Pennsylvania. He was a physician and a farmer. He engaged in numerous land transactions in Point. Pleasant, WVA. After his death, his widow married J. Bowling and had several sons.

The State Gazette, Thursday, April 2, 1908, written by Delia A. McCulloch: "PIONEERS OF MASON COUNTY, read before the Col. Charles Lewis Chapter, D.A.R., Tuesday, March 10,1908..... Morgan Moore came from the Shenandoah Valley, and located on a farm in Mercer Bottom, where he lived until his death in August 1869. He was the grandfather of Mr. G. Hooff......Dr. James Hooff came to Point Pleasant about 1854, and married Catherine, the daughter of Morgan Moore, of Mercer Bottom. After many years of successful practice, he bought the farm of John McMillen, who lived in the county for many years before the war and was the son-in-law of Major Andrew Bryan. On this farm, Dr Hooff died. He was the father of G.W.M. Hooff..."

Obituary - "Died at his residence near Point Pleasant, W.Va., November 25, 1871, after a brief illness, JAMES HAMMOND HOOFF, M.D, in the 47th year of his age. Dr. Hooff was born in Charles Town, VA on January 2, 1825. He was educated in his native town and in 1846 he entered Winchester Medical College, where he pursued the study of Medicine under the late Dr. McGuire. Removing to Point Pleasant in 1848, he began the practice of his profession with success. Ten years later, anxious to increase his knowledge of his favorite study, he entered, in the fall of 1858, the medical school of the University of Pennsylvania, at the close of his course receiving the usual diploma and degree of Doctor of Medicine. Returning to Point Pleasant, he resumed his practice with increased ardor and unwearied energies until his last illness. Naturally a man of warm heart and generous impulses, Dr. Hooff was a decided and constant friend, a devoted husband and affectionate father. Ambitious of success in his profession, and possessing an unusual degree of energy, he was a tender, faithful and..." the rest is missing.

Note: Obituary notice in *Weekly Register, Point Pleasant, WVA* on November 30, 1871 states he left wife and five children. Funeral by Rector of Christ Protestant Episcopal Church and buried by the Masonic Order.

Point Pleasant Daily Register, Friday, June 2, 1939:
"HOOFF RITES SUNDAY AT 2 - Funeral services for George William Moore Hooff. 79, who passed away at his home on Viand St., yesterday morning at a quarter to eleven, will be conducted from Franklin Funeral home on Main Street Sunday afternoon at 2 o'clock. Sepulture will be in Lone Oak Cemetery. The Rev. Rank T. Cady and the Rev. Chalmers McCutchen will officiate at the last rites. The deceased, long associated with Point Pleasant's business and political life, died from a combination of diseases induced by many disorders."

☙Lorenz - 1710 - 1779
Anna Muschler - 1726 - 1811

☙Laurence - 1754 - 1834
Ann Gretter - 1760 - 1836

☙William - 1796 -1850
Francis R.H. Packet - 1795 -1868

☙**Francis R.** - 1827 - 1896 —————— Susan R. Hammond
1825

William H.	Anna C.	Francis H.	Sarah B.	☙**Edward L.**	Bettie
1853	1854	1857	1860	1865	1866

Viola V. Gladding
1854

☙**Hammond F.**	Sarah I.	Anna L.	Francis H.	Asberry Fairfax	Gordon C.
1885	1886	1890	1892	1893	1896

Caroline L. Unsworth
1879

Thomas E. - 1911   ☙Jessie G. - 1913   Benjamin L. - 1918

Elona   Margaret E. Kirby - 1911   Jewel
                                                          No issue
Thomas E. Jr.   William A.

                  Janet   Edna L.   ☙Ronald L.
                                 1938   1939

William A. Jr.   Michelle   Kathleen M. Semega - 1945

          Kimberly M. - 1962   Lisa M. - 1964   Robyn M. - 1965

          1st - Alexander D. Thomson   Andre G. Francois   1st - Richard H. Weinstein
               Courtney M. - 1984   Ashleigh M. - 1996   Jamie L. Hooff -1986
                                                                    Brittany M.Hooff - 1987
          2nd - David V. Windell   2nd - Arthur Love
               Shannon M. - 1989   Michael Anthony - 1992
                                                                    Matthew Shaun - 1994

❧ Francis Rankin Hooff

Born: 1827 in Charles Town, WV
Christened/Baptized: June 10, 1855 at Zion Church, Charles Town, WV
Married: June 7, 1852 in Frederick, MD
Died: July 3, 1896 in Washington, D.C. at age 69, a widower.
Buried: Rock Creek Cemetery, Washington, D.C., Section H, Lot 16, Site 4
Father: William Hooff   Mother: Francis Rankin Hammond Packett

Spouse: Susan Rankin Hammond
Born: October 26, 1825
Christened/Baptized: August 29, 1852 at Zion Episcopal Church, Charles Town, WV
Died: We could not find when or where she died or where she is buried.
Father: Thomas Rankin Hammond   Mother: Maria Eleanor Conrad
     (Thomas was the brother of Francis R. Hammond Hooff)

They had six children:

William Hammond Hooff - Born April 1, 1853. Died June 27, 1853. Buried at Zion Episcopal Churchyard, Charles Town, WVA. The tombstone reads: William Hammond Son of Francis R. and Susan R. Born April 1, 1853. Departed this life June 27, 1853. Age 2 mos. And 28 days.

Anna Campbell Hooff - Born 1854. Baptized June 15, 1856 at Zion Episcopal Church. Died August 20, 1894. Buried at Rock Creek Cemetery, Washington, D.C. Sec. H, Lot 6, Site 8. Unmarried.

Francis Hammond Hooff - born August 5, 1857; baptized December 25, 1858 at Zion Episcopal Church. Had 1 son named Faulkner.

Sarah Brown Hooff - Born May 18, 1860. Baptized December 19, 1867 at Zion Episcopal ChurchCharles Town, WV. Died December 20, 1867. Buried at Zion Episcopal Churchyard. Tombstone reads: Sarah B. Hooff died December 20,1867 aged 7 years and 7 months. Daughter of Francis R. and Susan R. Hooff. Sarah was probably named for her great aunt, Sarah Hammond, sister of James Hammond, who married William Brown of Charles Town.

❧Edward Lee Hooff - Born 1865. See a separate chapter, page #109.

Bettie Hooff - Born 1866. Baptized December 19, 1867 at Zion Episcopal Church. Married with no issue.

Francis (Frank) Hooff was born and raised in Charles Town, West Virginia. He lived on the 75 acre wheat farm owned by his mother (by will of James Hammond) After the death of his father, he purchased from each of his brothers and his sister the interest they had in the property, and continued to farm the land. After the death of his mother (around 1878), he sold the property and moved to Fairfax County. He appeared in the 1860 and 1870 U.S. Census as living in Charles Town. He next appeared in the 1880 Census as living in Fairfax, VA with his wife and some of his children.

Charles Town land deeds show that Francis Rankin Hooff bought for $1000.00 each from James H. Hooff of Mason County in December 15, 1853, Edward Lee Hooff September 3, 1855; John Lawrence Hooff, Jane Hammond Hooff, William Albert Hooff, interest of ownership in land that was willed to them through their grandfather, James Hammond. (Note: We read the Will of James Hammond and cannot figure how this came about).

Obituary from a Charles Town newspaper: Mr. Francis Hooff a native of the county, brother of Mr. John L. Hooff of this town died in Washington City on Friday last at 2 p.m. Aged 66 years. Just prior to the Mexican War, Mr. Hooff and the present editor of the Free Press were pupils of "Jacky" Harding who went to Mexico with the Virginia Regiment under Col Hamtramck and Major Jubal A. Early and died there. All through this half century we have known Mr. Hooff to be a kindly and worthy man. We have the testimony of an affection able sister of the deceased that he was "a good man, a devoted husband and father." Sometime ago he was paralyzed and again Thursday last had another stroke which proved fatal after a few hours. He had relatives and friends in Point Pleasant, W. Va., Alexandria, VA., Lexington, VA, Baltimore, MD, and Holden, Missouri and papers in those places are requested to announce his death.

Partial roster of Co. G., 2nd Regiment, "Stonewall" Brigade dated April 1862 show Francis R. Hooff, 2nd Virginia Infantry, Co. G, Botts Greys, private. Also shown on this roster is his brother William Albert Hooff and his cousin James L. Hooff.

This is the only information we can find about Francis R. Hooff serving in the Civil War.

Francis Rankin Hooff
1827 - 1896

Ronald L. Hooff, great- great grandson of Francis Rankin Hooff had
a Civil War marker placed at Francis's unmarked grave in 1999.

❧ Edward Lee Hooff

Born: October 26, 1865 in Charles Town, WV
Christened/Baptized: December 19, 1867 at Zion Episcopal Church, Charles Town, WV
Married: October 30, 1884 in Fairfax, VA
Died: November 14, 1932, Falls Church VA, age 67 years and 18 days
Buried: Oakwood Cemetery, Falls Church, VA
Father: Francis R. Hooff   Mother: Susan R. Hammond

Spouse: Viola Victoria McMillian Gladding
Born: September 5, 1854 in Fairfax, VA
Christened/Baptized:
Died: December 4, 1932 in Falls Church, VA at age 78.
Buried: Oakwood Cemetery, Falls Church, VA
Father: William McMillian (PA)   Mother: Virginia Taylor (VA)

They had six children:

❧**Hammond Francis Hooff** - Born 1885. See a separate chapter, page #117.

Sarah Isabelle Hooff - Born June 29, 1886 in Fairfax City, Va. Died December 31,1974 in Shreveport, LA. Married _____ Cross. No issue.

Anna Lee Hooff - Born October 26, 1890. Married _____ Winslow. No issue. Died January 3, 1994 in Rossville, GA.

Frances Hammond Hooff - Born May 1892. Died April 13, 1956. Married _____ Schatz. No issue.

Asberry Fairfax Hooff - Born September 6, 1893.

Gordon Campbell Hooff - Born March 9, 1896. Died November 28, 1950 at Portsmouth, VA. Buried at Arlington Cemetery, Arlington, VA. He was a veteran of World War I. His service number was 1 299 904, Army of the United States from July 23, 1914 to June 15, 1919. His rank was a private. He entered service from Washington, DC and was discharged at Camp Meade, MD. He received an Honorable Discharge. All other military information was destroyed by fire at the record's center. We were told that he inhaled "mustard gas" and was sickly afterwards. Married Hallie Holt who was born August 20, 1899, and died December 7, 1998 in Richmond, VA. Gordon Campbell was called Richard, Uncle Dick, and Tango by various members of the family because he loved to dance.

Edward Lee Hooff had one step-daughter named Edith Mary Gladding, born June 16, 1876, died April 30, 1976. She married Howard Rothery and had five sons.

We have found conflicting birth dates for Edward Lee from the census records and from his marriage license, ranging from 1859 to 1865. He came to Fairfax, VA with his parents some time in the 1870's from Charles Town, WV. We cannot find a birth date in Charles Town for him because of a fire that destroyed the records between the 1860's and 1870's.

Edward Lee Hooff had a farm in Fairfax, VA, and was considered to be a "Virginia Gentleman" His wife cared for welfare children. He was retired as a farmer and at the time of his death, he lived at 301 Virginia Avenue, Aurora Heights, Arlington, VA, home of his daughter Frances Schatz.

Daughter Anna stated that Viola was sick in bed for nine years before she died. Illness was unknown. Viola's father was a Quaker from Pennsylvania, her mother from Virginia. Daughter Francis Schatz left her job at Kahns to care for her mother, and because of this, her husband left her.

MARRIAGE LICENSE

Virginia, _Fairfax County_ to wit:

To any Person Licensed to Celebrate Marriages:

You are hereby authorized to join together in the Holy State of Matrimony, according to the rites and ceremonies of your Church, or religious denomination, and the laws of the Commonwealth of Virginia,

E. L. Hooff

and _Victoria L. Gladden_

Given under my hand, as Clerk of the _County_ Court of _Fairfax Co._ this _30_ day of _Oct_ 1884

F. M. Richardson Clerk.

CERTIFICATE TO OBTAIN A MARRIAGE LICENSE.

To be annexed to the License, required by Acts passed 15th March, 1861, and February 27th, 1866.

Time of Marriage, _30 Oct. 1884_

Place of Marriage, _Fairfax C.H. Va_

Full Names of Parties Married, _E. L. Hooff_ _Victoria V. Gladden_

Color, _White_

Age of Husband, _22_

Age of Wife, _28_

Condition of Husband, (widowed or single)

Condition of Wife, (widowed or single)

Place of Husband's Birth, _West Va_

Place of Wife's Birth, _Fairfax "_

Place of Husband's Residence, _" "_

Place of Wife's Residence, _" "_

Names of Husband's Parents, _J. R. & S. R. Hooff_

Names of Wife's Parents, _W. N. & J. E. McMullen_

Occupation of Husband, _Farmer_

Given under my hand this _30_ day of _Oct_ 1884

F. M. Richardson Clerk.

MINISTER'S RETURN OF MARRIAGE.

I Certify, That on the _30_ day of _October_ 1884, at _Fairfax C.H. Virginia_ I united in Marriage the above-named and described parties, under authority of the annexed License.

L. Frank Euttler Minister

☞ The Minister celebrating a marriage, is required, within TEN days thereafter, to return the license to the Office of the Clerk who issued the same, with an endorsement thereon of the FACT of such marriage, and of the TIME and PLACE of celebrating the same.

Edward Lee Hooff
October 1865 - November 1932

Son of Francis Rankin Hooff &
Susan Rankin Hammond
Ballston, VA
June 30, 1918

Viola V. McMillian-Hooff
September 1854 - December 1932

Edward Lee & Viola V.
Hooff with daughter
Sarah I. Hooff-Cross on
Ballston, VA farm
June 30, 1918

Gordon Campbell Hooff
March 1896 - November 1950
Son of Edward Lee &
Viola V. Hooff

Gordon Campbell Hooff
March 1896 - November 1950
Son of Edward Lee & Viola V. Hooff

Left to right - Sarah Hooff-Cross, June 1986 - December 1974
Edith M. Gladding (half-sister), June 1876 - April 1976
Francis Hooff Schatz - May 1882 - April 1956

Left to right - Edith M. Gladding, Francis Hooff Schatz, and
Anna Hooff Winslow (October 1890 - January 1994)

Left to right -
Edith M. Sledding-Rothery
Sarah I. Hooff-Cross
Francs H. Hooff-Schatz
Anna L. Hooff-Winslow
Taken in 1975

❧ Hammond Francis Hooff

Born: July 29, 1885 in Fairfax, VA
Christened/Baptized:
Married: April 20,1910 in Washington, DC.
Died: September 12, 1964 in Washington, DC at age 79 years.
Buried: Oakwood Cemetery, Falls Church, VA
Father: Edward Lee Hooff   Mother: Viola Victoria McMillen Gladding

Spouse: Caroline Lolah Unsworth
Born: June 27, 1879 in Washington, DC
Christened/Baptized:
Died: February 5, 1966 in Fairfax, VA
Buried: Cedar Hill Cemetery, Suitland, MD
Father: Thomas Henry Unsworth   Mother: Kate E. A. Johnson

They had three children:

Thomas Edward Hooff - Born February 8, 1911 in Washington, DC. Died November 6, 1979 in Alexandria, VA. Buried at Cedar Hill Cemetery in Suitland, MD. Married Elona Christine Hebron, daughter of Edgar Hebron. Elona was born September 2, 1913 in Wisconsin; died April 25, 1968; buried at Cedar Hill Cemetery. Thomas (who was called Ed) was a blacksmith and lived in Alexandria, Va. He played pro football for Washington, Richmond and Baltimore during the early 1930's. Thomas and Elona had two sons:

Thomas Edward Hooff Jr. - Born December 28, 1949 in Wisconsin; died August 7,1997 in Virginia. He attended Fork Union Military Academy and University of Richmond. He was married with one child.

William Aaron Hooff - Born January 13, 1952 in Washington, DC. Married Dalene Braheny who was born January 16, 1953 in Washington, DC. They have two children: William A. Hooff Jr., born April 18, 1971, and Michelle Lynn Hooff, born May 8, 1973.

Obituary for Thomas Edward Hooff - On Tuesday, November 6, 1979, at Alexandria Hospital, THOMAS E. HOOFF of Alexandria, VA, beloved husband of the late Elona Hooff; father of William A. and Thomas E. Jr.; brother of Benjamin Hooff. He is also survived by three grandchildren. Friends may call at the Ives Funeral Home, 2847 Wilson Blvd., Arlington, VA, on Wednesday, November 7, and Thursday, November 8 from 2 to 4 and 7 to 9 p.m. Grave side services will be held on Friday, November 9, at 11 a.m. Interment Cedar Hill Cemetery, Suitland, MD.

Article from the Washington Star, October 31, 1965:
"BABY NEEDS A NEW PAIR OF SHOES, ED HOOFF is a blacksmith and his "village" is the Maryland and Virginia countryside within 100 miles of Washington. He is one of the some 50 blacksmiths serving this horse-conscious area with an estimated equine population of 25,000. There is a growing demand for the blacksmith, who at one time was threatened by automation in the form of the horseless carriage. But stables are on the increase in this affluent society. On the Potomac, MD farm named Astarte, owned by Mr. and Mrs. David Abse, there are 12 show horses. Hooff drives into Astarte in his air-conditioned baby blue Cadillac once every six weeks - more often in case of an emergency. "I have three daughters," say Mrs. Abse, "and you know what the crap-shooters say - "Baby needs a new pair of shoes. That's even more true about horses. Their hooves keep growing." Hooff has a number regular customers and they keep him busy. In addition, he is in demand at the big shows. He'll be on hand, along with others of his trade, at the Washington International Horse shows starting Thursday in the D.C. Armory. Each blacksmith will bring along a wide selection of styles and sizes in shoes. A show horse deserves and gets the best.

♨Jessie Gordon Hooff - Born 1913. See a separate chapter, page #123.

Benjamin Lee Hooff - Born June 5, 1918 in Washington, DC. He was a retired Lt. Col. U.S. Army. Married Jewell _____ . No issue. Lived in Chicago, IL. Died May 1984.

Per William Rothery, Hammond Francis was dead one week before Caroline Lolah Hooff would sign a release so that his sisters Sara, Annie, and Edie (half sister) could bury him.

Ronald Lee Hooff, grandson, doesn't remember much about Hammond. His father took him once to see Hammond at the People's Drug Store on Pennsylvania Avenue, Washington, DC, where Hammond and his friends would sit and drink coffee.

Hammond Francis Hooff was listed in the D.C. directory of 1910 as a carpenter, and in 1913 as a member of the fire department.

Caroline Lolah lived at the following addresses:
326 10th St., S.E., Washington, DC in late 1930s
1801 Ft. Davis St., Washington, DC in 1942-1964 with son Jessie
3705 80th Ave., Forestville, MD in 1964-1966

I, (grandson, Ronald Lee Hooff), would visit grandma Caroline Lolah often. She saw all three of my daughters at various times. My sister Lynn refused to let me take her children to visit grandma Caroline Lolah or Jessie (great grandmother and grandfather).

She died at the Fairfax Lodge (home for the old), 11140 Main St., Fairfax, VA of cerebral hemorrhage, hypertension cardiovascular disease and general arterosclerous. The funeral director was Simmons Funeral Home, 1661 Good Hope Rd., SE., Washington, DC.

Form SS-5
TREASURY DEPARTMENT
INTERNAL REVENUE SERVICE

U. S. SOCIAL SECURITY ACT
APPLICATION FOR ACCOUNT NUMBER 577-18 3785

1. Hammond *(EMPLOYEE'S FIRST NAME)* F. *(only)* *(MIDDLE NAME)* *(MARRIED WOMEN GIVE MAIDEN FIRST NAME, MAIDEN LAST NAME, AND HUSBAND'S LAST NAME)* Hooff *(LAST NAME)*

2. 2201 K St. N.W. *(STREET AND NUMBER)* Washington, DC *(POST OFFICE)* *(STATE)*

4. J. W. Chaalworth & Co *(BUSINESS NAME OF PRESENT EMPLOYER)* 5. Hyattsville Md. *(BUSINESS ADDRESS OF PRESENT EMPLOYER)*

6. 53 *(AGE AT LAST BIRTHDAY)* 7. July 30 1884 *(DATE OF BIRTH (MONTH) (DAY) (YEAR) (SUBJECT TO LATER VERIFICATION))* 8. Fairfax County Virginia *(PLACE OF BIRTH)*

9. Edward J Hooff *(FATHER'S FULL NAME)* 10. Victoria Viola Mullen *(MOTHER'S FULL MAIDEN NAME)*

11. SEX: MALE ✓ FEMALE *(CHECK J WHICH)* 12. COLOR: WHITE ✓ NEGRO OTHER *(CHECK J WHICH)* *(SPECIFY)*

10-11-37

13. IF REGISTERED WITH THE U. S. EMPLOYMENT SERVICE, GIVE NUMBER OF REGISTRATION CARD

14. IF YOU HAVE PREVIOUSLY FILLED OUT A CARD LIKE THIS, STATE no *(PLACE)* *(DATE)*

October 15 1937 *(DATE SIGNED)* Hammond F Hooff *(EMPLOYEE'S SIGNATURE, AS USUALLY WRITTEN)*

DETACH ALONG THIS LINE

Hammond Francis Hooff (1940's)
July 1885 -September 1964
Son of Edward Lee & Viola V. Hooff

On the right is
Caroline Lohla Unsworth
June 1879 - February 1966
taken August 1945

Sons of Hammond F. & Caroline L. Hooff taken in 1922

From left to right
Jessie Gordon Hooff - June 1913 - May 1975
Benjamin lee Hooff - June 1918 -May 1984
Thomas Edward Hooff - February 1911 - November 1979

๛ Jessie Gordon Hooff

Born: June 28, 1913 in Washington, DC
Christened/Baptized:
Married: April 14, 1937 in Alexandria, VA. Separated March 13, 1942. Divorced June 14, 1946
Died: May 28, 1975 in Lanham, MD at age 61 years and 11 months.
Buried: Cedar Hill Cemetery, Suitland, MD
Father: Hammond Francis Hooff   Mother: Caroline Lolah Unsworth

Spouse: 1st - Margaret Eleanor Kirby
Born: December 15, 1911 at Georgetown Hospital, Washington, DC
Christened/Baptized: Holy Trinity Church, Washington, DC
Died: July 29, 1992 at Prince George's Hospital, Cheverly, Md, 81 years, 11 months.
Buried: Cheltenham Veterans Cemetery, Cheltenham, MD.
After her divorce from Jessie, Margaret married Frederick W. McLeod in 1948.
Father: Frederick Lewis Kirby   Mother: Eleanor Irene Dove (Nellie Louise Dove)
                                      Served in WWI as Navy nurse and is buried at
                                      Arlington National Cemetery.

Jessie and Margaret had two children:

Edna Lynn Hooff - Born February 8, 1938 in Washington, DC.

๛Ronald Lee Hooff - Born 1939. See a separate chapter, page #129.

Jessie was in the U.S. Army April 15, 1942; Service #33189471, Social Security #579-05-0530. Hgt. Batry. 105th AAA P.F.C. Search Light Operator, North Apennines, PO Valley, Rome Anno. He received European, African, Middle East service, and Good Conduct Medals. He was discharged September 23, 1945, total service of 1 year 2 months U.S. and 2 years, 3 months and 9 days overseas service. Jessie joined the Army to avoid paying child support, but Margaret fooled him and had his Army pay seized.

He returned to live with his mother on 1801 Ft. Davis Street, SE Washington, DC. He then moved to 3705 80th Ave., Forestville, MD in 1964 where he lived with his mother until her death.

Spouse: 2nd - Audrey June Philyaw (nee Twilly)
b: May 30, 1926 - d: June 2, 1996, buried at Cedar Hill Cemetery.
Married: August 5, 1966 in Bowie, MD

Audrey June had two children by a previous marriage. Jessie moved into her home in Bowie, MD after their marriage. He sold the Forestville home that he inherited from his mother. There were no children to his marriage with Audrey.

LAST WILL AND TESTAMENT OF JESSIE G. HOOFF

I, Jessie G. Hooff, of Bowie, Maryland, declare this to be my Last Will and Testament, and revoke all prior Wills and codicils made by me.

Item I. I direct my Personal Representative to pay my legally enforceable debts and funeral expenses and have a marker erected at my grave, and I authorize her to expend for these purposes such sums as she deems proper, without any limit prescribed by law and without obtaining the prior, or subsequent order or ratification of any Court.

Item II. All of the rest and residue of my estate, real and personal, and all property over which I may have power of testamentary disposition, I devise, bequeath and appoint to my wife, Audrey J. Hooff, absolutely, if she survives me.

Item III. If my said wife predeceases me, I direct, authorize and empower my Personal Representative to distribute all of my tangible personal property including jewelry, clothing, books, pictures, silverware, china, household furniture and furnishings, and all other household and personal effects and any automobiles to such of my wife Audrey's children as may survive me in such proportions as my Personal Representative, in his sole and absolute discretion, may deem proper and to the best interests of such child or children. Any of such goods and chattels not so distributed may be sold or otherwise disposed of by my Personal Representative and if any sale is so made, the proceeds thereof shall form a part of the rest and residue of my estate. I authorize and empower my Personal Representative, in his sole discretion, to hold such proportionate share which my be distributed to any minor until he or she attains legal age or distribute the same to his or her legal Guardian or to such other person who in the opinion of my Personal Representative my be in proper charge of such minor to be held until such minor becomes of legal age, or if my Personal Representative deems best, to distribute the same directly to such minor and a release duly executed by any such person or minor to who distribution is made, shall be a full and complete acquittance and discharge to my Personal Representative.

Item IV. If my said wife predeceases me, all of the rest and residue of my estate, real and personal, and all property over which I may have power of testamentary disposition, I absolutely devise, bequeath, and appoint to my wife's issue, per stirpes, provided that at the time my wife's youngest living child is then of legal age, otherwise I devise, bequeath and appoint the same to my wife's sister, Lahoma D. Oliff (Mrs. Clarence M. Oliff), who presently resides in Edgewater, Maryland, in trust for the following uses and trust purposes:

A. Until the termination of this trust my Trustee shall pay so much or all of the net income and/or principal of the trust to or for the benefit of my said wife's children, in such proportions and in such manner as my Trustee, in her discretion, shall deem necessary or desirable to insure comfortable support, maintenance, education (including college education), general welfare and care for such children' provided, however, my Trustee may, in her absolute discretion, accumulate such income not expended during the calendar year in which the same may be received and shall add such accumulations to the principal of this trust. These payments shall be made according to the needs of my children and not necessarily equally, so that if any child has other sources of support, then the payments to such child may be reduced accordingly or suspended entirely in the discretion of my Trustee.

B. If any child or children of my wife shall die prior to the termination of this trust, my Trustee is authorized, in her sole discretion, to pay from the income and/or principal all or any portion of the expenses of the last illness and burial of any such child or children so dying and to have a suitable marker erected at his or her grave, is such expenses are not otherwise provided for.

C. I am especially concerned with the education of my wife's child or children and I direct my Trustee to be liberal in the use of the trust estate, both income and principal, for education since this is one of the primary reasons for the establishment of the trust estate.

D. The termination of the trust shall be at such time as there shall be no living child of my wife under twenty-two (22) years of age, at which time the trust estate as it then exists, both principal and undistributed income, shall be distributed to my wife's living descendants, per stirpes, absolutely.

Item V. Any property maturing for distribution from my estate or any trust created by this my Will in respect to which there be no person then living and qualified to take under the aforegoing provisions shall be distributed in accordance with the then laws of the State of Maryland as if I had then died intestate. (Note from Ron: I had been told all my life that he had no use for his natural children. If all of them die, including June's sisters family, the State of Maryland gets his estate; this is what he thought of his own children).

Item VI. All payments hereunder (whether of income or principal) are to be made into the hands of the respective beneficiaries direct and not into the hands of any other, whether claiming by their authority or otherwise, without power of anticipation and without being subject to execution or attachment; this provision, however, not to limit or restrict any discretionary powers conferred upon my Trustee nor to prevent the deposit of funds payable to beneficiaries to their credit in any bank or other financial institution.

Item VII. A. My Trustee shall have full power to receive insurance proceeds, to invest, reinvest and change the investments of the trust estate, real or personal, from time to time, and to subscribe to any stock or other securities to which the trust estate may be entitled from time to time to subscribe, and to compromise and settle any claims against or in favor of the trust estate, and for such purpose, or any other purposes which may be deemed by my Trustee to be advantageous to the trust estate, to sell, lease (including the power to lease for a period extending beyond the probable duration of the trust), mortgage, exchange or otherwise dispose of or deal with the assets of the trust estate; and whenever divisions are contemplated or necessary, to divide in kind and/or sell for the purpose of division the whole thereof or such portion thereof as my Trustee may deem necessary or desirable.

B. My Trustee is authorized to retain any investments acquired from my Personal Representative or otherwise, until such time as in her judgment it would be desirable to dispose of the same under the powers herein above conferred, and the decision of my Trustee shall be conclusive and without liability upon it for any loss occasioned thereby.

Item VIII. If my said wife and I shall die under such circumstances where there is insufficient proof to determine who predeceased the other, I direct that my said wife shall be deemed to have predeceased me.

Item IX. My failure to name as beneficiaries of this will the issue of my former marriage to Margaret E. Hooff, namely Edna Lynn Shymansky and Ronald Lee Hooff, was deliberate and intentional.

Item X. All estate, inheritance, succession and transfer taxes (including interest and penalties thereon, if any), payable with respect to all property includeable in my gross estate for federal estate tax purposes, or taxable by reason of my death, including inheritance taxes which may be prepaid by or on behalf of any person having a contingent or remainder interest therein, if my Personal Representative in her absolute discretion deems it advisable to prepay such taxes, shall be paid out of the principal of my residuary estate.

Item XI. I hereby appoint my wife Audrey J. Hooff, my Personal Representative, but if she predeceases me or is unable to any reason to complete the administration of my estate, then I appoint Daniel I. Sherry, Esquire, my Personal Representative. I request that my Personal Representative shall be excused from the necessity of giving bond.

I confer upon my Personal Representative full power and authority to sell, assign, transfer, convey, exchange, divide, invest, reinvest, mortgage, pledge, lease or otherwise dispose of any part of my estate, real or personal, and to compromise any
claims against or in favor of my estate for such sums and upon such terms and conditions as my Personal Representative may deem proper, without obtaining the prior or subsequent order of ratification of any Court.

IN TESTIMONY WHEREOF, I sign my name under seal this 11th day of October 1972,

/s/ Jessie G. Hooff   (SEAL)

SIGNED, SEALED and DECLARED by Jessie G. Hooff as his Last Will and Testament, in the presence of us, who, at his request, in his presence and in the presence of each other, sign our names as witnesses.

/s/   12406 Whitehall Drive
                          Bowie, Maryland

/s/   15518 Annapolis Rd.
                          Bowie, MD

LAST WILL AND TESTAMENT OF MARGARET E. HOOFF McLEOD

I, MARGARET E. McLEOD of Prince George's County, Maryland, being of sound and disposing mind, memory and understanding, do hereby make, publish and declare this as my Last Will and Testament, hereby revoking all Wills and codicils by me heretofore made.

First: I hereby direct my Personal Representative, hereinafter named, to pay all of my legally enforceable debts and funeral expenses as soon after my death as may be practicable. I direct that my funeral expenses including a suitable marker for my grave, may be paid in any amount notwithstanding and statutory limitation as to the amount of such expenses, and without the necessity of obtaining an Order of Court.

SECOND: I give and bequeath the sum of Fifty Thousand Dollars ($50,000.00) to my son, Ronald Hooff, should he survive me. Should he not survive me, I direct this legacy to lapse and the proceeds of the same pass under the residuary clause of this, my Last Will and Testament.

THIRD: All the rest, residue and remainder of my property and Estate, whether, real, personal or mixed, wheresoever situate, which, at the time of my death shall belong to me or be subject to my testamentary disposition, I give, devise and bequeath unto my son, Ronald Hooff, should he survive me and to my daughter, E. Lynn Shymansky, or her heirs, in equal shares, share and share alike, in fee simple and absolutely. (Note: Ron's wife and heirs were left out.)

FOURTH: I hereby nominate, constitute and appoint my daughter, E. Lynn Shymansky to be Personal Representative of my estate and Last Will and Testament. If she should fail or cease for any reason to serve as Personal Representative, I appoint my son, Ronald Hooff, to be Personal Representative of my estate and of this, my Last Will and Testament, and I direct that my Personal Representative be allowed to serve without the necessity of giving bond in any amount.

WITNESS, my hand and seal to this my Last Will and Testament this 9th day of September, 1991.

_____ (SEAL)
MARGARET E. McLEOD, Testatrix
12319 Stonehaven Lane, #S1
Bowie, MD 20715

SIGNED, SEALED, PUBLISHED AND DECLARED by the within named Testatrix, MARGARET E. McLEOD, as and for her Last Will and Testament, in our presence and in the presence of each other, who, at her request and in her presence and in the presence of each other, have hereunto subscribed our names and address as attesting witness, on the day and year last hereinbefore written.

Denise A. Ward
14507 Main Street
Upper Marlboro, MD

IN THE ORPHANS' COURT FOR

(OR)   Prince George's County_____, MARYLAND

BEFORE THE REGISTER OF WILLS FOR

IN THE ESTATE OF:

MARGARET ELEANORE McLEOD_____   ESTATE NO: ___39,698___

INFORMATION REPORT

1. At the time of death did the decedent have any interest as a joint owner (other than with a surviving spouse) in any real or personal property, including accounts in a credit union, bank, or other financial institution?

   ❏ No   XX Yes   If yes, give the following information as to all such jointly owned property:

Name, Address, and Relationship of Joint Owner	Nature of Property	Total Value
E. Lynn Shymansky, 12322 Flamingo Ln., Bowie, MD 20715 Daughter	Checking Acct. 80809080	4,282.36
E. Lynn Shymansky, 12322 Flamingo Ln., Bowie, MD 20715 Daughter	Savings Acct. 8-0705684	14,467.61

$18,749

Both accounts are located at Annapolis Federal Savings Bank, PO Box 751, Annapolis, MD 21404

2. Within two years before death did the decedent make any transfer, other than a bona fide sale, of any material part of the decedent's property in the nature of a final disposition or distribution, including any transfer that resulted in joint ownership of property?

   ❏ No   XX Yes   If yes, give the following information as to each transfer.

Date of Transfer	Name, Address, and Relationship of Transferee	Nature of Property Transferred	Total Value of Property
	SEE ATTACHED LIST		

3. At the time of death did the decedent have (a) any interest less than absolute in real or personal property over which the decedent retained dominion while alive, (b) any interest in any annuity or other public or private employee pension or benefit plan that is taxable for federal estate tax purposes, (c) any interest in real or personal property for life or for a term of years, or (d) any other interest in real or personal property less than absolute, in trust or otherwise?

   ☒ No   ❏ Yes   If yes, give the following information as to each such interest:

Description of Interest and Amount or Value	Date and Type of Instrument Establishing Interest	Name, Address, and Relationship of Successor, Owner, or Beneficiary

I solemnly affirm under the penalties of perjury that the contents of this report are true to the best of my knowledge, information, and belief.

Judith H. Mullen   Attorney   _E. Lynn Shymansky_   Personal Representative   Date
Judith H. Mullen   E. Lynn Shymansky

14842 Old Marlboro Pike
            Address   _____
                                                 Personal Representative   Date

Upper Marlboro, Maryland 20772
                                                 _____
                                                 Personal Representative   Date

(301) 627-8000
      Telephone Number

RW 24

PS-3580

Date of Transfer	Name, Address, and Relationship of Transferee	Nature of Property Transferred	Total Value of Property
09/25/91	E. Lynn Shymansky, Daughter 12322 Flamingo Lane Bowie, Maryland 20715	Cash	$140,170.00
03/19/91	E. Lynn Shymansky, Daughter 12322 Flamingo Lane Bowie, Maryland 20715	1991 Olds Cutlass	$ 15,000.00
02/25/92	Kathryn L. Tomey, Granddaughter 14150 Spring Branch Drive Upper Marlboro, Maryland 20772	Cash	$ 1,000.00
09/22/91	E. Lynn Shymansky, Daughter 12322 Flamingo Lane Bowie, Maryland 20715	Cash	$ 4,000.00
08/20/91	Ronald L. Hooff, Son 2208 Hideout Lane Bowie, Maryland 20716	Cash	$ 8,000.00
10/28/91	Ronald L. Hooff, Son 2208 Hideout Lane Bowie, Maryland 20716	Cash	$ 3,000.00
04/13/92	Ronald L. Hooff, Son 2208 Hideout Lane Bowie, Maryland 20716	Cash	$ 2,000.00

140
65
7 5,000

❧ Ronald Lee Hooff

Born: March 28,1939, Providence Hospital in Washington, DC
Christened/Baptized: May 21, 1939 at St. Francis Xavier Church, Pennsylvania Ave., Washington, D.C.
Married: 1st - March 9, 1962 in Easton, MD. Divorced July 23, 1972
Died:
Buried:
Father: Jessie Gordon Hooff   Mother: Margaret Eleanor Kirby

Spouse: 1st - Kathleen Marie Semega
Born: May 14, 1945 in Swickley, PA
Christened/Baptized: June 10, 1945 at Holy Trinity Church, Ambridge, PA
Died:
Buried:
Father: Bernard Paul David Semega   Mother: Francis Lillian Zganier
   Born: April 16, 1914   Born: February 28, 1924 in Ambridge, PA
   Died: December 10, 1967   Died: December 21, 1977
   In Hyattsville, MD

Both Bernard and Francis are buried in Arlington National Cemetery. It is interesting to note that death certificate for Francis Lillian Zganier shows her name as B. Lillian Gainer. Her parents were: Anthony Zgainer; born September 1, 1895 in Yugoslavia; died November 15, 1965 in Swickley Hospital, Swickley, PA. his father was Steve Zgainer; mother was Josephine (?). Mother was Katherine Rosic, born January 17, 1903 in Martins Ferry, OH; died July 5, 1964 in Swickley Hospital, Swickley, PA; buried at Mt. Olivet Cahtolic Cemetery, Hopewell Township, Beaver, PA.. Katherine's father was Anton Rosic; mother was Anna Katkic.

They had three children:

Kimberly Marie Hooff - Born November 15, 1962 in Washington, DC.. Baptized December 23, 1962 at Holy Trinity Church, Ambridge, PA. She first married Alexander David Thomson in Arlington County, VA on August 10, 1984, and divorced a few years later. They had one daughter, Courtney Marie Thomson who was born May 2, 1984, baptized October 21, 1984 at St. Bernard's Church, Riverdale, MD.

   Married 2nd - David Vincent Windell , son of William David Windell and Sue Louise Bush (an only child), on May 24, 1989 in Arlington County, VA. They had one daughter, Shannon Marie Windell (aka Kerry Leigh), who was born December 27, 1989 in Laurel, MD.

Lisa Marie Hooff - Born July 27, 1964 in Washington, DC. Baptized August 23, 1964 at St. Bernard's Church, Riverdale, MD. She married Andre Gustaaf Lambert Francois on November 20, 1995 in Upper Marlboro, MD. He was born in Belguim. They have one daughter, Ashleigh Marie Francois who was born June 13, 1996. Baptized December 5, 1996 at St. Bernards, Riverdale, MD

Robyn Marie Hooff - Born September 22, 1965 in Washington, DC. Baptized October 24, 1965 at St. Bernard's Church, Riverdale, MD. She married Richard Harry Weinstein, born October 8, 1951 to Max and Beatrice (Solomon) Weinstein, on September 23, 1988 in Upper Marlboro, MD. They have two children:
   Jamie Lee Hooff who was born November 3, 1986, at Montgomery General Hospital in Olney, MD. Christened at St. Ursala Catholic Church, Parkville, MD (Baltimore County).

   Brittany Marie Hooff who was born November 7, 1987 in route to Montgomery General Hospital, Olney, MD.

Robyn had these children before her marriage, and wanted Jamie and Brittany to have the family name of Hooff. She stated she wanted Jamie to carry on the Hooff family name. These 2 children were taken by Social Services; Brittany was adopted by Del and Pat Roy. As of this time (November 1999), Jamie remains in foster care.

Robyn had two more children by Arthur Charles Love, (b: February 18, 1965 in Fairfax, Va. Father was Frankin Baker Love, b: December 29, 1919 in Great Neck, NY; Mother: Janetta Haines Goddard, b: October 29, 1925 in Washington, DC, m: approx. 1954). Robyn and Arthur's children were born out of wedlock, but do carry their father's name of Love:

Michael Anthony Love, born April 24, 1992 in Montgomery County, MD, of which she gave up for adoption on February 4, 1993 to Julie Stinger. Michael tested positive for cocaine at birth.

Matthew Shaun Love, born October 30, 1994, at Washington Adventist Hospital in Takoma Park, MD. Matthew remains in Robyn's care.

Spouse: 2nd - Barbara Marie Carrick-Bell
Born: April 1, 1943 in Washington, DC
Christened/Baptized:
Married: December 31, 1974 in Bowie, MD
Died:
Buried:
There were no children from this marriage.
Father: Robert Elwood Carrick   Mother: Madeline Eleanor Robertson

Ron retired from National Security Agency May 6, 1971. He returned to work at U.S. Postal Service January 20, 1973. He retired from U.S. Postal Service.

Eleanor Irene Dove-Kirby (Nellie Louise Kirby)
April 1887 - June 1957
(Grandmother of Ron Hooff)

Daughter of James A. Dove & Margaret A. Burch

Picture taken in the 1920's

Margaret Eleanor Kirby-Hooff-McLeod
December 1911 - July 1992

Daughter of Eleanor Irene Dove-Kirby
(Nellie Louise Kirby)& Frederick Lewis Kirby

Picture taken in 1948

Ronald Lee Hooff
March 1938 -
Son of Jessie Gordon Hooff & Margaret Eleanor Kirby

Picture taken in 1941

Ronald Lee Hooff
1944

Ronald Lee Hooff
Early 1950's

Alter Boys of St. Bernard's Church, Riverdale, MD, 1951. *Rear* - Fred Kreamer, Bill Kreamer, unknown, unknown. *Front left to right* - Jerry Kirby, Larry Kreamer, Ron Hooff, unknown, unknown.

Ronald Lee Hooff

Picture taken in 1955

Wedding Day of Ronald L. Hooff & Kathleen M. Semega
March 9, 1962

Christening of Lisa Marie Hooff August 23, 1964
Rear - Buddy Semega holding Kim Hooff
Front - Bernard P. Semega, Sr., Anthony Zgainer, Carol Edwards holding Lisa Hooff

Caroline Lolah Unsworth-Hooff with great-granddaughters
Lisa M. and Kimberly M. Hooff.
Easter 1965

Jessie Gordon Hooff with granddaughters Lisa M. and Kimberly M. Hooff
Easter 1965

Anthony & Katherine-Rosic- Zgainer parents of Francis L. Zgainer-Semega
Easter 1964

Francis L. Semega & Bernard P.
Semega, Sr., grandparents of

Kimberly M. Hooff
Lisa M. Hooff
Robyn M. Hooff

August 1966

Margaret Hooff-McLeod grandmother of
Kim, Lisa and Robyn Hooff.
May 1970

Robyn, Ron, Lisa and Kim Hooff
December 1970

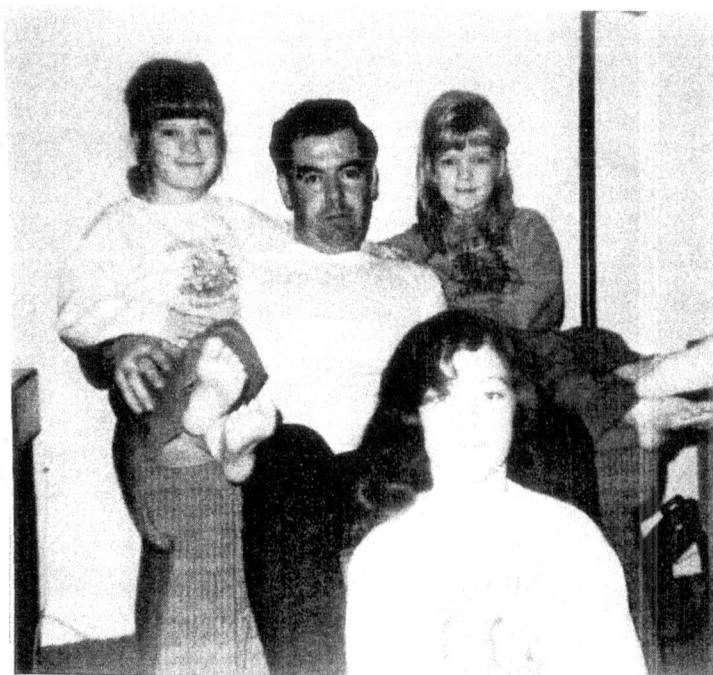

Grandmother Margaret Hooff-McLeod with Robyn, Lisa and Kim Hooff
Christmas 1974

Rear - Lisa Hooff, Barbara Carrick-Hooff, Kim Hooff
Front - Robyn Hooff
at Davidsonville home - Christmas 1974

Robyn Hooff, Kim Hooff, Barbara Carrick-Hooff, Lisa Hooff
at Davidsonville home - Christmas 1981

May 2, 1989

Seated - Fred McLeod, Lisa Hooff holding Jamie Hooff, Margaret Hooff-McLeod with Courtney Thomson standing in front of her, Kathy Semege Hooff- Henderson-Whyte, Kimberly Hooff-Thomson-Windell holding Brittany Hooff. *Standing in rear* - Ron and Barbara Hooff.

November 1989

Standing - Dave Windell, Ron Hooff, Lisa Hooff, Robyn Hooff holding Brittany Hooff, Rick Weinstein.
Middle row - Jamie Hooff, Kim Hooff-Thomson-Windell, Barbara Hooff.
Front row - Steven & Danny Windell, Courtney Thomson, Mike Windell

November 24, 1996 - Christening of Ashleigh Marie Francois

Rear - Bernard P.

(Buddy) Semega, Andre Francois, Ron Hooff
Front - Kathy Semega-Hooff-Henderson-Whyte, Lisa Hooff-Francois, Barbara M. Carrick-Hooff
Ashleigh Marie Francois

Christmas 1996

Standing - Dave Windell, Andre Francois, Shaun & Artie Love, Barbara Carrick-Hooff, Bob & Madeline Carrick.

Middle Row - Robyn Hooff-Weinstein-Love, Lisa Hooff-Francois & Ashleigh, Kimberly Hooff-Thomson-Windell, Ron Hooff (kneeling).

Sitting - Courtney M. Thomson, Shannon M. (Kerri L.) Windell.

Christmas 1996

Brittany M. Hooff

Jamie L. Hooff

Memorial Day, May 1997

Standing - Artie Love, Barbara Hooff holding Ashleigh Francois, Robyn Hooff, Kathy Hooff-Whyte, Andre Francois, Lisa Francois, Ron Hooff. *Front* - Kerri Windell, Shaun Love, Courtney Thomson, Kim Hooff-Windell.

From left to right
Kim Hooff-Windell
Ron Hooff
Lisa Hooff- Francois
Kathy Hooff-Whyte
Robyn Hooff

❦Lorenz
1710 - 1799

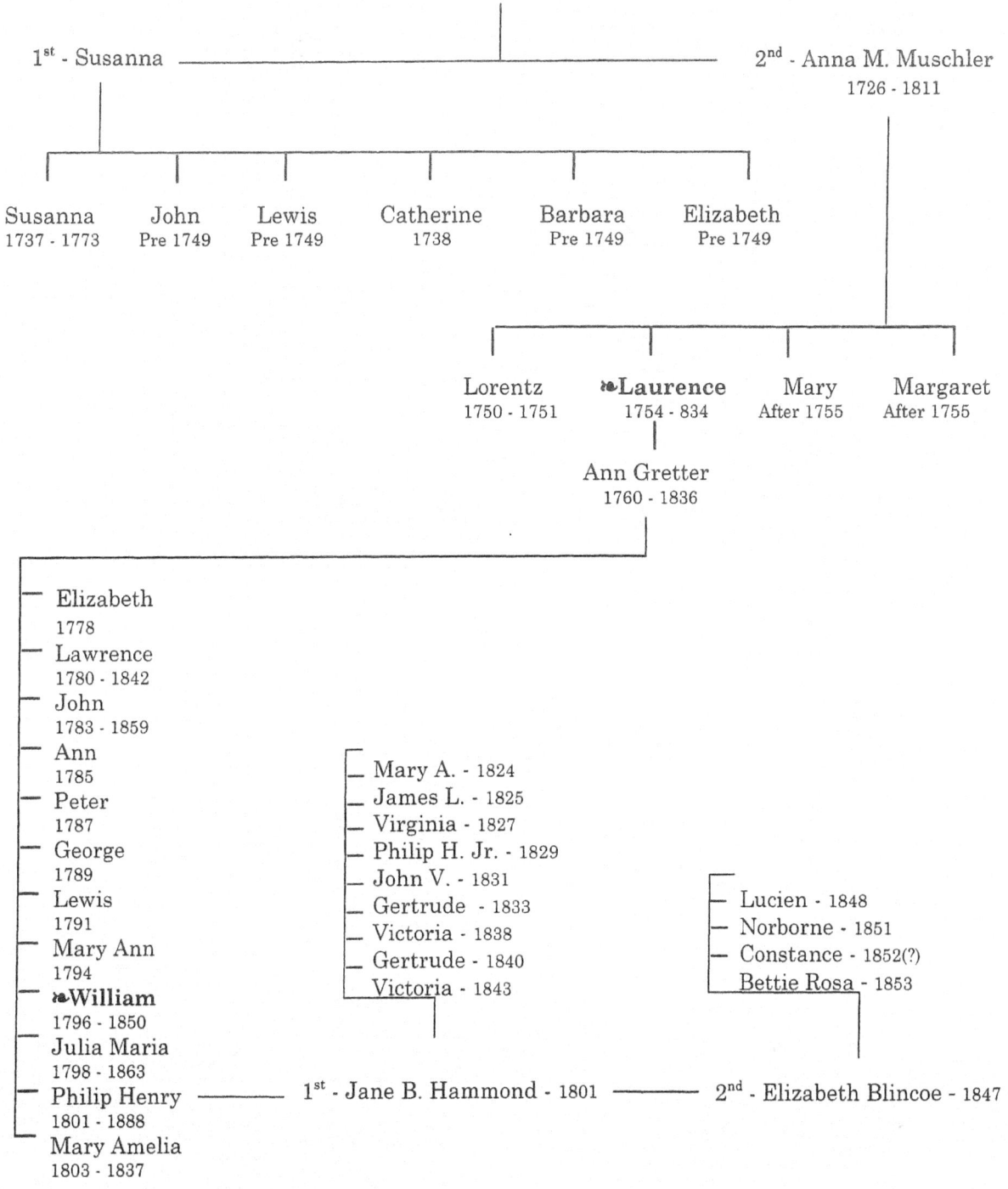

1st - Susanna ——————————————————————— 2nd - Anna M. Muschler
1726 - 1811

Susanna	John	Lewis	Catherine	Barbara	Elizabeth
1737 - 1773	Pre 1749	Pre 1749	1738	Pre 1749	Pre 1749

Lorentz	❦Laurence	Mary	Margaret
1750 - 1751	1754 - 834	After 1755	After 1755

Ann Gretter
1760 - 1836

Elizabeth
1778

Lawrence
1780 - 1842

John
1783 - 1859

Ann
1785

Peter
1787

George
1789

Lewis
1791

Mary Ann
1794

❦William
1796 - 1850

Julia Maria
1798 - 1863

Philip Henry ———————— 1st - Jane B. Hammond - 1801 ———————— 2nd - Elizabeth Blincoe - 1847
1801 - 1888

Mary Amelia
1803 - 1837

Mary A. - 1824
James L. - 1825
Virginia - 1827
Philip H. Jr. - 1829
John V. - 1831
Gertrude - 1833
Victoria - 1838
Gertrude - 1840
Victoria - 1843

Lucien - 1848
Norborne - 1851
Constance - 1852(?)
Bettie Rosa - 1853

Philip Henry Hooff I

Born: February 23, 1801 in Alexandria, D.C
Christened/Baptized:
Married: 1st - June 23, 1823 in Charles Town, WV
Died: February 7, 1888 in Alexandria at age 87
Buried: St. Paul's Episcopal Church Cemetery, Alexandria, D.C.
Father: Lawrence Hooff II   Mother: Ann Gretter

Spouse: 1st - Jane Baxter Hammond (Sister of Francis Rankin Hammond, his bother William's wife)
Born: 1801 at "Mt. Hammond" in Charles Town, WV
Christened/Baptized:
Died: June 7, 1844 in Alexandria, DC age 43
Buried:
Father: James Hammond   Mother Mary (Polly) Rankin

They had nine children:

Mary Ann Hooff - Born April 15, 1824 in Alexandria. Died January 26, 1899 in Washington, DC. Married Rufus Smith (b: August 12, 1822 in Middleburg, Loudoun Co. VA - d: December 1883 in Washington, DC, bur: in Georgetown, DC, son of Hugh Smith and Elizabeth Jones of Hill Farm, Middleburg, VA) on September 8, 1846. They had six children:

> Clarendon Smith - Born May 6, 1855 in Middleburg
> Virginia Smith
> Keyes Smith
> Julian Smith
> Heywood Smith
> Cuthbert Smith

James Lawrence Hooff - Born 1825. See a separate chapter, page #171.

Virginia Hooff - Born June 11, 1827. Baptized May 11, 1833 at St. Paul's Episcopal Church in Alexandria, VA. Died February 2, 1901, and buried at Zion Episcopal Churchyard in Charles Town, WV. She was unmarried. She lived in Charles Town and was the communicant of Zion Episcopal Church. Her tombstone reads: "Asleep in Jesus"

Philip Henry Hooff Jr. - Born 1829. See a separate chapter, page #191.

John Vowell Hooff - Born May 26, 1831. See a separate chapter, page #211.

Gertrude Hooff - Born December 25, 1833 in Alexandria, DC. Baptized April 11, 1837 at St. Paul's Episcopal Church. Died August 27, 1838 in Alexandria.

Victoria Hooff - Born July 12, 1838 in Alexandria, DC. Baptized August 6, 1838 at St. Paul's Episcopal Church, Alexandria, DC. Died September 4, 1839 in Alexandria.

Gertrude Heywood Hooff - Born June 1, 1840 in Alexandria, DC. Confirmed August 29, 1862 at Zion Episcopal Church in Charles Town, WV. Died 1899. She married John Royster Armistead, Jr. of Marengo County, Alabama on December 6, 1883 in Charles Town. They had no children. (The 1860 Census, Loudoun Co., VA shows Gertrude Hooff, age 19, living in the household of Mary Ann and Rufus Smith).

Victoria Hooff - Born April 15, 1843 in Alexandria, DC. Died September 5, 1843.

"Mt. Hammond"
built ca. 1745
Jefferson County, WVA (formerly Berkeley County)
Birth place of Jane Baxter Hammond Hooff (Mrs. Philip Henry Hooff) and
Frances Rankin Hammond (Mrs. William Hooff)
Benjamin Rankin left this house to his daughter "Polly" after her marriage to James Hammond.

Spouse: 2nd - Elizabeth Blincoe (Bettie) on February 19, 1847 in Loudoun Co., VA. Elizabeth is the sister of Martha Jones Blincoe, 2nd wife of John Hooff, 2nd
Born: ca. 1820, probably Leesburg, VA (Loudon County)
Christened/Baptized:
Died: December 28, 1899 in Baltimore, MD
Buried: St. Paul's Church Cemetery, Alexandria, VA.
Father: Samson Blincoe   Mother Martha Jones

They had four children:

Lucien B. Hooff - Born January 20, 1848. Died May 6, 1886 in Panama of smallpox and is buried there. Monument in St. Paul's Cemetery reads: "To my beloved son, Lucien, Born 1848" Member of Capt. Frank Adams Boys Co. C.S.A. 1861. He attended VMI, class of 1870. Lucien was unmarried. See Interesting Notes on page 124.

Norborne Hooff - Born June 6, 1851 in Alexandria, VA. Baptized June 21, 1861 at St. Paul's Church, Alexandria, VA. Died 1861 at 10 years old. Buried at St. Paul's Church Cemetery, Alexandria, VA, with sister Constance. Member of Capt. Frank Adams Boys Co. C.S.A.

Constance J. Hooff - Buried with Norborne at St. Paul's Church Cemetery in Alexandria, VA. Inscription on tomb reads: "Their Mother's Darlings", Constance age 8 months.

Bettie Rosa Hooff (Rose) - Born June 1853 in Alexandria, VA. Baptized May 6, 1855 at St. Paul's Church; died April 27, 1889. Monument at St. Paul's Church Cemetery next to Lucien reads, "Bettie Rosa Hooff - This Sister Bettie Rosa Hooff Fell Asleep and Awoke With God - 27 April 1889.

Philip Henry Hooff lived at 916 Prince Street, and owned property on Quaker Lane and at the corner of King and Henry Sts., Alexandria, VA. He was a commission merchant, exporting and importing sugar flour, coffee, etc., from a warehouse on the river front at the foot of Prince Street, and from a warehouse and store on Fayette Street. His business ledger was maintained by his nephew, James Wallace Hooff, and reflects an extensive business among the inhabitants of Alexandria. In 1828 he purchased 200 acres of land in Jefferson County, VA from his brother William, and in 1839, he and his brother John, purchased a house and lot in Union, Loudoun County, VA from their sister and brother-in-law, Mary Amelia and James Bennett.

After the death of his first wife, Jane, he entered into a pre-marital contract with Elizabeth Blincoe in which he stipulated that she could retain her 1/6 interest in her father's estate. Soon after the marriage, the three boys left home and by 1860, the two remaining girls had also left the Alexandria area, and settled among relatives in Jefferson County, WV.

On September 30, 1848, Philip executed a Deed of Gift to his daughter Mary Ann Smith, giving her his piano, furniture, and personal property. In December of the same year he gave his son, James Lawrence, a storehouse and lot in Middleburg, Loudoun Co., VA. In 1855 he and his partner, Hugh Smith, father-in-law of Mary Ann, deeded their "house of private entertainment" in Middleburg to Mary Ann Smith for her "exclusive use", to take effect at the close of business on December 31, 1855.

After the death of Philip, Elizabeth moved to Baltimore, MD, where she had numerous relatives. Her will contained nine codicils, and was valued at $20,000. It was contested by several of her nieces and nephews, including John J. Hooff and some of the Bealls. It was finally probated in Baltimore, MD and in Leesburg, VA.

Jane Baxter Hammond (first wife of Philip Henry Hooff) was the granddaughter of Henry Hammond and Jane Baxter, and was named for her grandmother (d: 1794, bur: in Churchyard of "Old Church" at Soldierstown, near Belfast, Ireland). James Hammond, Jane's father was born in Aghalee, Ireland, and came to America in 1785. In 1790 he married Mary (Polly) Rankin, owner of a large estate left to her by her father, Benjamin Rankin, later called "Mt. Hammond." James Hammond died in 1803, leaving a farm to each of his daughters, and large tracts of land to each of his sons, Thomas Hammond and Henry James Hammond. The four children were also beneficiaries under the will of their grandmother, Judith Rankin.

Of the six children of Henry Hammond and Jane Baxter Hammond, four came to America. John Hammond settled in Baltimore, MD; Thomas in Jefferson, Co.,VA (married Mildred Washington, daughter of Col. Charles Washington), and Sarah Hammond married William Brown of Charles Town, WV in 1810.

Obituary - *Alexandria Gazette, June 8, 1844*: DIED Yesterday morning, MRS. JANE B. HOOFF, wife of Philip H. Hooff, of this place, in the 43rd year of her age. The friends and acquaintances of the family are requested to attend the funeral from the Hooff's residence, upper end of Prince Street, this afternoon at 5 o'clock.

Obituary - *Alexandria Gazette, February 7, 1888*: DEATH OF AN OLD CITIZEN - Mr. Philip H. Hooff, after a lingering illness, died at his home at the upper end of Prince Street at an early hour this morning, aged 87 years. Up to the breaking out of the war, Mr. Hooff was actively engaged in mercantile pursuits and did an extensive business on Union Street. Soon after the war, his health failed and he has been for a long time a confirmed invalid. Mr. Hooff was twice married and while several of his children are dead, he leaves a large family. Maj. J. Vowell Hooff of Nicaraguan fame was one of his sons.

Interesting Notes: We obtained copies of letters in the **VMI Archives** specific to Lucien. Mr. Joseph Reid Anderson, Jr. was a member of the VMI Class of 1870, same as Lucian, and devoted most of his life to gathering biographical information about VMI alumni. As a result, VMI has a file of information concerning every 19th century VMI student. Anderson corresponded with alumni, relatives, descendants, and friends in order to collect accurate data. In the case of Lucian Hooff, he seems to have contacted family friends. Following are contents of letters from Isabella Smith and Mary Powell regarding Lucien written to Mr. Anderson. Additionally, there is a letter of resignation from VMI written by Lucian. We have copies of the originals, however, they are dark and reproduction for this book was not possible.

Mattie Brooke Beall wrote a letter dated February 26, 1951, in which she stated "Lucien went to Africa and had yellow fever - his body was sent home in a metallic casket with a notice to bury at once." We do not know to whom this letter was sent.

2nd April (written in the upper left corner of the letter is Apr 5/12)
317 N. Washington St.,
Alexandria, VA

Dear Mr. Anderson,
I have gained the information you asked for with the exception of the date of his death. This I will send as soon as the weather changes so that Mrs. Fawcett can go to the Cemetery.
Lucian Hooff was unmarried.
He was employed by the Pacific Steamship Co.
Went from Hong Kong to Panama where he died of yellow fever in 1886. He was convalescent but during the night he had a relapse and died very suddenly. Was buried in Panama but his name is on the family stone in St. Paul's Cemetery Alexa. He was universally beloved by friends, acquaintances and employees. A remarkably handsome man _____ and well formed so says his cousin. I must thank you for the address you kindly sent me. I read with interest and pride and forwarded bo my brother George in Los Angeles. I have recently spent seven delightful months with him stopping afterwards on my way home in Washington and Michigan. Enjoyed it all especially Golden Cal. But I am too loyal to Virginia to care for any other place as home.

Very sincerely

Isabella R. Smith (Isabella was a historian who wrote a book about Alexandria, VA)

July 9, 1912 (written in the upper left corner of the letter is July 13, 1912)
20 N. Washington St.,
Alexandria, VA

Col. J.R. Anderson

Dear Sir:

I am pleased to learn from your letter that Mrs. P____ has written you. Her brother died <u>here</u>. I think I was a child at the time but have vague memory of a schoolmate's loss of a brother. In my record of Milton F___ I failed to give his grandmothers name "Eleanor Williams."
Lucian Hooff was born about 1845 middle name Blincoe. His father was Mr. Philip Hooff, quite an old man when he married 2nd wife Miss Betty Blincoe. She came of a very eccentric family. I think from Loudoun Co. She had four children, Lucian, Rose Elizabeth, Norburne & Constance. Mrs. H was one of towns privileged ones. She said & did exactly what she chose. Touching the tenderest subjects with perfect effronty. No one minded her & her legacy will out last the next generation. But her poor old husband & her really nice children!
Rose was a lovely girl & would have married well but for her mother. Lucian soon left Alex. Va. No one blamed him and I never knew him after ward - only heard that he married & died in the west.
Mrs. H became notorious soon after, for maltreating her senile old husband was arrested on the complaint of some carpenters who were at work on the adjoining property. The old gentleman was removed from town by his son Phil Hooff. But on Rose's return from the country she took her father back home where he soon died.
She did not long survive him. During her last days her friends one or two at a time kept constantly at her bed side to see that she was properly fed & cared for & she passed away in the bloom of her beautiful girlhood leaving her mother to an unloved old age. The only excuse for Mrs. H was of course the family tendency, insanity. She died some years ago. I think in Baltimore. Sometime when I visit the cemetery I will get the date of Lucian's birth & death.
The gentleman who recently was so lucky in escaping the penitentry was the son of a first cousin of Lucian's. He will be tried again in April and ought to be punished for his defaults $185 000 totally gone & nothing to show for it & that sum represented the savings of the shop girls, sterographers & poor colored people.
It really affected more seriously the humble & poor classes than Rixeys swindling did. How these people manage to escape punishment I don't know. Fortunately for me I drew out all the money I had in their banks a few months previous to their failure. I was buying some suburban property at the time & just finished the transactions at a happy moment. I think I know a way of successful approach to Capt. G. Brown. I will try it.

With best wishes I am truly

Mary G. Powell

Alex. VA
February 15, 1867

Gen. J.H. Smith

Dear Sir.

I hereby tender you my resignation as a Cadet of the Virginia Military Institute owing to the delicate state of my father's health, my presence is absolutely necessary at home. My fathers age hinders him from tending to business and all though I am willing and would be delighted to remain yet I am compelled necessary to resign. I am the only one now at home qualified to tend to the family affairs. I have only been at the Institute a few short months yet I am as much attached to the place as if I had been there for years. Such bond of sympathy out of love rising among so great a number of young men I have never witnessed before. Hoping that the Institute may flourish and that her endeavors here after may be blessed with the greatest success.

I remain

Very Respectfully
L.B. Hooff
Late Cadet, V.M.I.

My son hs written this at my request.
Very Resptf. P.H. Hooff

Theological Seminary
Fairfax co. Va.
Sept. 7th 1885

Gen. F.H. Smith
Supt. V.M.I.

D' Sir:

I have on file at the State Department an application to be appointed Consul to Sidney, Australis and with it the endorsements of all the prominent business men of Alexandra, backed by one member of Congress, letters from California and other states. Now Sir, if I could procure a letter from you to the Secretary of State Washington D.C. also endorsing my application, it would be a favor which I should not forget in a hurry. I have been for ten years traveling in the Pacific, china, Japan, Australis in the service of the Pacific Mail Steamship Co. (from which I have a very strong letter) and by experience and education as well as socially, am thoroughly capable of filling a Consul's position. One ex cadet already fills a prominent foreign appointment and I am anxious that the same good luck should fall to another one. Trusting my request may meet with your favor.

I have the honor
To be
Very Respectfully
Lucien B. Hooff '70
Ex cadet V.M.I.

St. John's Academy,
ALEXANDRIA, VA.

Instituted September 8, 1833.   Reorganized September 13, 1847.

September 22d 1866

This certifies that
Lucien B. Hooff, who entered
this school as a member of
the Senior Class, on the 9th
of December, 1861, withdrew
in good standing, at the close
of the 25th Session, on the 1st
of July, 1864, having obtained
the gold medal for application
to study, with the highest honors
of the school.

His deportment, while in at-
tendance, was such as to deserve
and obtain the approbation of
his teachers and fellow students.

Richard L. Carne, jr.
Principal.

Letter from James Lawrence Hooff (Philip Henry's son)
to Elizabeth Blincoe prior to her marriage to his father.
Courtesy of Ann Hooff-Kline

Alexandria Decbr 1st 1846

Madam,

    You may think my acquaintances will not justify me in thus addressing you but hope the circumstances of the case may prove a sufficient reason for my so doing.

    We are all aware of an existing engagement between our Father and yourself, and at the same time so opposed by us, I now consider it my duty, being an age so to do, to let you know our opinion the same being that of others concerning it.

    Let me say to you it is something we can never become reconciled to an affair that will blast forever the happiness of a family bound together by the stingiest feelings of attachment, we cannot for one moment suppose you are aware of our opposition, or that you will place yourself in a family where by so doing you incur the hatred of all. Imagine yourself in the same position and see what your feelings dictate. It is not in accordance with human nature thus to act. We all desire the esteem of those with whom we associate and to place yourself in a numerous body holding no converse with you, is a situation in my opinion not be courted. There is no need of saying more. From the above you will _____ our opinion never to be changed. In conclusion let me add, we'll respect you a connexions(?), but as a wife you will render yourself despicable, and of this, are all persons of this place aware.

        J.L. Hooff

The letter you addressed my father, I saw this eve, on the subject there spoken of, say to you. As far as my knowledge serves me, am not aware of saying anything derogatory of your sister. At this time of writing her it was not my intention to give insult, but to inform her of our opposition.

        Resply Yours
        J.L. Hooff

To
C.H. Blincoe Esq
Jany 19th

Information on back of the miniature of Philip Henry Hooff (1801-1888) now owned by Fontaine B. Hooff. "Painted by Weinedel, from Saxony, August 26, 1819, Charlestown, VA"

Mrs. Harris Loewy identified the subject as Philip Henry Hooff as a young man of 18 years.

Courtesy of Ann Hooff-Kline

Philip Henry Hooff
1801 - 1888

Courtesy of Ann Hooff-Kline

Philip H. Hooff 1st

Home of Philip Henry Hooff
ca. 1812
916 Prince St., Alexandria, VA.

Mary Ann Hooff (1824-1899)
Daughter of Philip Henry Hooff I
and Jane Baxter Hammond

Courtesy of Ann Hooff-Kline

Gertrude Heywood Hooff (1840-1899)
Daughter of Philip Henry Hooff I
and Jane Baxter Hammond

Courtesy of Ann Hooff-Kline

Lucien Hooff (1848-1886)
Son of Philip Henry Hooff I
and second wife Elizabeth Blincoe

Courtesy of Ann Hooff-Kline

P.H. Hooff - 20th Sept. 1844 ground marker behind the three uprights shown on the next page.
We are unable to correlate this marker to any of the P.H. Hooff's know to us.

Asleep with Jesus To my beloved son, Lucien, born 1848 On side of the tombstone: Their Mother's Darlings, Norborne lived 10 years, Constance lived 8 months.	Bettie Rosa Hooff - This sister Bettie Rosa Hooff fell asleep and awoke with God - 27 April 1889.	Elizabeth Blincoe wife of Philip H. Hooff Died December 28, 1899.

Fifth Codicil: I leave to Marion N. Poor, if she continues attentive and affectionate to me the use of my house 1416 Street, Baltimore, Maryland while she lives and at her death I give the house to her daughter Lillie Johnson Poor my house 1416 Bolton Street my other property hereinafter I will dispose of Harry Poor to have a monument like my daughter erected to my memory and administer on my Estate and repair the graves of my mother, father, brother and sister Virginia in the yard of the Church in Leesburg. I being of sound mind and body as all who know me will testify. $100 to be put in the Trustee of St. Paul's Church at my death, the interest of which is to be paid for keeping up my yard in the Cemetery and pay the superintendent yearly while he lives to keep my yard in cemetery in repair he to see while he lives to see it is keep in good repair Harry Poor to put the $100 in Trustee of St. Pau'ls Church, Alexandria, the interest of which is to pay my lot repairs he to see it done while he lives.

> /s/ Elizabeth P. Chancellor Annan
> /s/ Nellie V. Rogers Feb.24, 1895
> /s/ W.B. Safford Feb. 24, 1895
> /s/ Bettie L. Smith
> /s/ Marie M Annan March 24, 1899
> /s/ Elisabeth P. Annan
> /s/ Lillie Johnson Poor
> /s/ Louisa Ogle Beall Sep. 10, 1899
> /s/ Ida G. Kerr

Baltimore City S.S.

On 25th day of August 1903 personally appeared Elisabeth P. Chancellor Annon, Marie M. Annon, Elizabeth P. Annon and Lilly J. Poor and made oath in due form of Law that they did see the Testatrix, Elizabeth B. Hooff, sign the 5th Codicil to a paper purporting to be a Will, that the signature of Elizabeth B. Hooff to the 5th Codicil is the true and genuine signature of Elizabeth B. Hooff, that at the time of her signing said Codicil she was to the best of their apprehension of sound and disposing mind, memory and understanding. Eliza P. Annon made oath in due form of law that she is well acquainted with the signatures of Nellie V. Rogers and W.B. Saffold; also subscribing witnesses to the fifth Codicil whose presence cannot be obtained and that the same are the true and genuine signatures of said Nellie V. Rogers and W.B. Saffold; and also appeared Lilly Johnson Poor and made oath in due form of law that she is well acquainted with the

signatures of Louisa Ogle Beall, Ida G. Keer and Bettie L. Smith also subscribing witnesses as to said 5th Codicil whose presence cannot be obtained and that the same are the true and genuine signatures o Louisa Ogle Beall, Ida G. Keer and Bettie L. Smith.

Sworn to in Open Court

Teste: Stephen R. Mason, Register of
          Wills for Baltimore City

Friday mourning Oct. 13, 1899

The above will is to remain as written that concerning Marion Poor, my elder sister Lally's daughter and her daughter Lilly J. Poor after he is to have $500 of Alex. Stock investment to pay the $500 mortgage on my Bolton Street, Baltimore, house, the mirror over mantle to Marion, the large mirror to Lilly, the linen & cotton sheets are also everything else in my house to Lilly, the balance of my property I leave to Lilly and Harry t. Poor with the exception of $1000 to Upton Beall, my nephew, son of Mattie Beall.

> /s/ E.B. Hooff
> /s/ Marion M. Poor   )
> /s/ Lilly J. Poor   )
> /s/ W. Casey Barry) Oct. 13. 1899
> /s/ George I. Barry   )
> Alphonse M. Barry   )

Baltimore City S.S.

Made Oath; On the 4 day of January, 1900 came Harry T. Poor & made oath in due form of law that he does not know of any will or Codicil of Elizabeth B. Hoof, late of said City deceased, other than the above Instrument of Writing, that about the first part of December 1899 that he received the will and Codicils from Elizabeth B. Hoof, that he has kept them continuously in his custody and that she died on the 28th day of December 1899.
Sworn to in Open Court

Teste: Stephen R. Mason, Register of
Wills for Baltimore City Sworn to in

On the 25th day of August 1903 came Marion N. Poor and Lilly Johnson Poor and made oath in due form of law that they did see the Testatrix sign the 6 Codicil to a paper writing purporting to be a Will, that the signature of Elizabeth B. Hoof is her true and genuine signature, that at the time of her signing said Codicil she was to the best of their apprehension of sound & disposing mind, memory & understanding and that they signed the said Codicil in her presence; and that they are well acquainted with the signature of said W. Casey Barry, Alphonse M. Barry & George I. Barry; also subscribing witnesses to the 6th Codicil, whose presence cannot be obtained and that the same are the true and genuine signatures of the said W. Casey Barry, Alphonse M. Barry and George I. Barry, as witnesses to the 6 Codicil.
Sworn to in Open Court

Teste: Stephen R. Mason, Register of
Wills for Baltimore City

Will of Elizabeth B. Hooff

In the Matter of the Estate of   )   In the Orphans Court of
Elizabeth B. Hooff, Deceased   )   Baltimore City

DECREE

The matter of the Petition and Caveat of Henry T. Ward and others filed to all the papers writing brought into this Court on January 4th, 1900 by Harry T. Poor, purporting to be the Last Will and Testament of Elizabeth B. Hooff, and Codicils thereto (the first of them being dated Alexandria, Virginia, December 15, 1888, and the last of them being dated Friday morning October 13, 1899, and all, excepting the last mentioned, being written upon one sheet of paper, and the last mentioned being written upon a separate piece of paper from the others, but being pinned thereto at the bottom of the last of said Codicils), standing ready for hearing, and the parties having consented that the Court should determine the validity of each & all of said paper writings and the Court having heard the evidence and the Counsel for the several parties, and the parties having failed to prove the execution of any of said paper writings preceding the Fifth Codicil and it appears to the Court that all of them were revoked, and it further appears to the Court that the Fifth Codicil consists of the following language, which is in the genuine handwriting of the Testatrix:

Fifth Codicil

I leave to Marion N. Poor, if she continues attentive and affectionate to me the use of my house 1416 Street, Baltimore, Maryland while she lives and at her death I give the house to her daughter Lillie Johnson Poor my house 1416 Bolton Street my other property hereinafter I will dispose of Harry Poor to have a monument like my daughter erected to my memory and administer on my Estate and repair the graves of my mother, father, brother and sister Virginia in the yard of the Church in Leesburg. I being of sound mind and body as all who know me will testify. $100 to be put in the Trustee of St. Paul's Church at my death, the interest of which is to be paid for keeping up my yard in the Cemetery and pay the superintendent yearly while he lives to keep my yard in the cemetery in repair while he lives to see it is keep in good repair Harry Poor to put the $100 in Trustee of St. Paul's Church, Alexandria, the interest of which is to pay my lot repairs he to see it done while he lives.

And that it and also the codicil dated Friday morning October 13, 1899, in the following language; which is in the genuine handwriting of the Testatrix
"Friday mourning Oct. 13, 1899

The above will is to remain as written that concerning Marion Poor, my elder sister Lally's daughter and her daughter Lilly J. Poor after he is to have $500 of Alex. Stock investment to pay the $500 mortgage on

---

my Bolton Street, Baltimore, house, the mirror over mantle to Marion, the large mirror to Lilly, the linen & cotton sheets are also everything else in my house to Lilly, the balance of my property I leave to Lilly and Harry T. Poor with the exception of $1000 to Upton Beall, my nephew, son of Mattie Beall." were duly executed as required by the Laws of Maryland and Virginia to pass both real and personal estate, and the Testatrix, Elizabeth B. Hooff, was at the time of the execution thereof, respectfully, of sound and disposing mind, and capable of executing a valid deed of contract, and that no undue influence or fraud was practiced upon her, and that said two paper writings last mentioned remain unrevoked, and that the contents thereof were understood by her at the time of the execution thereof, and that they are all respects valid as her complete and final last testamentary dispositions of her property real and personal.

It is therefore by the Orphan's Court for Baltimore City this 26 day of August 1903 Adjudged, Ordered that Decree that the Order heretofore passed herein directing issues concerning the validity of said paper writing to be transmitted to a Court of Law for trial before a Jury be and the same is hereby rescinded; and that the Caveat and petition be and the same is hereby dismissed with costs; that probate of all said paper writings preceding the Fifth Codicil and said Codicil dated Friday Morning October 13, 1899, be and they are hereby admitted to probate as, and as constituting, the complete and final last Will and Testament of Elizabeth Blincoe Hooff.

And it is further ordered and Decreed that Letters Testamentary be issued to Harry T. Poor, upon his filing a Bond in the usual form in the penalty of $4300, with two sureties, to be approved by the Resister of Wills or this court, and that the Letter of Administration pende lite heretofore granted to Henry T. Ward and said Harry T. Poor, be and they are hereby revoked and said Admin's are directed to account with the said Executors and pay over to him all the personal estate in their hands.

/s/   George Savage
Myer J. Block
Wm. J. O'Brien

(S E A L)   The State of Maryland
Baltimore City, Sc.

I, Stephen R. Mason, Register of Wills, and by law, Keeper of the Seal, and the Records, and of the Original Papers of the Orphans Court of Baltimore City, do hereby certify that the afore going is a true and full copy of the Fifth Codicil and said Codicil dated Friday Morning October 13, 1899, as constituting the complete & final last Will & Testament of Elizabeth Blincoe Hooff, late of said city, deceased, together with the proof and probate thereof taken from Wills, Liber S.R.M.No. 91, Folio 495 and being one of the records kept in the Office of Register of Wills for Baltimore City.

(S E A L)   In Testimony Whereof, I hereunto subscribe my name, affix the Seal of Said Court & Offices this thirty-first day of August in the year of our Lord nineteen hundred and three.

/s/   Stephen R. Mason
Register of Wills for Baltimore City Maryland, Sct

I, George Savage, Chief Judge of the Orphans' Court of Baltimore City, in the State aforesaid, do certify that the foregoing Attestation of Stephen R. Mason, Register of Wills for said City, is in due form, and by the proper Officer.

Given from under my hand, at the City of Baltimore, this Thirty first day of August in the year of our Lord nineteen hundred and three.

/s/   Geo. Savage

State of Maryland, Baltimore City, Sct.

I hereby certify that the Honorable George Savage, by whom the above certificate was given, and who hath thereto subscribed his name, was at the time of so doing, Chief Judge of the Orphans' Court of Baltimore City, duly elected, commissioned and qualified.

In Testimony Whereof, I hereunto subscribe my name and affix the seal of the said Court this thirty first day of our Lord nineteen hundred and three.

/s/　　　　　Stephen R. Mason, Register of Wills
　　　　　　　For Baltimore City

At a County Court held for Loudoun County, September 14, 1903

A proper purporting to be an authenticated copy of the last will and testament of Elizabeth Blincoe Hooff deceased and the certificate of the probate thereof in the Orphans' Court of the City of Baltimore, State of Maryland, was this day produced in this court for probate and it appearing therefrom that said will was proved in said Court to have been so executed as to be a valid will of land in this State by the laws hereof the Court doth order that said paper so certified be admitted to probate and recorded in this County as the last will and testament of the said Elizabeth Blincoe Hooff, deceased, both as to real and personal estate of said decedent therein devised and bequeathed.

A Copy Teste:　　　W.D. Hempstone, cc

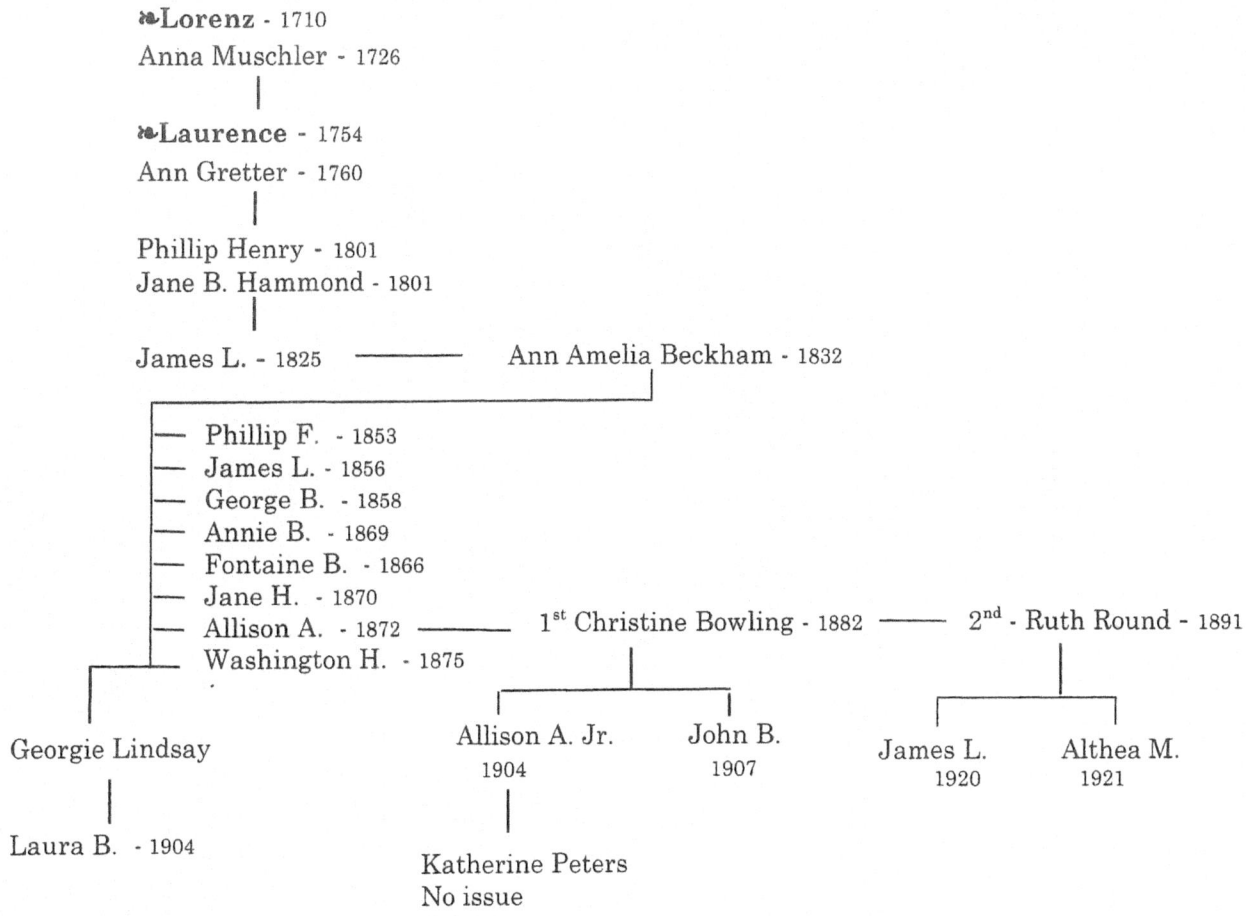

&Lorenz - 1710
Anna Muschler - 1726

&Laurence - 1754
Ann Gretter - 1760

Phillip Henry - 1801
Jane B. Hammond - 1801

James L. - 1825 ——————— Ann Amelia Beckham - 1832

—— Phillip F. - 1853
—— James L. - 1856
—— George B. - 1858
—— Annie B. - 1869
—— Fontaine B. - 1866
—— Jane H. - 1870
—— Allison A. - 1872 ——————— 1st Christine Bowling - 1882 ——————— 2nd - Ruth Round - 1891
—— Washington H. - 1875

Georgie Lindsay

Laura B. - 1904

Allison A. Jr.   John B.
1904   1907

James L.   Althea M.
1920   1921

Katherine Peters
No issue

James Lawrence Hooff

Born: October 2, 1825 in Alexandria, D.C.
Christened/Baptized: May 11, 1833 at St. Paul's Episcopal Church, Alexandria, VA
Married: April 15, 1851 in Charles Town, WV
Died: September 24, 1887 at his home in Charles Town, WV
Buried: Zion Episcopal Churchyard, Charles Town, WV
Father: Philip Henry Hooff I   Mother: Jane Baxter Hammond

Spouse: Ann Amelia Beckham
Born: August 8, 1832 in Charles Town, WV
Christened/Baptized:
Died: December 16, 1915, 82 years old
Buried: Zion Episcopal Churchyard, Charles Town, WV
Father: Fontaine Beckham   Mother: Anne Amelia Stephenson
(Fontaine Beckham was killed during "John Brown's Raid" at Harpers Ferry when he and a colored man who was also killed, refused to open a gate to the train yard for John Brown and his men).

They had eight children:

Philip Fontaine Hooff - Born June 27, 1853 in Charles Town, WV. Baptized 1858 and Zion Episcopal Church in Charles Town, WV. Died September 15, 1862 in Charles Town of scarlet fever.

James Lawrence Hooff - Born January 7, 1856 in Charles Town, WV. Baptized 1858 at Zion Episcopal Church, Charles Town WV. Died February 17, 1931 in Altoona, PA and is buried at Edgehill Cemetery, Charles Town, WV. Unmarried. His will is in Charles Town, Will Book F, page 187, leaving everything to his sister Annie Beckham Brown.

George Beckham Hooff - Born February 11, 1858 in Charles Town, WV. Baptized 1858 at Zion Episcopal Church, Charles Town, WV. Died November 21, 1928 and is buried Edgehill Cemetery in Charles Town, WV. His will is in Charles Town, leaving everything to his sister, Annie Beckham Brown.

Annie Beckham Stephenson Hooff - Born September 11, 1869 in Charles Town, WV. Baptized June 20, 1869 at Zion Episcopal Church, Charles Town, WV. Died June 15, 1953 in Manassas, VA and is buried at Manassas Confederate Cemetery, Center St. and Lee Ave., Manassas, VA. Married William Hill Brown on February 23, 189? at Zion Episcopal Church, Charles Town, WV. William died in 1932. They had three children.

Fontaine Beckham Hooff - Born 1866. See a separate chapter, page #181.

Jane Hammond Hooff - Born February 21, 1870 in Charles Town, WV. Baptized July 3, 1870 at Zion Episcopal Church, Charles Town, WV. Died January 20, 1884.

Allison Armstead Hooff - Born 1872. See a separate chapter, page #185.

Washington Hammond Hooff - Born 1875. See a separate chapter, page #187.

James Lawrence Hooff attended Episcopal High School in Alexandria, VA, and Trinity College, Hartford, Conn. In 1848 he received a storehouse and lot in Middleburg, VA from his father, the use and rents of which he traded to his sister, Mary Ann Smith, for her 1/9 interest in property in Jefferson Co., WV. He settled on the property adjacent to his uncle, William Hooff.

Before the outbreak of the Civil War he was a Major in the 2nd Virginia Regiment, a volunteer organization, and he continued in that position until his regiment was attached to the Confederate Army. Later (186-63), he enlisted in the Botts Grays, Co. G, 11th VA Cavalry, where he served as captain for 12 months, after which he was promoted to the rank of major in the 11th Virginia Regiment. Between 1863 and 1865, he was regimental quartermaster of Rosser's Brigade.

At the close of the Civil War he returned to Charles Town, and entered the mercantile business and in 1875 was elected a representative to the West Virginia Legislature, which position he held until 1878. Between the years 1881 and 1887, he served as county commissioner of Jefferson Co., WV. Several years afterward he became president of the Jefferson County Court.

Zion Episcopal Church, Charles Town, WV records of 1852 show James L. Hooff of Smithfield Park as a communicant of the Church. In 1867 he purchased "Richwood Hall" in Jefferson Co., WV, which remained in the family until 1902.

James Lawrence Hooff
1825 - 1887

Richmond Hall, Jefferson County,
WVA. Home of James Lawrence
Hooff. 1867

Commissioned: June 21, 1860 as Lieutenant Colonel of the 2nd Regiment Virginia Volunteers, 16th Brigade, and 3rd Infantry Division, Virginia Militia. Signed by John Letcher 20th August 1860. Also in the 55th Regiment as Maj. J. L. Hoof of Charles Town, W. VA.

The following information is from the records the Virginia Library in Richmond, VA.

A partial roster of Co. G., 2nd Regiment, "Stonewall" Brigade dated April 1862, shows a James L. Hooff as being a private in this company for three years. Also shown on this roster are his two cousins, Francis R. Hooff and William A. Hooff, also privates.

A partial roster (no date) of the 2nd Regiment "Stonewall" Brigade, Field & Staff, General James A. Walker, shows Lawrence Hoof as a Com. Sgt.

Partial roster (no date) of Company E, 11th Regiment, Cavalry Brigade "Potomac Mounted Rifleman" - Shenaudoah Co. shows J. L. Hooff as a Captain.

The following statement is from The Virginia Regimental Histories Series, 11th Virginia Cavalry by Richard L. Armstrong, page 151

HOOFF, JAMES LAWRENCE: Capt. Co. E/AQM, 11th Virginia Cavalry. Born in Jefferson Co., WV, October 2, 1825. Merchant, Charles Town, W. Va. Prior service, Co. G, 2nd Va. Inf., Enl. Fishers Hill, May 20, 1863(?). 1st Lt., commanding Co. E, January 30, 1863; April 30, 1863 - June 30, 1863. When Capt. Hess resigned, July 14, 1863, Col. L. L. Lomax wrote: "I consider the 1st Lieut. of this company better qualified as a commander of this company." Promoted to Capt. Commanding Co. E, June 9, 1863 and July 10, 1863. Present, September 1 through October 31, 1863, appointed reg'tl QM October 1, 1863. Recommended for the post of AQM, by Lt. Col. M.D. Ball, October 2, 1863. Appointed reg'tl QM October 19, 1863 to be effective from October 2, 1863. Serving as Acting Brigade QM, October 22, 1863. Present, Field and Staff Muster Roll, March 31, 1864. A Board of Examiners on February 8, 1863 found him to be "qualified in every respect" for the post of Brigade QM. Recommended for promotion to Brigade QM February 27, 1864 by Gen. R.E. Lee. Appraised horses, March 6, 1864. Relieved of duty as AQM, 11th Va. Ca., 4/29/1864, and directed to report to the QM Gen. At Richmond. Relieved due to a break down in communication over some reports that he submitted. Ab. Sick, febris remitten. billious, July 5 - July 11, 1864. Learned of his being relieved of duty on March 4, 1865, he wrote QM Gen. A.R. Lawton, requesting a court of inquiry or Court Martial to determine the facts surrounding his being relieved. Gen. Lawton recommended that he be re-instated at once. Reinstated as AQM, 11th Va. Cav. March 17, 1865. Paroled, Winchester, April 19, 1865. Desc.: age 38, 5'8", fair comp., dark hair and blue eyes, a resident of Charles Town, W. Va. Post war source shows that he held the rank of Major. Post war merchant and resident of Charles Town, W. V. Member W.Va. Legislature, 1875. President of Jefferson Co. Court. Died in Charles Town, W.Va., September 24, 1887. Buried at Edge Hill Cemetery in Charles Town, WVA.

National Archives Veterans Records

The following is information typed directly from copies of Company Muster Records. The actual copies are included.

Undated Register	Shows Jas. Law. Hooff Asst. Q.M. State of Virginia. To report to 11th VA Cav. Regt. Date of appointment is October 19, 1863. Date of confirmation is February 17, 1864. To take rank October 2, 1863. Date of acceptance is October 30, 1863. Delivered Q.M. Genl.
Sept/Oct 1863	Capt. Hooff, Co. E, 11 Reg't VA Calvary was enlisted May 20, 1863 at Fishers Hill by Capt. Hess for war. Appointed Regt QM October 1, 1863.
Oct. 2, 1863	Register (commissioned officers) shows Jas. Law. Hooff relieved, then a note states he is restored March 17, 1865. (I an not sure what he was relieved of).
October 20, 1963	There is a copy of a letter to Gen. Cooper nominating James Law. Hooff as quartermaster. The signature on the letter cannot be read because of the quality of the xerox copy.
March 31, 1864	Field and Staff Muster Roll shows him commissioned October 2, 1863 and present on this date.
April 29, 1864	Special Order Number 100/16 shows Capt. and A.Q.M. Jas. Law. Hooff is to report for duty.
Undated	Appointment card recommends J.L. Hooff for major and q.m. in 1864.
April 19, 1865	Capt. J. L. Hooff of 2nd Rossers Brig signed a quartermaster document. He wrote that he is 38 years old, 5-8 tall, fair complexion, dark hair and blue eyes.
March 17, 1865	Special Order Number 63/28 states: Hooff, J.L., Capt. and A.Q.M. is revoked.
April 1865	List of prisoners of war paroled April 18 and 19, 1865, at various places in Virginia and West Virginia given by E.B. Parsons(?) in Winchester, show J. L. Hooff, Capt. and Q.M.

National Archives

Prior service: Co. G 2nd VA Infantry.

James Lawrence Hooff, born October 2, 1825. Enlisted 2nd VA Infantry July 6, 1861 at Darkesville in Co. G as Pvt. Last official entry shows him present November and December 1861.

J. Law. Hooff, Co. E, F& S, 11 VA Cavalry, formed in February 1863 by the addition of 2 companies of the 5th Regiment VA Cavalry to the 17th (also known as the 1st) Battalion VA Cavalry which battalion was made up of 7 companies, which had previously served in the 7th Regiment VA Cavalry and one company, which has previously served in the 24th Battalion VA Cavalry. Captain/AQM. Originally filed under Hoof, James L.

War Department, Niter and Mining Bureau
Richmond, November 20, 1964
Col. I.M. St. John, Chief of Bureau:

Col: Your questions on the iron service are hereinafter replied to in their order:

Sixth: State what essentials of labor, stock, and supplied must be demanded to guarantee a supply of iron for the next year.

The iron force was much too small before one-fifth of the men were taken away under General orders, No. 82. These men must be replaced and an addition of 300 men fully be made to the previous force, with an increase of from 100 to 150 horses or mules. Should this labor be furnished promptly, and the service placed upon a proper footing before all army officers, but little apprehension need be felt for the iron supply, for all difficulties of fuel and ore will in that event be overcome. But it is absolutely essential that the iron masters shall have more support from the Government than heretofore. The manufacture of pig-iron in Virginia was a very hazardous enterprise, even before the war, and but two men are known to me whoever met with success. All the difficulties have been much increased by the war, and the much greater difficulty of securing supplies added to them. But all these could have been overcome if the iron masters had been properly protected against the interference of Government officers. Ample general orders exist on this subject, but they are not respected, and it has never been found possible to have any officer punished for their violation. It will suffice to mention one notable case where a quartermaster, **Capt. Hoof, of Gen. Rosser's Brigade**, not only impressed supplies from the contractors, but from the Government furnaces, thereby causing the actual starvation of some of the furnace mules, and making it necessary to hire out the furnace labor to prevent a similar result. On hearing the facts the Secretary of War immediately ordered **Capt. Hoof** to be relieved from duty and to report in Richmond, but this order, now some months old, has never been obeyed, and **Capt. H.** remains on his original duty.

The iron master is a necessity, and should be cherished as such, and allowed the same facilities for securing subsistence and forage as are enjoyed by commissaries and quartermasters; and his supplies once secured should not be touched for any other purpose.

Unless this encouragement and protection is afforded the contractors will become disheartened and give up. They cannot possibly carry on their operations under the present system of protection, which exists only on paper.

Very respectfully yours,

Richard Morton,
Lieut.-Col.
Niter and Mining Bureau
Richmond, VA, November 21, 1864

THE

Commonwealth of Virginia,

To *James L. Hoof* Greeting

Know You, That from special trust and confidence reposed in your fidelity, courage and good conduct, our GOVERNOR, in pursuance of the authority vested in him by the Constitution and Laws of this Commonwealth, doth commission you a *Lieutenant Colonel of the Second Regiment Virg.ᵃ Volunteers* ~~Regiment~~ of the *16th* Brigade and *3d* Division of the **VIRGINIA MILITIA** to rank as such from the *twenty third* day of *June* 18 *60*

In testimony whereof, I have hereunto signed my name as Governor, and caused the Seal of the Commonwealth to be affixed, this *20th* day of *August* 18 *60*

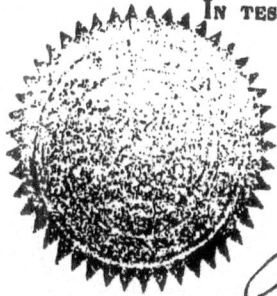

John Letcher

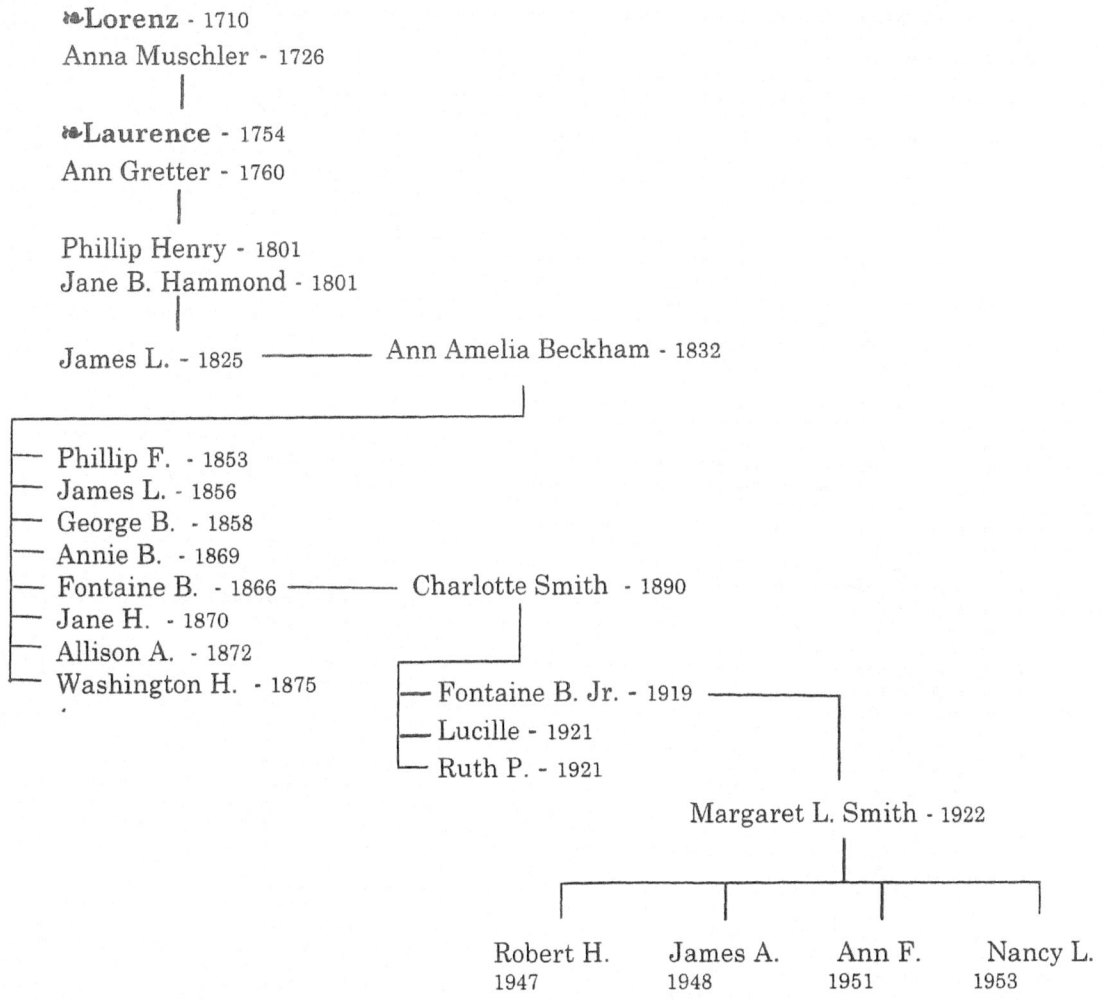

▪Lorenz - 1710
Anna Muschler - 1726

▪Laurence - 1754
Ann Gretter - 1760

Phillip Henry - 1801
Jane B. Hammond - 1801

James L. - 1825 ———————— Ann Amelia Beckham - 1832

— Phillip F. - 1853
— James L. - 1856
— George B. - 1858
— Annie B. - 1869
— Fontaine B. - 1866 ———————— Charlotte Smith - 1890
— Jane H. - 1870
— Allison A. - 1872
— Washington H. - 1875

— Fontaine B. Jr. - 1919 ———————
— Lucille - 1921
— Ruth P. - 1921

Margaret L. Smith - 1922

Robert H.   James A.   Ann F.   Nancy L.
1947   1948   1951   1953

Fontaine Beckham Hooff

Born: October 12, 1866 in Charles Town, WV
Christened/Baptized:
Married: December 27, 1917 in Washington, DC
Died: July 22, 1941, 74 years old
Buried: Edgehill Cemetery, Charles Town, WV
Father: James Lawrence Hooff   Mother: Ann Amelia Beckham

Spouse: Charlotte Lucille Smith
Born: August 24, 1890
Christened/Baptized:
Died: January 1, 1983 in Wheeling, WV at age 93.
Buried: Manassas City Cemetery from Trinity Episcopal Church
Father: George Hancock Smith   Mother: Mary Roberta Brown

They had three children:

> Fontaine Beckham Hooff Jr. - Born 1919. See a separate chapter, page #183.

> Lucile Smith Hooff (twin) - Born May 2, 1921. Died 1993. Married Harris Loewy at All Saints Episcopal Church in Chevy Chase, MD on December 4, 1943. Harris died October 17, 1967 in Washington, DC. They had two children:
> > Elizabeth Loewy - Born August 6, 1949
> >
> > Faith Loewy - Born March 18, 1953. Died 1992.

> Ruth Powell Hooff (twin) - Born May 2, 1921, died young.

Fontaine Beckham Hooff attended Shepherdstown Academy and graduated from West Virginia University. He was a pharmacist in Charles Town, WV.

Wedding Announcement from *Charles Town Newspaper*: "SMITH-HOOFF. Mr. Fontaine Beckham Hooff, popular businessman of Charles Town, and a member of the well known drug firm of Brown & Hooff, was married on Thursday, December 27, to Miss Charlotte Lucile Smith, daughter of Mr. and Mrs. George Hancock Smith of Manassas, VA. The ceremony was performed in Calvary Baptist Church in Washington, DC, Rev. S.J. Green uniting them in marriage. Mr. and Mrs. Hooff will reside in Charles Town. The Advocate joins Mr. Hooff's many friends in town and country in extending to him and his fair bride, congratulations."

Obituary from *Washington Post, January 2, 1983*; "HOOFF, CHARLOTTE SMITH of Manassas, VA on January 1, at Peterson Hospital in Wheeling, WV. She was preceded in death by her husband, Fontaine B. Hooff, Sr. Mother of Fontaine B. Hooff Jr. of Wheeling and Mrs. Harris (Lucile) Loewy of Chevy Chase, MD; six grandchildren and may be one great-granddaughter. Visitation at Baker Funeral Home, 9320 West St., Manassas, Sunday from 2 to 8 p.m. Funeral services in Trinity Episcopal Church, Manassas, Monday at 2 p.m. Interment Manassas City Cemetery. Contributions made to the Discretionary Fund of the Clergy at Trinity Episcopal Church of the Montgomery County Association of Retarded Citizens, 11600 Nebel St., Rockville, MD 20852."

Fontaine Beckham Hooff, Sr.
1866 - 1941

Fontaine Beckham Hooff Jr.

Born: December 26, 1919 in Charles Town, WV
Christened/Baptized: May 23, 1920 at Zion Episcopal Church in Charles Town, WV
Married: November 10, 1944 in Wheeling, WV
Died:
Buried:
Father: Fontaine Beckham Hooff   Mother: Charlotte Smith

Spouse: Margaret (Peggy) Louise Smith
Born: April 21, 1922 in Wheeling, WV
Christened/Baptized:
Died:
Buried:
Father: Sidney Clement Smith   Mother: James Clinton Perkins (She is a female named James)

They had four children:

> Robert Hancock Hooff - Born January 21, 1947, graduated from West Virginia University, sales manager for R.M. Wilson Co., Wheeling, WV. Married Sarah Stevens Hupp, b: 1948. They have one child named Sarah Beckham who was born 1988.

> James Allison Hooff - Born June 3, 1948, graduated from West Virginia University, industrial engineer with the firm of Charles H. Tompkins Co., Washington, DC. Had one daughter, Meghan Allyson Colloton, born 1973. Second wife is Mary Elizabeth Champley who was born in 1956. They have one son named John Lawrence Hooff who was born in 1987.

> Anne Fontaine Hooff - Born August 7, 1951, graduated from University of Maryland. Married Jack Leroy Hewitt on June 3, 1972. Second husband is Kirk James Mortimer who was born in 1954. They have one child named Bryant James Mortimer who was born in 1987.

> Nancy Louise Hooff - Born March 1, 1953, graduated from Dickinson College, Phi Beta Kappa, graduate work at University of Bologna, Italy, attended Fletcher College of Law and Diplomacy, Boston, Mass. Married C.M. Kamara who was born in 1949. They have one daughter, Anya Hooff Kamara who was born in 1981.

Fontaine Beckham Hooff Jr. graduated from West Virginia University, and received his Lieutenant commission and "wings" in 1942. He was attached to the U.S. Army Air Corps Transport Command, and served in Burma and India, achieving the rank of Captain before his discharge in 1946.

Fontaine Beckham Hooff, Jr.
1919 -

Allison Armstead Hooff

Born: October 23, 1872
Married: 1st - July 30, 1902
Christened/Baptized:
Died: December 28, 1944 in Mansassas, VA at age 72 years old.
Buried: Trinity Episcopal Church Cemetery, Manassas, VA
Father: James Lawrence Hooff   Mother: Ann Amelia Beckham

Spouse 1st - Christine Bowling
Born: January 6, 1882
Christened/Baptized:
Died: March 28, 1914 at age 32 years.
Buried: Mt. Carmel Cemetery in Upper Marlboro, MD. The tombstone reads: "Sacred to the Memory of Christine Bowling Hooff, Beloved Wife of Allison Armstead Hooff, born January 6, 1882, died March 28, 1914, Love Makes Life Eternal, He Shall Give His Beloved Sleep."

They had two children:

> Allison Armstead Hooff Jr. - Born April 25, 1904. Died October 1983 in Chantilly, VA. Graduated from College of William and Mary, married Katherine Peters, no issue.

> John Bowling Hooff - Born October 7, 1907. Died November 26, 1920 and is buried at Mt. Carmel Cemetery in Upper Marlboro, MD. The tombstone reads:" John Bowling Hooff, Son of Christine Bowling and Allison Armstead Hooff, Born October 7, 1907, Died November 26, 1920, He Giveth His Beloved Sleep." We were told that he died in a hunting accident.

Spouse 2nd - Ruth Round
Born: September 5, 1891
Christened/Baptized:
Married: October 7, 1917 in Manassas, VA
Died:
Buried:
Father: George Carr Round   Mother: Emily Caroline Bennett

They had two children:

> James Lawrence Hooff - Born July 18, 1920. Died July 19, 1920 and is buried at Confederate Cemetery in Manassas, VA.

> Althea Maitland Hooff - Born December 19, 1921. She married Lt. Howard Cooksey of the USN (he was born June 21, 1921), on March 1, 1947 in Tokyo, Japan. He is the son of Carl Jackson Cooksey and Norma Young. Althea was graduated from Wheaton College, and Howard Cooksey from V.I.P. Lt. Gen. Howard Cooksey retired in 1977 and devotes his full time to Cooksey Corporation, a consulting firm located in Alexandria, VA. They had two children:
>> Paul Hooff Cooksey - Born August 13, 1948. A graduate of Hampton-Sidney. He married Emily Lewis Ford who was born in 1958.
>>
>> Allyson Maitland Cooksey - Born July 6, 1950. A graduate of Washington College, Chestertown, MD. She married Larry Hyland on November 18, 1972.

Obituary, 1944: "Allison A. Hooff, 72, Died at Home in Manassas: Allison Armstead Hooff Sr, 72, a resident of Manassas, VA for 47 years, died last night at his home. Funeral services will be held at 2 P.M. Sunday in Trinity Episcopal Church, Manassas, with burial in the cemetery there. Mr. Hooff was born in Charles Town, W.VA in 1872.

He moved to Manassas in 1897 to become a partner in the lumber firm of Brown & Hooff. He was master of the Masonic Lodge there in 1927, and president of the Kiwanis club in 1932. Survivors are his widow, the former Ruth Round, a son, Allison, Jr., and a daughter, Althea."

Before the establishment of the Brown & Hooff lumber yard in Manassas, VA, Allison Armstead Hooff taught at Miami University in Oxford, Ohio. The Carillonic Bells of Trinity Episcopal Church were dedicated in memory of A.A. Hooff Sr., and his brother-in-law, William Hill Brown, Sr., among others.

The tombstone cross on the left is John Bowling Hooff.
The one directly beside the cross is Christine Bowling Hooff.

Washington Hammond Hooff

Born: February 22, 1875 in Charles Town, WV
Christened/Baptized: Confirmed March 24, 1907 at Zion Episcopal Church, Charles Town. WV
Married:
Died: January 29, 1954, 79 years old
Buried: Edgehill Cemetery, Charles Town, WV
Father: James Lawrence Hooff   Mother: Anne Amelia Beckham

Spouse: Georgie Hildegard Lindsay
Born:
Christened/Baptized: Confirmed March 24, 1907 at Zion Episcopal Church, Charles Town, WV
Died:
Buried:

They had one child:

> Laura Beckham Hooff - Born November 4, 1904. Baptized March 30, 1907 at Zion Episcopal Church in Charles Town, WV. Confirmed May 23, 1920 at Zion Episcopal Church. Married William Harry Beard of Washington, DC and had one child, William Harry Beard Jr. born ca. 1929 and lives in Washington, DC.

> Zion Church records indicate that Washington Hammond Hooff, Georgie Lindsay Hooff and Laura B. Hooff transferred their Church memberships to Washington, DC around 1920.

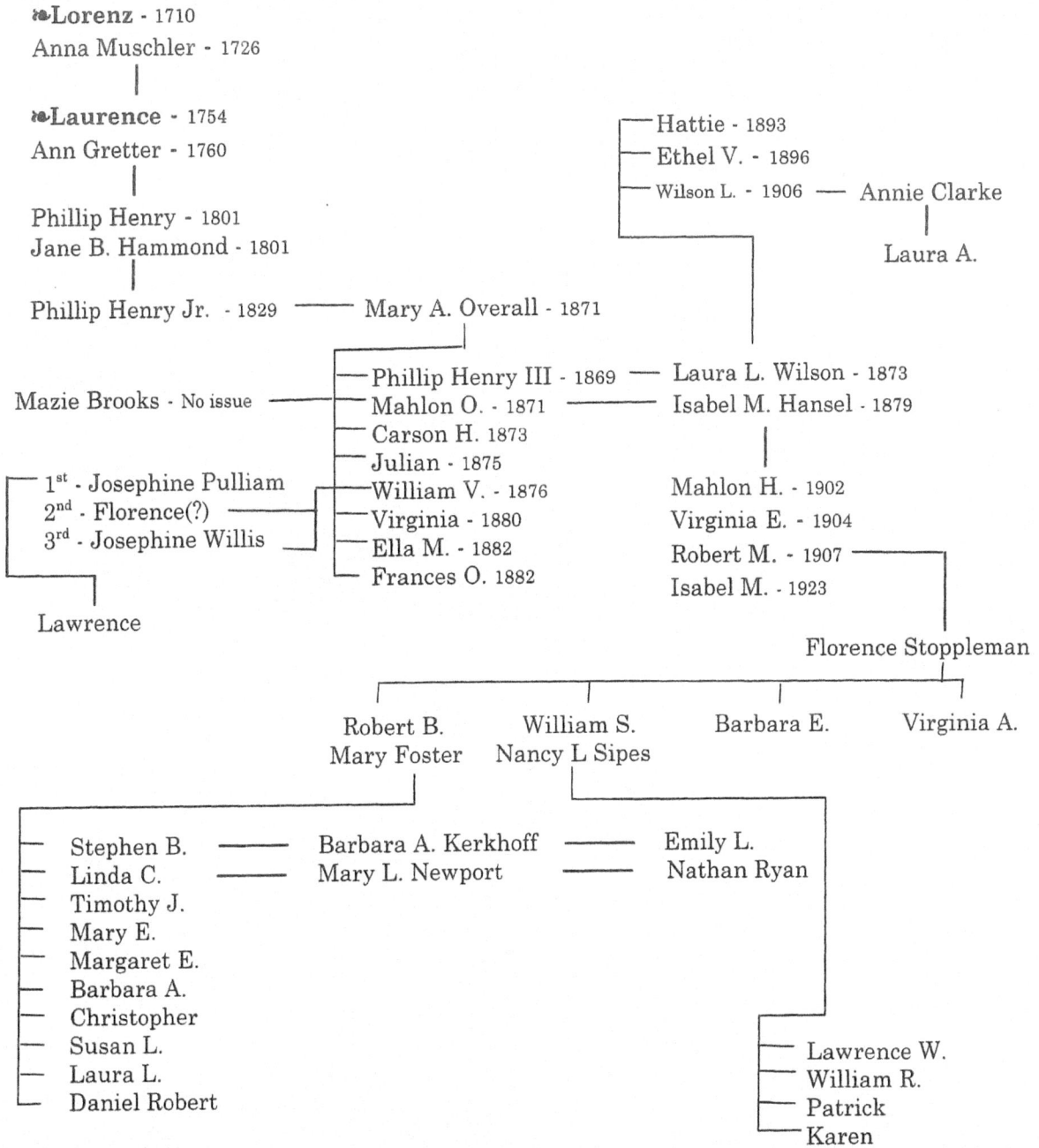

Lorenz - 1710
Anna Muschler - 1726

Laurence - 1754
Ann Gretter - 1760

Phillip Henry - 1801
Jane B. Hammond - 1801

Phillip Henry Jr. - 1829 ——— Mary A. Overall - 1871

Hattie - 1893
Ethel V. - 1896
Wilson L. - 1906 ——— Annie Clarke

Laura A.

Mazie Brooks · No issue ———

Phillip Henry III - 1869 ——— Laura L. Wilson - 1873
Mahlon O. - 1871 ——— Isabel M. Hansel - 1879
Carson H. 1873
Julian - 1875
William V. - 1876
Virginia - 1880
Ella M. - 1882
Frances O. 1882

1st - Josephine Pulliam
2nd - Florence(?)
3rd - Josephine Willis

Mahlon H. - 1902
Virginia E. - 1904
Robert M. - 1907 ———
Isabel M. - 1923

Lawrence

Florence Stoppleman

Robert B.   William S.   Barbara E.   Virginia A.
Mary Foster   Nancy L Sipes

Stephen B.   ——— Barbara A. Kerkhoff ——— Emily L.
Linda C.   ——— Mary L. Newport   ——— Nathan Ryan
Timothy J.
Mary E.
Margaret E.
Barbara A.
Christopher
Susan L.
Laura L.
Daniel Robert

Lawrence W.
William R.
Patrick
Karen

Philip Henry Hooff, Jr.

Born: January 26, 1829 in Alexandria, VA
Christened/Baptized: April 11, 1833 at St. Paul's Episcopal Church, Alexandria, VA
Married: November 25, 1868
Died: March 22, 1913 in Washington, DC at age 84 years old.
Buried: Glenwood Cemetery, Washington, DC
Father: Philip Henry Hooff I   Mother: Jane Baxter Hammond

Spouse: Mary Ann Overall
Born: January 29, 1847 in Overall, VA (near Front Royal)
Christened/Baptized:
Died: December 26, 1938 in Washington, DC at age 91.
Buried: Glenwood Cemetery, Washington, DC
Father: William Carson Overall   Mother: Selina Jolliffe

They had eight children:

Philip Henry Hooff III - Born 1869. See a separate chapter, page #199.

Mahlon Overall Hooff - Born 1871. See separate chapters, page #205.

Carson Hammond Hooff - Born June 24, 1873. Died March 26, 1944 and is buried at Oakwood Cemetery in Falls Church, VA. Married Maizi Brooks. No issue.

Julian Hooff - Born August 1, 1875, and died young

William Vowell Hooff - Born December 3, 1876. Died October 23, 1959 and is buried in Waterloo, Indiana. He married 1st - Josephine Pullian and had one child, Lawrence Hooff who died in 1971. Married 2nd Florence _____ of Ridgewood NJ. No issue. Married 3rd Josephine Willis of Indiana. No issue. We believe he changed his name to Walter Hoffman and moved to New Jersey to avoid his first wife.

Virginia Hooff - Born November 11, 1880. Died October 8, 1942 and is buried at Rock Creek Cemetery, Washington, DC. Married W.C. Bond. No issue

Ella Mercer Hooff - Born July 25, 1882 in Overall, VA. Died August 11, 1976 and is buried at Glenwood Cemetery in Washington, DC. Married Elwood Custer Franklin (b: July 25, 1879 in Philadelphia, son of George Franklin and Sadie Pyle) Died January 28, 1920 and buried at Glenwood Cemetery. They had four children:
    Adeline Virginia Franklin - Born January 28, 1906 in Washington, DC.

    Francis Willis Franklin - Born June 13, 1913 in Washington, DC. (Was adopted by Booth family). He married and had one son.

    Robert Elwood Elijah Franklin who was born December 28, 1914 in Hyattsville, MD. Married and had one daughter, Deborah.

    John Daniel Franklin - Born September 20, 1917 in Falls Church, VA. Died in 1923 and is buried at Glenwood Cemetery.

Frances Overall Hooff Franklin - Born July 25, 1882. Died August 22, 1933 in Washington, DC and is buried at Glenwood Cemetery in Washington, DC. Married Harry Stites, and had one son, Harry Stites Jr. Divorced before 1914.

Philip Henry Hooff Jr. was about 20 years of age when he left Alexandria to participate in the California gold rush. It is not known how long he stayed in California, but it is said that he established a trading post there (later raided and burned by the Indians). After his marriage he farmed the Overall land for approximately 30 years. The family moved to Washington, D.C. between the years 1895 and 1897. In 1897-98, Philip left to join the Yukon gold rush, returning to Washington, D.C. around 1901. All of the children were born in Overall, VA, and began their education in the one-room, one-instructor schoolhouse in Overall. It was during this period that the spelling of the last name changed to "Hoff", and was used by all his children except Philip Henry III.

Obituary, *The Washington Star, December 1938*: "Mrs. Mary Ann Hooff Funeral Rite's Held: Funeral services for Mrs. Mary Ann Hooff, 93, who died Monday at her home, 6007 Broad Branch Road, NW, were held today in Chambers Funeral Home. The Rev. Dr. G.E. Lensky, pastor of Grace Lutheran Church officiated. Burial was in Glenwood Cemetery. Mrs. Hooff was the widow of Philip Henry Hooff, former Alexandria, VA commission merchant, who died in 1913. They were married in 1868. Born on a Virginia plantation, Mrs. Hooff witnessed several skirmishes between Confederate and Union veterans during the Civil War. Her father was the late William Carson Overall, who owned a large estate, a section of which was taken over by the government to form a part of the Shenandoah National Park. Mrs. Hooff had been a resident of this city for 50 years. During the World War she was employed in the government services. She was a member of St. Stephen's and Incarnation Episcopal Church. Surviving are two daughters, Mrs. Ella M. Franklin and Mrs. Virginia Bond, both of this city, four sons, Philip Henry Hooff, Carson Hammond Hooff and Mahlon O. Hooff, all of Virginia, and William V. Hooff of New Jersey; a sister, Mrs. Clarendon Smith, of this city, seven grandchildren and several great-grandchildren."

Mary Overall Hooff and her daughter-in-law, Isabelle Hansell Hoff, were among the many women who marched in Washington, DC to gain the right to vote (Constitutional Amendment 19 finally passed in 1920).

Philip Henry Hooff, Jr.
1829 - 1913

Courtesy of Ann Hooff-Kline

Mary Ann Overall Hooff
1847 - 1938

Philip Henry Hooff
1829 - 1913

Photo taken on their wedding day, November25, 1868

Courtesy of Ann Hooff-Kline

Standing - Carson Hammond Hooff
Left to right - Philip Henry Hooff III, Mazie B. Hoff, Mahlon O. Hoff, Isabel H. Hoff,
Laura W. Hooff, Virginia Hoff Bond

Ella M. Hooff
1882 - 1976

Elwood C. Franklin
1879 - 1920

Frances Hoff- Stites
1882 - 1933
Twin sister of Ella M. Hooff

Philip Henry Hooff, III

Born: September 18, 1869 in Overall, VA
Christened/Baptized:
Married: 1891 in Washington, DC
Died: May 19, 1952 in Arlington, VA at age 81 years, 8 months.
Buried: Presbyterian Cemetery, Alexandria, VA
Father: Philip Henry Hooff, Jr.   Mother: Mary Ann Overall

Spouse: Laura Lee Wilson
Born: February 13, 1873 in Paris, VA
Christened/Baptized:
Died: June 28, 1958 in Arlington, VA at age 85 years old.
Buried: Presbyterian Cemetery, Alexandria, VA
Father: Jeremiah DeBelle Wilson   Mother: Harriet Cornelia Brown
Jeremiah was a member of "Mosby's Rangers" C.S.A.

They had three children:

Hattie Hooff - Born March 31, 1893. Married Clarence C. Melville, no issue.

Ethel Virginia Hooff - Born March 2, 1896. Married Henry H. Freeman, no issue.

Wilson Lee Hooff - Born 1906. See a separate chapter, page #201.

Philip Henry Hooff, III left Overall, VA before the age of twelve, and lived with his aunt and uncle, Selina Overall and Clarendon Smith in Washington, DC, assisting them in their wholesale feed and grain business. In 1906 he was a partner in the firm of Bushley & Hoff, and between the years 1910 and 1913, was associated with Edwin E. Overholt in Hoff & Co., a used furniture business. In 1918 or 1919 he was employed by the Veterans Administration, from which he retired in 1939.

Article, *Washington Star, February 18, 1951*: "Honored on Anniversary: Mrs. And Mrs. Philip H. Hooff of 748 Albermarle Street, Arlington, were guests of honor yesterday at a sixtieth wedding anniversary party given for them by their son, Wilson L. Hooff, at his home, 3312 Fessenden St., N.W., here. Natives of Virginia, Mrs. and Mrs. Hooff lived in Washington for many years and were married in Mt. Pleasant. Hooff retired from government service in 1939 when he was 70. Mrs. Hooff, now 78, and her husband are in excellent health and both attend Mount Olivet Methodist Church in Arlington."

Obituary, *Washington Star, May 20, 1952*: "Funeral Rites for Philip Hooff to be held tomorrow: Philip Henry Hooff III, 82, member of an old Virginia family that settled in Alexandria before the Revolutionary War, died yesterday at his home. 748 North Albermarle Street, Arlington, following an illness which lasted several months. Mr. Hooff, a retired clerk with the Veteran's Administration, was born on his grandfathers country estate in Overall, VA, named after his mother's family. The estate is now part of the Shenandoah National Park. He was a member of the Mount Olivet Methodist Church. Mr. Hooff is survived by his wife, Mrs. Laura Wilson Hooff, two daughters, Mrs. Ethel H. Freeman of the home address, and Mrs. C.C. Melville, Brookline, PA; a son, Wilson L. Hooff, 3312 Fessenden St., NW, Washington, DC, and two brothers, and one granddaughter. Funeral rites will be held tomorrow at 2 P.M. at the Ives Funeral Home, 2847 Wilson Blvd., interment will be in Presbyterian Cemetery, Alexandria."

Obituary, *Washington Star, June 1958*: "Laura W. Hooff: Laura W. Hooff, 84, widow of Philip Henry Hooff, died at her residence, 748 N. Albermarle St., Arlington, Saturday, after a brief illness. Mrs. Hooff was born in Paris, VA, but spent most of her life in Washington, Alexandria, and Arlington. Her husband was a retired Veterans Administration employee, and a member of an old Virginia family whose ancestors settled in Alexandria before the Revolutionary War.

Mrs. Hooff is survived by a son, Wilson L., 3312 Fessenden St., NW; two daughters, Hattie H. Melville, Brookline, PA, and Ethel H. Freeman, of the home address, and a granddaughter. The funeral service will be at the Ives funeral home, 2847 Wilson Blvd., Arlington, at 2 p.m. Tuesday. Burial will be at the Presbyterian Cemetery in Alexandria.

Philip Henry Hooff, III
1869 - 1952
The son of P.H. Hooff, Jr.
and Mary Ann Overall

Courtesy of Ann Hooff-Kline

Wilson Lee Hooff

Born: August 7, 1906 in Washington, DC
Christened/Baptized:
Married: 1929 in Washington, DC
Died: July 31, 1993 in Gaithersburg, MD at age 87.
Buried: Old Presbyterian Cemetery, Alexandria, VA
Father: Philip Henry Hooff III   Mother: Laura Lee Wilson

Spouse: Annie Laura Clark
Born: April 3, 1908
Christened/Baptized:
Died:
Buried: Father: Clifton P. Clark   Mother: Alta S. Kelly

They had one child:
    Laura Ann Clark Hooff - Born February 3, 1938. Married Robert Cornelius Kline (born January 7, 1937 to Sydney D. and Leona Kline). Laura Ann is a graduate of Dickinson College and a professional water color artist. Robert is a graduate of Dickinson College and is in banking. They have two children:
    Frederick DeLong Hooff Kline, born February 10, 1967

    Laura Lee Kline, born July 16, 1964.

An article from the *Washington Post*: 'WILSON L. HOOFF - FEDERAL RESERVE COUNSEL. Wilson L. Hooff, 87, a retired attorney at the Federal Reserve Board and a collector of early American lighting devices, died July 31 at Asbury Methodist Village in Gaithersburg, where he had lived since 1985. Hie death was attributed to head injuries he sustained in a fall at his residence three days earlier.

Mr. Hooff, a native of Washington and a resident of the city for most of his life, graduated from Western High School. He received bachelors' and law degrees from George Washington University.

In 1931, he went to work for the Federal Reserve Board. He was assistant general counsel in the legal division when he retired in 1973.

Mr. Hooff was a member of the Early American Glass Club, and he lectured about his collection of early American lighting devices. He was a past chairman of the pastoral committee of Mount Vernon Place United Methodist Church and a past president of its Rustin Couples Class, a Sunday school group. Survivors include his wife of 64 years, Laura Clark Hooff of Asbury Methodist Village; a daughter Ann Hooff-Kline of Phoenixville, PA; two sisters, Ethel Hooff Freeman and Hattie Hooff Melville, both of Alexandria; and two grandchildren."

Obituary from *Washington Post*: "HOOFF, WILSON L. On Saturday, July 31, 1993, of Gaithersburg, MD; beloved husband of Laura Clark Hooff; father of Ann Hooff-Kline of Phoenixville, PA; brother of Hattie Hooff Melville and Ethel Hooff Freeman, both of Alexandria, VA; grandfather of Frederick Hooff Kline and Laura Lee Kline. Memorial service will be held at the Asbury Methodist Home Chapel, 211 Russell Ave., Gaithersburg, MD on Tuesday, August 3, at 11 a.m. Private interment to follow at Old Presbyterial Cemetery, Alexandria, VA. In lieu of flowers, memorial contributions may be made to the Asbury Benevolent Fund, 210 Russell Ave., Gaithersburg, MD 20877. Arrangements by Devol Funeral Home, Gaithersburg, MD."

Four generations:

Left to right is Philip Henry Hooff, III (69) Nary Ann Overall Hooff (91)
Wilson Lee Hooff (32)
Laura Ann Hooff (1 month)
Photo taken March 20, 1938 - Mary Ann died in December of that same year.

Courtesy of Ann Hooff-Kline

Wilson Lee Hooff (1906 - 1993)
(son of P.H. Hooff, III and Laura Lee Wilson) and Laura Ann Hooff (1938 -

Photo taken January 22, 1939

Courtesy of Ann Hooff-Kline

Left to right: Wilson lee Hooff, Laura Ann Hooff Kline, Laura Clark Hooff
Photo taken 1989.

Courtesy of Ann Hooff-Kline

Mahlon Overall Hoff (Changed name from HOOFF)

Born: July 3, 1871 in Overall, VA
Christened/Baptized:
Married: October 19, 1901, Church of the Advent, Washington, DC
Died: November 7, 1953 in Arlington, VA at age 82.
Buried: Columbia Gardens Cemetery, Arlington, VA
Father: Philip Henry Hooff, Jr.   Mother Mary Ann Overall

Spouse: Isabel McGill Hansel
Born: October 4, 1879 in Philadelphia, PA
Christened/Baptized:
Died: May 6, 1968 in Fairfax, VA at age 89 years old.
Buried: Columbia Gardens Cemetery, Arlington, VA
Father: Wilbert Fisk Hansel   Mother: Isabel Amelia Goodyear

They had four children:

Mahlon Hansel Hoff - Born August 18, 1902 in Washington, DC. Died December 6, 1950 and is buried in Long Island, NY; married Adele Mathews, no issue.

Virginia E. Hoff - Born July 1904. Died August 26, 1904 and is buried at Glenwood Cemetery, Washington, DC.

Robert McGill Hoff - Born 1907. See a separate chapter, page #207.

Isabelle Mary (Betty) Hoff (deceased) - Born October 25, 1923 in Dayton, Ohio. Married Joseph Whatley Lemons (born June 4, 1923 in Bristol, TN, son of Joseph Abraham Lemons and Dorothy Rogers Lundy) on January 15, 1943 in Arlington, VA. They have two children:
Donald Wayne Lemons - Born February 22, 1949 in Washington, DC.

Janet Gail Lemons - Born July 7, 1952 in Arlington, VA.

Mahlon Overall Hoff (Hooff) attended school in Overall, Va, and came to Washington, DC in 1895. He was a carpenter and a building contractor for many years before being employed with the Library of Congress. In 1913 he moved the family to Dayton, Ohio, where he was active in the Masonic Lodge and the Carpenters Union. In 1931 he moved to Arlington, VA with his wife and daughter. He retired from Government service on November 1, 1953 at age 82.

Isabel McGill Hansel came to Washington, DC in 1896 after the death of her parents. She lived with her married sister, and was employed for a short time with the Census Bureau. Most of her family were Quakers and she claimed to the first "Yankee" bride in the family. She and her mother-in-law were among the ladies who marched in Washington, DC for passage of the 19th Amendment giving women the right to vote.

Obituary, *The Washington Star, November 1953*: "Hoff, Mahlon O.: On Saturday, November 7, 1953, at Arlington Hospital, Mahlon O. Hoff of 1826 N. Stafford St., Arlington, VA, beloved husband of Isabel H. Hoff. He also is survived by one son, Robert M. Hoff of Dayton, Ohio; one daughter, Mrs. J.W. Lemons of Falls church, VA; one daughter-in-law, Mrs. Mahlon Hoff of Wyckoff, NJ; a brother, W.V. Hoff of Lake Worth, Fla., and six grandchildren. Friends may call at the Ives Funeral Home, 2847 Wilson Blvd., Arlington, VA, where funeral services will be held Tuesday, November 10, at 2 p.m. Interment, Columbia Gardens Cemetery."

Obituary, *Northern Virginia Sun, May 1968*: "Isabel Hoff, 89, Dies in Fairfax: Funeral services for Isabel Hoff, 89, were to be held today. Mrs. Hoff lived at 2439 Luckett Ave., Vienna. She died Sunday at Fairfax Hospital following a heart attack after having been in poor health for many years. The former Isabel Hansel, Mrs. Hoff was born in Philadelphia. She went to public schools in Philadelphia, and married the late Mahlon Overall Hoff. Funeral services were to be held at 10 a.m. today at the Money & King Funeral Home, followed by interment at Columbia Gardens Cemetery. Mrs. Hoff is survived by a son, Robert M. Of Dayton, Ohio; a daughter, Mrs. Betty H. Lemons, of the home; 6 grandchildren and 19 great-grandchildren."

Robert McGill Hoff

Born: January 10, 1907 in Washington, DC
Christened/Baptized:
Married: August 12, 1929 in Dayton, OH
Died: May 11, 1975 in Dayton, OH at age 66.
Buried: Calvary Cemetery, Dayton, OH
Father: Mahlon Overall Hoff (Hooff)   Mother: Isabel McGill Hansel

Spouse: Florence Stoppelman
Born: January 9, 1906 in Dayton, OH
Christened/Baptized:
Died:
Buried:
Father: William S. Stoppelman   Mother: Elizabeth Byrne

They had four children:

Robert Byrne Hoff - b: 1930. See a separate chapter, page #209.

William Stoppelman Hoff - Born May 3, 1934 in Dayton, OH. Married Nancy Lee Sipos (b: December 15, 1936 in Dayton, daughter of John Sipos and Ethel Schuran) January 26, 1957 in Dayton. They had four children:
   Lawrence William Hoff - Born January 27, 1959. Married Darlene Unger.

   William Robert Hoff - Born December 1, 1960. Married Sheila Gunter. They have one child named Abigail Lee Hooff, born 1994.

   Patrick Hoff - Born March 14, 1965

   Karen Hoff - Born January 26, 1969

Barbara Elizabeth Hoff - Born August 31, 1938 in Dayton, OH. Married Michael C. Laukhart (born January 10, 1936, son of Charles Francis Laukhart and Martha M. Geiss) in 1957 at St. Agnes Church in Dayton. Barbara is a graduate of Illinois University and is a teacher in Arnold, Maryland. They had four children:
   Michael Charles Laukhart - Born August 15, 1957

   Lisa Geiss Laukhart- Born April 21, 1959

   Laurel Ann Laukhart - Born February 1,1961

   Jennifer Isabel Laukhart - Born November 1, 1963

Virginia Ann (Ginni) Hoff - Born January 29, 1943 in Dayton, OH. Married (1st)Ronald Blaine Nolan (b: July 25, 1938). They had three children:
   Ronald Blaine Nolan Jr. - Born April 1961 in Providence, RI

   Elisabeth Florence (Betsy) Nolan - Born June 15, 1962

   Robert McGill Nolan - Born June 19, 1964 in New Orleans, LA

   NOTE: Ginni's Ann's 2nd husband, Richard Meyers adopted her three children. Ginni is a nurse.

Robert McGill Hoff graduated from Roosevelt High School in Dayton and played semi-pro baseball for the National Cash Register Co. during the depression years. He was employed for a short while with the Frigidaire Corp., and later established Hoff Refrigeration Sales & Service. He was active for many years in coaching and sponsoring youth activities in the Dayton area.

Florence Stoppelman Hoff taught in the public school system of Dayton for many years before receiving her Bachelor of Science Degree from the University of Dayton in 1958.

Obituary, May 1975, Dayton, Ohio: "Hoff, Robert M., died Sunday, May 11th at his home, 405 Redhaw Rd. He was born in Washington, DC and was a son of the late Mahlon O. Hoff and Isabel Hansel Hoff of Alexandria, VA. Mr. Hoff was president of Hoff Refrigeration Sales and Service, and a charter member of Refrigeration Service Engineers Society. He was a member of Corpus Christi Parrish. He is survived by his wife, Florence (Stoppleman), 2 sons, Robert Bryrne of Ft. Mitchell; KY, William Stoppleman Hoff of Dayton, Ohio; two daughters, Mrs. Michael Laukhart (Barbara Hoff of Annapolis, MD), and Mrs. Richard Meyers (Virginia Hoff of Kettering, MD). Twenty-one grandchildren survive, and a sister, Mrs. Joseph W. Lemons, (Bette Hoff) of Vienna, VA. Mr. Hoff was interested in youth activities for many years, and was active in sponsoring and managing CYO baseball and basketball teams for boys and girls in the Dayton area, particularly at St. Agnes Parrish. Friends may call at the Harris Funeral Home, 49 Linden Ave., Tuesday from 3:30 -5:00 p.m. and 7:00 - 9:00 p.m. Funeral will be held at 11:30 a.m Wednesday, followed by mass of Christian Burial in Corpus Cristi Church at 12 noon. Interment at Calvary Cemetery. The family suggest contributions may be made to the Montgomery County Cancer Society in lieu of flowers."

Robert Byrne Hoff

Born: December 9, 1930 in Dayton, OH
Christened/Baptized:
Married: 1952 in Dayton, OH
Died:
Buried:
Father: Robert McGill Hoff   Mother: Florence Stoppelman

Spouse: Mona Foster
Born: July 16, 1933
Christened/Baptized:
Died:
Buried:
Father: Herman Fricke   Mother: Margaret Mohan

They had ten children:

Stephen B. Hoff - Born August 24, 1952. Married Barbara Ann Kerkhoff, May 31, 1975 at Our Lady of Lourdes Church, Cincinnati, Ohio. They have one daughter, Emily Lynn Hoff, born November 20, 1978 in Cincinnati. Second wife is Joan (?). They have 2 children, Madeline and Charles.

Linda C. Hoff - Born August 31, 1953. She is a graduate of University of Kentucky.

Timothy Joseph Hoff - Born January 4, 1955. Married Mary Lisa Newport in 1978 in Ft. Mitchell, KY. They have a son, Nathaniel Ryan Hoff, born January 14, 1979 in Ft Mitchell.

Mary Elaine Hoff - Born November 28, 1956. She is a graduate of University of Kentucky

Margaret Elizabeth Hoff - Born August 26, 1958. She is a graduate of University of Oregon

Barbara Ann Hoff - Born January 30, 1961. She is a graduate of St. Thomas More College in Kentucky

Christopher Hoff - Born September 23, 1962. Married Margaret Fahey.

Susan Lynn Hoff - Born October 29, 1963

Laura Lee Hoff - Born September 3, 1965

Daniel Robert Hoff - Born October 8, 1968

Robert Byrne Hoff graduated from the University of Dayton and shortly thereafter, established Byrne Development Corp., a building and development firm in Ohio and Kentucky, which now has several subsidiaries. He is a former vice president of the National Home Builders Assoc., and a former president of the National Home Builders of Kentucky.

John Vowell Hooff

Born: May 26, 1831 in Alexandria, DC
Christened/Baptized: May 11, 1833 at St. Paul's Episcopal Church, Alexandria, DC
Married: Unmarried
Died: April 23, 1874 in Cerro Gerdo, Inyo County, CA
Buried:
Father: Philip Henry Hooff I   Mother: Jane Baxter Hammond

Obituary in Alexandria Gazette, May 12, 1874: DIED. In Cerro Gerdo, California, on the 23rd of April last, in the 43rd year of his age, after a short illness, JOHN VOWELL HOOFF, son of P.H. Hooff of this city.

John Vowell Hooff
1st Lieut. C.S.A.
May 26, 1831 - April 23, 1874

He served in Nicaragua with General William Walker on his 1855 through 1857 Filibuster Campaign. The name Hooff is mentioned several times in the book *The War in Nicaragua by Gen. William Walker*, as being an aide-de- camp. He may have been with General Walker on his other filibuster campaigns into South America. This could be where he obtained the rank of major. Walker was captured and shot in Honduras in 1860.

Note: We believe the following two men are one in the same. The information we have was a John V. Hooff also recorded as John V. Hough and J.J./J.V. Haugh came from Texas to Richmond in 1861 to get a commission. He was not qualified. He joined the Gen. Henry Wise Legion.

The entire legion was captured on Roanoke Island, Nags Head, NC. On a list of prisoner's that were exchanged in early 1862 is a 1st Lieut. J.V. Hooff, 59th Virginia Volunteer Aide. We don't know if this is the same man or our John Vowell Hooff that was a 1st Lieut. in the 2nd Reg. Texas/Arizona Brigade later in 1862.

After his release he joined Co. D. of Smith's Legion (Partisan Rangers) of Floyd County, Georgia on August 6, 1863, and was detailed to the Quartermaster Department in Knoxville, TN as a private. Later called Fain's Reg. Which was then redesigned in March 1863 as the 65th reg. Georgia Volunteer Army of Tennessee.

John Hoff, Co. G, 60 VA Infantry (34 Regiment of Infantry, Wise Legion), Private
J.V. Hooff, Co. D, 65 Georgia Infantry, Private.

We found a John V. Hooff in the 2nd Texas Cavalry (2nd Regiment Arizona Brigade) as a 1st Lieutenant. We don't know for sure if this is the same John V. Hooff or how he got to Texas. He may have stayed in Texas after his return from South America.

John G. Johnston Hooff of the 4th Maryland Artillery, in one of his letters asks that they try and find out where Vowel Hooff is and what rank he holds.

John Vowell Hooff's service records show that he was a 1st Lieutenant in Co. B, Baylor's Regiment Texas Cavalry (2nd Regiment Arizona Brigade). Company B was formed mostly from Bexar County, San Antonia, TX. Baylor's Reg't Cav. Co. B, 2nd Battalion Arizona Brigade Company Muster Rolls show him present on Sept. 8th ; Dec. 31,1862 as a 1st Lt. In for the war.

Roster of Commissioned Officers of the Arizona Brigade, Columbus, Texas dated March 1, 1863 show a J. A. Hoff 1st Lieut. Co. B 2nd Regt. was commissioned on Sept. 8, 1862.

His name also appears in the body of a letter addressed to Maj. Gen. J. B. Magruder, Comdg. Dept. of Texas, New Mexico and Arizona, and was signed by 1st Lieut. Jno. V. Hooff, Comdg. Spy Comp. dated Feb. 16,1863 at Camp Bernard.

Two pay records show a Jno. V. Hooff 1st Lt. Arizona Brigade signing for pay.
From 8 Sept. 1862 - 8 Feb. 1863 - $500.00 ++ From Capt. Francis Mullen
From 8 Feb. 1863 - 28 Feb. 1863 - $66.66 ++From Capt. Francis Mullen

The following information was received from *Robert Perkins* a historian of the Civil War in the Texas - Arizona area. I believe this information to be more accurate that what I received from Hill College in Hillsboro, Texas. Mr. Perkins explains his reasoning in his summary.

The organization of Baylor's Regiment Texas Cavalry (also known as the 2nd Regiment Arizona Brigade) was authorized by S.O. No. 74, Headquarters, District of Texas, New Mexico and Arizona dated February 13,1863. It was formed by the addition to Baylor's 2nd (also called 1st)Battalion Arizona Brigade of two independent companies and two of which Lieut. Col. Mullen's Unorganized Battalion Arizona Brigade was composed. The two independent companies do not appear to have ever joined this organization and the regiment was completed in 1865 by the addition of two other companies.

History of the Second Texas (Arizona Brigade) Cavalry

The Second Texas (Arizona Brigade) Cavalry was organized on February 21, 1863 per S.O. # 81 by the consolidation of two battalions. These two battalions, the Second Texas Cavalry Battalion and Mullen's Texas Cavalry Battalion, had been mustered into Confederate service only a few weeks before their consolidation. After the consolidation, the unit was still short companies to constitute a regiment and a number of additional men were recruited in and around San Antonio to bring the unit up to strength.

As was the case with almost all Civil War units, they were frequently named for their commanding officer. Because of this The Second Texas (Arizona Brigade) was also called:

George W. Baylor's Cavalry
Sherod Hunter's Cavalry
John W. Mullen's Cavalry
D.C. Carrington's Cavalry

The regiment served in the Trans-Mississippi Department throughout its career. Listed below are the specific higher command assignments of the regiment.

September 30,1864 2nd - Texas Cavalry Brigade, 1st Texas Cavalry Division, 2nd Corps, Army of Trans-Mississippi

The 2nd Texas (Arizona Brigade) Cavalry participated in more that thirty various types of engagements during its career. Numbers following the engagements locate them on the map after this history.

June 20, 1863	Skirmish	Jackson's Cross Roads, LA
June 23, 1863	Battle	Brashear City,
July 12 - 13, 1863	Battle	Cox's Plantation
September 14, 1863	Skirmish	Vidalia, LA
September 14, 1863	Skirmish	Cross Bayou, LA
Oct. 3 - Nov. 30, 1863		Campaign in Wester Louisiana and Operations in Teche County
March 13, 1864	Skirmish	Los Patricios, TX (detachment)
Mar. 13-May 22, 1864		Operations against Banks's Red River Campaign

April 7, 1864	Engagement	Wilson's Farm (8) near Pleasant Hill (9), LA
April 8, 1864	Skirmish	Bayou de Paul (Carroll's Mills (10) near Pleasant Hill (9), LA
April 8, 1864	Battle	Sabine Cross Roads (11), Mansfield (12) near Pleasant Hill (9)
April 9, 1864	Engagement	Pleasant Hill, LA (9)
April 23-24, 1864	Skirmish	Cloutiersville, LA (13)
April 27, 1864	Skirmish	Alexandria, LA (14)
April 28, 1864	Skirmish	Alexandria, LA (14)
April 29, 1864	Skirmish	Alexandria, LA (14)
May 3, 1864	Skirmish	David's Ferry, LA
May 5, 1864	Action	Graham's Plantation, LA
May 6, 1864	Skirmish	Bayou LaMourie, LA
May 13, 1864	Skirmishes	Alexandria, LA (14)
May 13-20, 1864		Operations against the Retreat from Alexandria (14) to Morganza (15), LA
May 18, 1864	Engagement	Yellow Bayou, Bayou de Glaze (16), Norwood's Plantation (Old Oaks), LA
May 30, 1864	Action	Steamer "City Belle", LA
June 19, 1864	Affair	Eagle Pass, TX (detachment) (17)
June 25, 1864	Skirmish	Rancho Las Rinas, TX (detachment) (18)
September 6, 1864	Skirmish	Palmetto Ranch near Brazos, Santiago, TX (19)
October 14, 1864	Skirmish	Bocca Chico Pass, TX (20)
June 2, 1865	Surrender	Galveston, TX (6)

The following battle statistics are Northern reports from Matthew Brady's Illustrated History.

June 23, 1863 Brashear City, LA. Detachments of the 114th and 176th New York, 23rd Conn., 42nd Mass., and 21st Indiana, were northern units that fought at Brashear City.
 Union - 46 killed, 40 wounded, 300 missing.
 Confederate - 3 killed, 18 wounded. It appears that the 2nd Texas did well in this engagement.

July 13, 1863, Donaldsonville, LA. Portions of Weitzel's and Grover's Divisions, 19th Corps. Of the Union Army fought in this engagement.
 Union - 450 killed, wounded and missing.

April 9, 1864, Pleasant Hill, LA and Sabine Crossroads. Portions of the 13th, 16th, and 19th Corps and Calvary Divisions, Army of the Department of the Gulf of the Union fought this engagement. Union - 300 killed, 1600 wounded, 2100 missing. Maj. Gen. Franklin and Brig. Gen. Ranson wounded. Confederate - 600 killed, 2400 wounded, 500 missing. Maj. Gen. Mouton and Brig. Gen. Parsons killed.

The Second Texas (Arizona Brigade) Cavalry was included among the Confederate Trans-Mississippi troops surrendered at Galveston in early June 1865. The unit probably ceased to exist by that time, however, the regiment was reported stationed near Houston in April 1865, and it probably disbanded there in May 1865 when the news of the surrender of eastern Confederate forces reached the Trans-Mississippi Department. Surrender by Gen. E. K. Smith commanding Trans-Mississippi Department, May 26, 1865.

Major John Vowell Hooff (1831 - 1874)
Son of Philip Henry Hooff I and Jane Baxter Hammond
Photo taken by Blessing & Bros. Gallery
Main Street, Houston, TX - no date

Courtesy of Ann Hooff-Kline

ACKERMAN Dorothy 74
ALLEN Mary 101
ARMISTEAD John R 149
ARMSTRONG Jonathan WC 101
ASHBY I 99
BARNES Harriet V 65
BARNWELL Carlton 65 Mary Janney 65
BAUSERMAN John 73 John Jr (1963) 73
BEALL Aquila Brooke 31 Upton 31 Brook 31
    John Hooff 31 Louise 31 Mattie 31
BEARD William H 187 William H Jr (1929)187
BECKHAM Ann A (1832) 171 Fontaine 171
BENNETT Charles Jr 16 Clara Soares (1831)
    16 87 Emily C 185 James H (1797) 16
    Julia Delaney (1834) 16 Mary Ann (1825)
    16 69
BIERMAN Gary S 71 Gary S Jr (1974) 71
BIGELOW Cynthia L (1932) 41
BLINCOE Elizabeth (1820) 151 Martha J 31
    Sampson 31 151
BLOCHER Anna R 35
BOND WC 191
BOWLING Christine (1882) 185 Katie 77
BROOKS Maizi 191
BROWN Harriett C 199 Janett (1824) 53 John
    D 53 Mary R 181 William H 171
BURNETT Elizabeth 13
BUSH Sue L 129
BYRNE Elizabeth 207
CARRICK Barbara M (1943) 130 Robert 130
CARTER Mary E (1849) 87 Issac N 87
CHAMPLEY Mary E (1956) 183
CHEESEMAN Lewis 53
CLARK Annie L (1908) 201 Clifton 201
COLE Frank 59 John M Jr 60 Robert A 60
CONRAD Maria E 105
COOKSEY Howard (1921) 185 Paul H (1948)
    185 Allyson M (1950) 185
CRICKENBERGER William (1947) 73
    Campbell D (1979) 73 Cassie B 73
    William A 73
CROSS 109
CULLUM Andrew 99
DARREN 3
DAVIDSON Archie 99 Rebecca H (1907) 99
DeNEAL Jennett (1787) 31 William 31
DOVE Eleanor I (Nellie L) 97
DOYLE Conrad 4 Margaret 4 Henry 4
    Lawrence 4 John 4 George 4
DUNN Elizabeth T (1918) 71 Houston 71
FAHEY Margaret 209
FAWCETT Edward S 53 Ellen D (1886) 53
    Janet B 83 John D 53 Laurence G 53 Lewis
    H (1888) 53 Malcolm G (1891) 53 Richard
    H (1892) 53 Mary G (1894) 53

FAWCETT Laurence G (1898) 53 Susan S 53
    Wallace H 53 Willis 53
FORD Emily (1958) 185
FOSTER Mona (1933) 209
FRANKLIN Elwood C (1879) 191 Adeline V
    (1906) 191 Deborah 191 Francis W (1913)
    191 Franklin O H 147 Robert E E (1914)
    191 George 191 John D (1917) 191
FRANCOIS Andre GL 129 Ashleigh Marie
    129
FRICKE H 209
FREEMAN Harry H 199
GARDNER Caroline G 54
GEISS Martha 207
GLADDING Edith M (1876) 109 Viola V
    (1854) 109
GOODYEAR Isabel A 205
GRETTER George M 13 Mary Ann (1760) 13
    Mary G 53
GRIFFITH Nancy 73
GUNTER Sheila 207
HAMILTON Mary 16
HAMMOND James 77 149 Jane B (1801) 149
    Susan R (1825) 105 Thomas R 105
HANSEL Isabel M (1879) 205 Wilbert F 205
HEBRON Elona C 117
HEINSTANCE Hobart 65
HERBERT James R 69 Sarah C F(1880) 69
HEWITT Jack L 183
HOFF/HOOFF
    Abigail L (1994) 207 Albert C (1869) 101
    Alexander R (1984) 73 Allison A (1872)
    171 185 Allison A Jr (1904) 185 Allyson C
    (1973) 183 Althea M (1921) 185 Ann
    Amelia (1834) 77 Ann (1785) 16 Anna
    Campbell (1854) 105 Anna DC (1881) 88
    Anna L (1890) 109 Anne F (1951) 183
    Annie BS (1869) 171 Asberry F 109
    Barbara (before 1749) 3 Barbara Ann
    (1961) 209 Barbara E (1938) 207
    Benjamin L (1918) 118 Bettie (1866) 105
    Bettie B (1883) 88 Bettie Rosa (1853) 151
    Brittany Marie (1987) 129 Carlyle (1981)
    71 Carlyle FH (1950) 73 Caroline (1945)
    71 Caroline (Carrie) (1854) 61 Caroline A
    (1829) 49 Caroline J (1823) 49 Carson H
    (1873) 191 Charles 209 Charles R (1826)
    49 61 Charles R (1864) 61 Charles R III
    (1940) 71 Charles R Jr (1911) 69 71
    Charles R Sr (1882) 65 69 Christopher
    (1962) 209 Churchill H (1972) 71 Clara S
    (1876) 87 Clara S (1831) 57 Constance
    151 Courtland H 53 Daniel R (1968) 209
    Douglass (1858) 54 Edna L (1938) 123
    Edward L (1865) 105 109 Edward Lee
    (1829) 77 Elizabeth (before 1749) 3

Elizabeth (1778) 13 Elizabeth J (1976) 71
Ella M (1882) 191 Ellen C (1878) 88
Ellen D (1864) 54 Elona (1913) 73 Emily L
(1978) 209 Ethel V (1896) 199 Eugene P
(1954) 73 Eugene Jr. (1982) 73 Evelyn
(1946) 73 Faulkner 105 Fontaine B (1866)
171 181 Fontaine B Jr (1919) 181 183
Francis H (1857) 105 Frances O H (1882)
191 Francis H (1892) 109 Francis L (1861)
87 Francis R (1827) 77 105 Frank Loney 35
(George 1789) 16 George B (1858) 171
George WM (1860) 101 Gertrude (1833)
149 Gertrude H (1840) 149 Gordon C
(1896) 109 Hammond F (1885) 109 117
Hattie (1893) 199 Ida(?) (1857) 101 Isabel
M (1923) 205 James A (1948) 183 James H
(1825) 77 101 James H (1869) 87 James L
(1825) 149 171 James L (1856) 171 James
L (1920) 185 James L (1987) 183 James M
(1867) 101 James W (1825) 49 53 Jamie
Lee (1986) 129 Jane H (1831) 77 Jane H
(1870) 171 Jennie M 101 Jessie G (1913)
118 123 John (before 1749) 3 John (1783)
16 31 John B (1907) 185 John CH (1918)
69 73 John CH Jr (1948) 73 John CH III
(1976) 73 John GJ (1844) 31 35 John J
(1866) 35 John L (1866) 87 John L (1987
John LC (1823) 77 87 John Vowell (1831)
149 211 Julia A (1827) 49 Julia Maria
(1798) 16 Julian (1875) 191 Karen (1969)
207 Kimberly M (1962) 129 Laura AC
(1938) 201 Laura B (1904) 187 Laura L
(1965) 209 Laurentius (1754) 4 13
Lawrence (d: 1971) 191 Lawrence III
(1780) 13 Lawrence W (1959) 207 Lewis
(before 1749) 3 Lewis (1852) 61 65 Lewis
(1791) 16 49 Linda C (1953) 209 Lisa
Marie (1964) 129 Lorentz (1750) 4 Lorenz
(before 1714) 3 Louise (1885) 65 Louise N
(1979) 73 Lucien B (1848) 151 Lucille S
(1921) 181 Madeline 209 Mahlon H (1902)
205 Mahlon Overall (1871) 191 205
Maremi (1972) 71 Margaret (after 1755) 4
Margaret E (1958) 209 Maria Catharina
(1738) 3 Mark A 53 Martha Blincoe (1847)
31 Mary (after 1755) 4 Mary (1887) 65
Mary Ann (1824) 149 Mary AB (1856) 87
Mary Amelia (1803) 16 Mary Ann (1794)
16 Mary E (1956) 209 Mary F (1854) 101
Mary G (1853) 53 Mary H (1887) 33 Mary
M (1905) 99 Mary M (1941) 99 Mary S
(1863) 87 94 Meghan 183 Michelle 117
Nancy L (1953) 183 Nannie T (1900) 99
Nathaniel R (1979) 209 Norborne (1851)
151 Patrick (1965) 207 Peter (1787) 16

HOFF/HOOFF
Philip F (1853) 171 Philip Henry (1801)
16 149 Philip Henry Jr (1829) 149 191
Philip Henry III (1869) 191 199 Rebecca
A (1935) 99 Robert B (1930) Robert B
(1930) 207 209 Robert E (1985) 73 Robert
H (1947) 183 Robert M (1907) 205 207
Robyn Marie (1965) 129 Ronald Lee
(1939) 123 129 Royal L 35 Ruth P (1921)
181 Sarah B (1860) 105 Sarah B (1988)
183 Sarah I (1886) 109 Sarah V (1828) 49
Stephen B (1952) 209 Susan L (1963) 209
Susanna (died before 1749) 3 Susanna
(1734) 3 Thomas E (1911)117 Thomas E
Jr (1949) 117 Timothy J (1955) 209
Unnamed female possibly Ida (1857) 77
Victoria (1838) 149 Victoria (1843) 149
Virginia (1827) 149 Virginia (1880) 191
Virginia A (1943) 207 Virginia E (1904)
205 Virginia Looney 35 Washington H
(1875) 171 187 William (1796) 16 77
William (died young) 77 William A (1839)
62 William A (1952) 117 William A Jr
(1971) 117 William H (1853) 105 William
L (1859) 87 99 William L Jr (1907) 99
William R (1960) 207 William S (1934)
207 William V (1876) 191 Wilson L
(1906) 199 201
HOLT Hallie 109
HUPP SarahS (1948) 183
HYLAND Larry 185
JANNEY Rebecca M (1829) 61
JOHNSON Kate E A 117
JOLLIFFE Selina 191
JONES Elizabeth 149 Martha 31
KAMARA C M (1949) 183 Anya H (1981) 183
KATKIC Anna 129
KEARSLEY Ann M 87
KELLY Alta S 201
KERKHOFF Barbara A 209
KIRBY Frederick L 97 Margaret E (1911) 123
KLINE Robert C (1937) 201 Frederick
    DH (1964) 201 Laura L (1967) 201
KULPS Gudrun (1943) 71
LAUKHART Charles 207 Michael C (1936)
    207 Michael C (1957) 207 Lisa G (1959)
    207 Laurel A (1961) 207 Jennifer I (1963)
    207
LECHE, JG 16
LEMONS Joseph W 205 Donald W (1949) 205
    Janet G (1952) 205
LEWIS Henry 13 Mary Ann 13
LINDSAY Georgie H 187
LLOYD Mary E 43
LOEWY Harris 181 Elizabeth (1949) 181
    Faith (1953) 181

LONEY Fannie 35
LOVE Arthur C (1965) 130 Michael A (1992)
    130 Matthew S (1994) 130
MAHONE Lana 101
MARSHALL Dorothy C (1929) 59
MATHEWS Adele 205
McCullum Andrew 51
MCDONALD Alexander 3
McEWEN Mary H (1869) 99 James NP 99
McMILLIAN William 109
McTYEIRE Holland N III 99 Holland IV
    (1930) 99
MELVILLE Clarence C 199
MEYERS Richard118
MILES Adelia 101
MILLER Joseph M 77 Katie R 77 Ruben 77
    Joseph S (1848) 77 Morgan 77
MOHAN Mona 209
MOON Letitia 49
MOORE-MILLER Mary C (ca 1827) 101
MOORE Morgan 101 Rebecca 77
MORTIMER Kirk J (1954) 183 Bryant J
    (1987) 183
MUSCHLER Anna M 3
MEYERS Richard 207
NEWPORT Mary L 209
NOLAN Ronald B (1938) 207 Ronald B
    Jr (1961) 207 Elizabeth F (1962) 207
    Robert M (1964) 207
NUNNALLY Lynn (1950) 73 Moses 73
OVERALL Mary A (1847) 191 William C 191
PACKETT Frances R H (1795) 77 John B 77
    Mary Ann (1818) 77
PAULSULT Michael 3
PERKINS James C (female) C 183
PETERS Katherine 185
PHILYAW Audrey June (1926) 123
PRINCE Elizabeth (1923) 73 John R 73
PULLIAN Josephine 191
PYLE Sadie 191
RANKIN Mary (Polly) 77
RAPLEY Abraham 49 Elizabeth M (1798) 49
RICHARDSON R Perry 54
ROBERTSON Madeline 130
ROBBINS Chandler 54 Mary D (1855) 54
ROSIC Anton 129 Katherine 129
ROTHERY Howard 109
ROUND George 185 Ruth (1891) 185
RUDDEROW Benjamin J 65 Elizabeth 65
RUSSELL Evelyn 73
SANDERS Cora 77 Henry M 101
SCHATZ 109
SCHURAN Ethel 207
SCOTT Gustavas 13 Robert J 13
SEMEGA Bernard 129 Kathleen M (1945)
    129

SHACKLEFORD Hudson Z 65 Mary A
    (1858) 65
SHARP Frank 101
SHAW Mattie 77
SHIPLEY Floyd C 31
SHUTE Nannie 99
SIPOS John 207 Nancy L (1936) 207
SMITH Charlotte (1890) 181 Clarendon
    (1855) 149 Courtland H 69 Cuthbert 149
    George H 181 Heywood 149 Hugh 149
    Julian 149 Keyes 149 Margaret L (1922)
    183 Mark A 69 Rufus (1822) 149 Sidney
    183 Virginia 149
STABLER Alban G 16 Susan 53
STEPHENSON Anne A 171
STITES Harry 191 Harry Jr 191
STOPPLEMAN Florence (1906) 207
    William 207
TATE Erasmus 77
TATESBAUGH (1795) 4 George 4 Elizabeth 4
    Lawrence 4 Peter 4
TAYLOR Elizabeth E 71 Virginia 109
THOMSON Alexander D 129 Courtney M
    (1984) 129
UNGER Darlene 207
UNSWORTH Caroline L (1879) 117
    Thomas 117
URQUHART Anselm B (1869) 88
    John C (1913) 88 Mary F (1922) 88
WALLACE Benjamin L (1866) 30 54
    Benjamin L (1797) 16 Caroline G (1892)
    54 Jane Eliza (1829) 16 James L (1903)
    54 Janet H (1893) 54 Margaret D (1895)
    54 Mary Ann (1826) 16 Robert Redfield
    (1833) 16 William Lawrence (1824) 16 49
    William Lawrence 54 William W 16
WALTON Atlantic O 71
WASHINGTON Lucy 77 Samuel 77
WILLIAM William L (1824) 38
WEINSTEIN Richard H (1951) 129
WILLIAMS Peter C 73
WILLIS Josephine 191
WILSON Jeremiah D 199 Laura L (1873) 199
WINDELL David V 129 Shannon Marie
    (1989) 129 William 129
WINSLOW 109
YORK Clinton W (1929) 75
ZGAINER Anthony 129 Frances L 129 Steve
    129

www.ingramcontent.com/pod-product-compliance
Lightning Source LLC
Chambersburg PA
CBHW080236270326

41926CB00020B/4265